Management of Business
for CAPE®

Johoan Chambers-Blackwood
Rob Dransfield
Geoffrey Sankies
Margaret Scott-Thompson
Lilith Wilson

Contents

Introduction   1

Module 1   Business and its environment   2

1.1   Types of economic activity   4

1.2   Types of business organisation: sole traders and partnerships   6

1.3   Types of business organisation: private and public limited companies   8

1.4   Types of business organisation: cooperative enterprises   10

1.5   Types of business organisation: franchises and joint ventures   12

1.6   Types of business organisation: public sector organisations   14

1.7   Types of business organisation: not-for-profit organisations   16

1.8   Privatisation and nationalisation   18

1.9   Setting business objectives   20

1.10   The hierarchy of business objectives   22

1.11   Business ethics and corporate social responsibility   24

1.12   Business ethics: obligations to stakeholders and good corporate governance   26

1.13   Decision making   28

1.14   Quantitative and qualitative decision making   30

1.15   Stages of decision making   32

1.16   Factors affecting decision making   34

1.17   The impact of globalisation and multinationals   36

1.18   The role of government in globalisation   38

1.19   The impact of globalisation: consumer behaviour   40

1.20   The impact of globalisation: domestic business   42

1.21   The impact of globalisation: increasing trade liberalisation   44

1.22   Practice exam-style questions: Business and its environment   46

Module 2   The management of people   48

2.1   Evolution of management theories: the classical model   50

2.2   Evolution of management theories: the human relations model   52

2.3   Evolution of management theories: systems approach and contingency approach   54

2.4   Functions of management   56

2.5   Application of management functions   58

2.6   Organisational structure: by function, product and geographical market   60

2.7   Organisational structure: the matrix structure and team working   62

2.8   Organisational structure: network and virtual organisational structures   64

2.9   The characteristics of formal organisational structure   66

2.10   The characteristics of formal organisational structure: centralisation and decentralisation   68

2.11   Factors that influence motivation   70

2.12   Theories of motivation   72

2.13   Applying motivational theories   74

2.14   Financial and non-financial motivational strategies   76

2.15   Leadership   78

2.16   Leadership styles   80

2.17   Transformational leadership and skills required for effective leadership   82

2.18   Informal leadership   84

2.19   Group and team management   86

2.20   The characteristics and composition of effective teams   88

2.21	Group cohesiveness and advantages and disadvantages of teams to an organisation	90
2.22	Causes of conflict	92
2.23	Conflict management strategies	94
2.24	Managing change: the nature of change	96
2.25	Managing change: resistance to change	98
2.26	Strategies to manage change	100
2.27	Communication in business: the communication process	102
2.28	Communication channels and methods	104
2.29	Lines of communication	106
2.30	Barriers to effective communication	108
2.31	Human resource management	110
2.32	Functions of the HR department: recruitment and selection	112
2.33	Functions of the HR department: training and development	114
2.34	Functions of the HR department: compensation and performance management	116
2.35	Practice exam-style questions: The management of people	118

Module 3 Business finance and accounting   120

3.1	The need for capital	122
3.2	Sources of finance	124
3.3	Criteria for seeking finance and short-term finance	126
3.4	Medium- and long-term finance	128
3.5	Money and capital markets and sources of capital	130
3.6	Functioning and workings of money and capital markets: the stock exchange	132
3.7	The need for accounting information	134
3.8	Components of financial statements: income statement	136
3.9	Components of financial statements: balance sheet	138
3.10	Components of financial statements: cash flow statement	140
3.11	Relationship between the statement of financial position and the statement of comprehensive income	142
3.12	Financial statements analysis: use of accounting ratios	144
3.13	Calculation and interpretation of types of ratio: liquidity ratios	146
3.14	Calculation and interpretation of types of ratio: profitability ratios	148
3.15	Calculation and interpretation of types of ratio: efficiency ratios	150
3.16	Calculation and interpretation of types of ratio: gearing ratio	152
3.17	Calculation and interpretation of types of ratio: investor/shareholder ratios	154
3.18	Types of budget	156
3.19	Cash and sales budgets	158
3.20	Production, materials and labour budgets	160
3.21	The importance of budgeting	162
3.22	Budgetary control	164
3.23	Need for investment appraisal	166
3.24	Analytical methods of appraisal: average rate of return	168
3.25	Analytical methods of appraisal: payback period	170
3.26	Analytical methods of appraisal: net present value	172
3.27	Reviewing investment appraisal and comparing investment appraisal methods	176
3.28	Practice exam-style questions: Business finance and accounting	178
Glossary		180
Index		186

Introduction

This Study Guide has been developed exclusively with the Caribbean Examinations Council (CXC®) to be used as an additional resource by candidates, both in and out of school, following the Caribbean Advanced Proficiency Examination (CAPE®) programme.

It has been prepared by a team with expertise in the CAPE® syllabus, teaching and examination. The contents are designed to support learning by providing tools to help you achieve your best in CAPE® Management of Business and the features included make it easier for you to master the key concepts and requirements of the syllabus. *Do remember to refer to your syllabus for full guidance on the course requirements and examination format!*

Inside this Study Guide is an interactive CD that includes the answers to practice exam-style questions and electronic activities to assist you in developing good examination techniques:

- **On Your Marks** activities provide sample examination-style short answer and essay type questions, with example candidate answers and feedback from an examiner to show where answers could be improved. These activities will build your understanding, skill level and confidence in answering examination questions.

- **Test Yourself** activities are specifically designed to provide experience of multiple-choice examination questions and helpful feedback will refer you to sections inside the study guide so that you can revise problem areas.

This unique combination of focused syllabus content and interactive examination practice will provide you with invaluable support to help you reach your full potential in CAPE® Management of Business.

General objectives

On completion of this module, you should be able to:

- understand the nature and scope of business and its role in society
- understand how different business organisations function
- appreciate the importance of maintaining high ethical standards in business practices
- appreciate the process of decision making and its impact on the environment
- show an awareness of the impact of the external environment on business.

KEY TERMS

Gap in the market: an opportunity to meet existing and potential customer requirements that nobody else has spotted.

Business plan: a detailed description of a business and its plans for the next one to three years. A business plan explains what the business does (or what it will do if it is a new business): that is, what it will produce or services it will provide. It also provides financial assessments and forecasts to demonstrate the business's viability.

Introduction

A business organisation is a decision-making unit that produces a product in the form of a good or service. There are many different types of business organisation. These include:

- large and small businesses, such as a global drinks manufacturer or a local ice-cream cone seller
- businesses that seek to maximise profits, such as a large international bank, and those that just want to provide a useful service to the community, such as a credit union
- businesses run by the government and those run privately – for example, a government bus service or a private bus service.

In this module you will learn about the many different types of business organisation.

Setting up a business

Where does the idea to set up an enterprise come from? Many people, at some time or another, think about setting up a business of their own. You will hear people say things like 'Someone could make a fortune out of selling …' or 'If I had some money, I could make a business out of producing …'.

All businesses start out from a business idea. Some people copy ideas that they have seen elsewhere, such as selling bottles of aloe vera on the beach. Other people spot a **gap in the market**, such as a mobile hairdressing service in a particular area where there is no competition. Others turn a hobby into a business – for example, someone who enjoys making wooden toys might set up a toy company.

These are just a few of the ways in which people come up with a business idea. However, an idea on its own does not create a business. Ideas need to be turned into activities that can be maintained over a period of time and carried out effectively. In addition to an idea, organisation and planning are needed. Businesses also need a structure in order to organise and plan their activities.

Business plans

Businesses require the following inputs: time, effort, information, raw materials, capital, labour and paperwork. These inputs need to be combined in a detailed and organised way, and this is usually described in a **business plan**.

A business plan includes details such as: information on the experience and background of the owner; the name of the business and where it is situated; the market to which it is selling; how it will carry out advertising and promotional activity; how finance will be raised; how the business will be organised; and expected sales, costs and profits (see more about business plans in CAPE® Management of Business Unit 2).

Organisational structure

The business also needs to have an organisational structure, showing who is responsible for decision making within the organisation.

There are a number of different types of business organisation. The most widespread type of business enterprise in the Caribbean is the sole trader, with just one owner. In order to grow and share the workload the owner may change the form of the business to a partnership, working together with one or more additional partners. To expand further it is possible to create a company which will be owned by shareholders (who appoint managers to act as agents on their behalf) and have a board of directors with responsibility for running the company. In this module we will examine these and other types of businesses, including cooperative and franchise organisations.

Business ethics

Ethical principles are important in the success of a business. **Business ethics** are rules of conduct that should be followed by a business, and the people working within the business, to avoid activities that may have a negative impact on the environment or on people outside of the business. Businesses should benefit society as a whole, not just the owners. A business should therefore take into consideration all of the stakeholders in the business (such as shareholders, directors, managers, employees, customers, suppliers, local communities in which the business operates, and the government). An ethical business seeks to identify and meet the expectations of all of these groups while recognising that some conflicts of interests between groups might arise.

Factors that influence business decisions

Businesses do not exist in isolation but are part of a wider environment. The following factors influence the decisions that a business makes:

- governmental, political and legal influences
- economic influences
- social and cultural influences
- technological influences
- ecological influences
- human and natural constraints.

Business people need to be aware of how these influences impact on every decision that the business makes.

Did you know?

Each of the organisations mentioned here are in the private sector of the economy, i.e. they are owned by private citizens on their own behalf. There are also government owned businesses including public corporations and statutory boards.

KEY TERMS

Business ethics: principles that incorporate a sense of 'doing the right thing'. A business that takes ethics seriously will make business decisions that benefit the wider society.

Figure 1.1.1 *Farming itself is a primary activity, but it provides the basis for the food-processing industry – a secondary activity*

Economic activity involves the production of items that are of value. The terms 'adding value' and 'value added' refer to increasing the value to a user of a raw material, a semi-finished product or a finished product.

Economic activity is often broken down into three types:

- primary industries (extractive industries and farming)
- secondary industries (manufacturing and construction industries)
- tertiary industries (services).

Primary industries

Primary industries extract and use natural resources. Examples include farming, mining and oil drilling. Farmers throughout the Caribbean grow and harvest crops, such as sugar, maize, peppers and bananas, as well as farming livestock. Mining of bauxite and other materials, such as asphalt, is also carried out in Guyana and Trinidad, for example, and oil is drilled and piped to terminals in Trinidad.

Secondary industries

Secondary industries make and assemble products. Examples include manufacturing and construction industries. Manufacturers use raw materials and parts from other industries. A semi-manufactured good is one that is only partly made. For example, component manufacturers might produce parts (semi-manufactured goods) that will be assembled into a finished car. Most products go through several stages of production. Examples of manufactured products are furniture, cars, chocolate and oil rigs. A & F Manufacturing Co. Ltd in Antigua is an example of a business in a secondary industry. It takes raw materials, such as canvas and steel, and manufactures awnings and shutters for export across the Caribbean.

Tertiary or service industries

Tertiary industries provide people with a service that is not a physical good: you cannot actually touch it. For example, the protection provided by the police, the services provided by banks for safeguarding savings, and a haircut are all services. Other examples are insurance and public transport.

Services are sometimes classified as:

- direct services, which are provided to everyday people – for example, the police and hairdressers
- commercial services, which are provided to businesses – for example, insurance and banking.

However, the distinction is not always clear-cut. Some commercial services, like banking, are used by individuals as well as businesses.

Quaternary industries

In addition to the three types of industry described above, people sometimes refer to **quaternary industries**. These are intellectual, knowledge-based industries, such as scientific research, some government jobs (for example, collecting and analysing statistics) and the media. This sector is sometimes described as comprising the **knowledge-based economy**.

How the different types of industry interrelate

While it is helpful to distinguish between different types and stages of industry, particularly to monitor changing patterns of industry over time, in some cases the distinction between stages is blurred. For example, a restaurant engages not only in some food-processing activities (secondary) but also in providing a personal service to customers (tertiary). Figure 1.1.2 shows how the different types and stages of industry are involved in the oil industry.

The changing face of economic activity

Most countries go through three waves of economic development:

1 Activity is dominated by agriculture and farming. In the Caribbean this took the form of plantation agriculture with the growth of cash crops, such as sugar and bananas, for export.

2 Activity is focused on manufacturing. In the Caribbean this took the form of sugar processing and canning of food products for example.

3 Services become the most important sector in the economy, with many people working in insurance, banking, office administration and leisure, for example. Today, many parts of the Caribbean, such as Barbados, Jamaica and Trinidad (where the majority of people are involved in service sector employment, including tourism and government administration), are in the third wave.

The Caribbean also has quaternary industries. The development of quaternary industries represents a fourth wave of economic development. For example, the Scientific Research Council in Jamaica includes researchers examining new solar technologies for the agricultural industry.

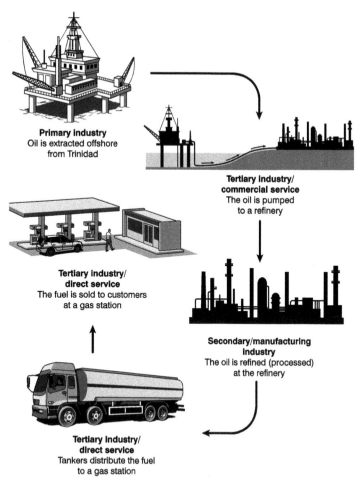

Primary industry
Oil is extracted offshore from Trinidad

Tertiary industry/ commercial service
The oil is pumped to a refinery

Tertiary industry/ direct service
The fuel is sold to customers at a gas station

Secondary/manufacturing industry
The oil is refined (processed) at the refinery

Tertiary industry/ direct service
Tankers distribute the fuel to a gas station

Figure 1.1.2 *The different types of industry involved in oil extraction, processing and distribution*

Summary table

Primary industry	Secondary industry	Tertiary industry	Quaternary industry
Extraction or gathering of raw materials	Manufacturing and construction	Services (e.g. insurance and banking)	Knowledge-based industries

Summary questions

1 Hotels are important tertiary sector businesses in the Caribbean. In what ways are hotels and tourism dependent on goods provided by the secondary and primary sectors of the economy?

2 Classify the following occupations according to the sector into which they fit: hairdresser, insurance clerk, factory machine operative, farmer, personal fitness trainer, building worker and sports coach.

Types of business organisation: sole traders and partnerships

1.2

Specific objective

On completion of this section, you should be able to:

- compare the different types of business organisation based on economic sectors and legal structures – sole traders and partnerships.

KEY TERMS

Sole trader: a business owned by one person. The sole trader may, or may not, employ other people.

Did you know?

Being made redundant from a large company often provides the impetus for starting up a business. Employees who have been made redundant can use the skills they have learned and the capital from any redundancy payout.

KEY TERMS

Debt: capital that is borrowed from outside the business, which must be repaid with interest.

Unlimited liability: situation in which owners of a business have no limits on the sums that they may be required to pay to settle the debts of their business.

When setting up a business, it is important to decide on the type of business organisation you are going to establish. The type of business organisation will vary depending on the nature, legal status and size of the business. How the owner will access capital also has some bearing on the type of organisation.

Sole trader

This is the most common form of business ownership and the easiest to set up. A **sole trader** is a business owned by one person – though this business may employ a large number of people.

Table 1.2.1 shows some of the advantages and disadvantages of setting up as a sole trader.

Table 1.2.1 Advantages and disadvantages of setting up as a sole trader

Advantages	Disadvantages
- Easy to set up as no special paperwork is required - Generally these are small businesses, so less capital is required - Speedy decisions can be made as few people are involved - Personal attention is given to business affairs - Bespoke services can be offered to customers - Sole traders can cater for the needs of local people - Profits do not have to be shared - Business affairs can be kept private	- Having unlimited liability (see below) is a risk – if the business is unsuccessful, the owner can lose their personal possessions - Finance can be difficult to raise - The small-scale nature of the business limits discounts available and other benefits of large-scale production - Prices are often higher than those of larger organisations - Ill-health, holidays, etc. may affect the running of the business

Sole traders only have their own resources to draw on. A sole trader therefore has to use his or her savings and may need to borrow money – usually from credit unions and commercial banks.

Sole traders hope to make a profit. However, if they run into **debt**, they will have to pay any money they owe from their own pocket.

The business term we use to describe a sole trader's position is **unlimited liability**. For example, if a sole trader has a business and equipment worth $15,000 and runs up debts of $75,000, the debt is not limited to the $15,000 already put into the business. The sole trader may have to sell his or her house and other possessions to meet the debts.

Partnership

A partnership is a business relationship between two or more owners. Partnerships usually have between 2 and 20 members, although today this rule is more relaxed and some professional partnerships (such as international accountancy firms) may have many more partners.

At the start of a partnership, a solicitor draws up a Deed of Partnership. This sets out the details by which the partnership is governed, such as how the profits (and/or losses) will be shared and the key duties of each partner – for example, how much capital they should contribute, their roles and responsibilities, and procedures for introducing new partners and settling disputes.

Partners can form either a general partnership or a limited partnership. In a general partnership all partners have unlimited liability. In a limited partnership there has to be at least one limited partner (who has **limited liability**) and one general partner (who has unlimited liability). **'Sleeping' partners** can also be introduced to a partnership. They take no active part in the running of the business.

Limited liability means that if a partnership runs into debt, the maximum amount in law that a limited partner is likely to lose is what he or she put into the business. In other words, the limited partner will not be required to sell his or her house and possessions to meet the business's debts.

Table 1.2.2 shows some of the advantages and disadvantages of setting up as a partnership.

Did you know?

A partnership can be formed orally, in writing or by conduct. However, it is usually recommended that it be set out in writing by drafting up a Deed of Partnership.

KEY TERMS

Limited liability: a restriction on the amount of debt in a company that owners can be expected to pay. Liability is limited to the value of their shares.

'Sleeping' partner: an individual who contributes capital to a business but who is not involved in the day-to-day decision making or running of the business.

Table 1.2.2 Advantages and disadvantages of setting up a partnership

Advantages	Disadvantages
▣ Capital is introduced by partners ▣ Larger-scale opportunities than for a sole trader ▣ Members of family can be introduced to the business ▣ Affairs can be kept private ▣ Risks and responsibilities can be spread among the partners	▣ Unlimited liability (except for special partnerships) ▣ Potential disagreements between the partners ▣ Limitations on the number of partners ▣ Partnerships have to be re-formed if a partner dies

Summary table

Sole trader	Partnership
■ Little paperwork is required to set up ■ One owner ■ Unlimited liability ■ Limited capital ■ All profits go to the sole owner	■ To establish a legal footing it is helpful to set up a Deed of Partnership ■ Two or more owners ■ Unlimited liability ■ Access to more capital than a sole trader ■ Profits are shared among partners – disputes may arise

Summary questions

1 Which type of business organisation would be most suitable for each of the following businesses? Give reasons for your choice.
   a A car wash business
   b A market stall business
   c A small website design business
   d A veterinary business
   e A small accountancy practice
   f A tourist shop

2 Hovill Lawes is hoping to set up a mobile sound system music business to provide a service to people wanting to organise functions where a little music is required. What advice would you give her about the relative merits of setting up as a sole trader or entering a partnership agreement with someone else?

Specific objective

On completion of this section, you should be able to:

■ compare different types of business organisation based on economic sectors and legal structures – private limited companies and public limited companies.

KEY TERMS

Company: a business that is owned by shareholders, who contribute capital in return for a share in the company and its profits. The US term for company is corporation.

Shareholder: someone who owns shares in a company. A share represents a portion of the total capital of the company. A shareholder therefore part owns the company.

Dividend: the return (reward) paid to a shareholder out of the profits made by a company.

Certificate of Incorporation: states that a company has been incorporated as a company.

Did you know?

To register a company in Jamaica, the main document that the company needs to submit to the Registrar of Companies is the Articles of Incorporation. Other forms provided include the Declaration of Compliance, details of directors and details of the registered office of the company. The forms that need to be filled in can be accessed online.

The word '**company**' suggests a group of companions who have come together to set up a business. In reality, many companies are large organisations where the owners (**shareholders**) are quite far removed from the decision making. A key feature of a company is that it is protected by limited liability (see p7). Limited liability limits the financial obligations of the shareholders to the value of the shares they have contributed to the business. Should the business be faced by demands from creditors, the maximum amount a shareholder can lose is the value of his or her shareholding in the limited company.

Figure 1.3.1 TCL is an example of a public company whose shares can be bought and sold on the Trinidad Stock Exchange

Private limited companies

Private limited companies are often family-owned businesses. Private limited companies are owned by the shareholders and every shareholder owns a share in the business. There must be at least two shareholders but there is no upper limit on the number of shareholders. Companies can grow by selling more shares.

The shares of private limited companies are not quoted on the stock exchange and cannot be advertised for sale publicly. Shares can only be traded with the permission of the board of directors.

Shareholders in a private limited company share in the profits by receiving a regular **dividend** – usually every six months.

A company must follow a particular procedure to be registered as a limited company. This procedure may vary across the Caribbean (see the 'Did you know?'), although in most cases the company must first submit its Articles of Association and Memorandum of Association to the Registrar of Companies. The Articles of Association set out the internal rules governing the organisation of the company (for example, rules about when meetings will be held and the voting rights of shareholders) that the board of directors must follow. The company should then be issued with a **Certificate of Incorporation** by the Registrar of Companies.

Public limited companies

Public limited companies (plcs) are generally the largest type of privately owned company and are usually larger than private limited companies. They are able to raise capital through buying and selling shares publicly on the stock exchange. A minimum of two shareholders (who may also be directors) is needed to form a public limited company. This number can differ for some Caribbean countries, but there is no legal limit on the maximum number of shareholders.

A public limited company must be registered with the Registrar of Companies. If the Registrar of Companies is satisfied that the company is likely to have a good trading record, and that it has sound Articles of Association, the company will be issued with a Certificate of Incorporation.

Once it has received a Certificate of Incorporation, a public limited company then normally issues a prospectus. This is an advertisement or invitation to the public to buy shares. The issuing of shares then takes place, and the Registrar of Companies issues a **Certificate of Trading**. Business can then commence and the share price is quoted on the stock market.

Sometimes companies are able to operate on a sufficient scale as private limited companies (for example, hotel chains such as Sandals). If a private company wants to become a public limited company they must follow certain legal procedures set out by the Companies Act. Good examples of public companies are GraceKennedy, the publicly listed Jamaican consumer goods company, and TCL (see the case study).

> **KEY TERMS**
>
> **Certificate of Trading:** states that a company can commence trading.

CASE STUDY

Trinidad Cement Limited (TCL)

TCL is an example of a public limited company. Its shares can be bought and sold on the Trinidad Stock Exchange and it currently has more than 6,000 shareholders. It is a holding company – that is, a company with a majority ownership of other companies. TCL owns eight companies, including Arawak Cement in Barbados and companies in Jamaica, Anguilla, Guyana and Trinidad. The core business of the company is the manufacture and sale of bulk and bagged cement that is extracted from local raw materials. TCL operates as a public limited company because it needs lots of capital for such large-scale production.

1 Carry out some online research. Find the website of TCL and find out the main companies that it owns. When was it set up originally and how was it set up?

2 Is it involved in the primary sector of the economy or the secondary sector of the economy?

Did you know?

A limited company can be either a public limited company (plc) or a private limited company (Ltd). In either case, the company has limited liability. If a limited company gets into financial difficulty, only the company's assets can be taken by the creditors. The personal assets of the directors and shareholders cannot be taken.

Summary table

Private company	Public company
■ Often a family company or a relatively small company ■ Needs a Certificate of Incorporation (after registering Articles of Association) to trade ■ Can raise more capital than a sole trader or partnership ■ Has limited liability and is run by a board of directors	■ May have thousands of shareholders who can buy and sell shares through the stock exchange ■ Needs a Certificate of Incorporation and Certificate of Trading ■ Can raise more capital than any other form of business ■ Has limited liability and is run by a board of directors

Summary questions

1 Which of the following statements apply to **i** private limited companies and **ii** both private and public companies?

   a Shareholders are only liable to the value of their shares in the company.

   b A family is able to retain control of a business.

   c The rules of the company are based on the Articles of Association.

   d It can raise more capital than smaller forms of business.

   e The owners are termed shareholders.

2 Produce a table showing the advantages and disadvantages of private and public limited companies.

Specific objective

On completion of this section, you should be able to:

■ compare different types of business organisation based on economic sectors and legal structures – cooperative enterprises.

Figure 1.4.1 *Cable television companies can benefit from cooperatively purchasing access to programming from television networks*

Did you know?

The Caribbean Cable Cooperative has over 40 member companies. The company is a registered Bahamas corporation run by a board of directors.

Did you know?

Marketing cooperatives enable groups of cooperators to jointly market their products (often agricultural products). The cooperative will promote and distribute the products on behalf of cooperators and engage in advertising and selling activities such as talking directly to customers and arranging sales. It will also ensure the quality of the products being sold.

Cooperatives in the Caribbean

Cooperative businesses are a particularly important part of Caribbean heritage. Cooperatives are not only economic enterprises but also social and political enterprises. They are often created by cooperators (with relatively limited income or land) to enable them to achieve shared objectives in the face of competition from larger organisations. Cooperation involves sharing resources, sharing work responsibilities and ultimately sharing the benefits. Cooperatives in the Caribbean span many industries, such as credit unions, fishing, agriculture, marketing and taxi driving.

The need for resources is often the impetus for setting up a cooperative, as individuals on their own only have limited resources. As part of a cooperative their resources can be pooled and shared.

CASE STUDY

Television cooperative

Any licensed cable television company in the Caribbean can benefit from being a member of a television cooperative. A company can join a cooperative by becoming one of its shareholders. The cooperative's objective is to give each of the hundreds of cable television companies access to resources that they might not be able to access on their own (see the 'Did you know?'). The cooperative negotiates directly with television networks on behalf of its members. Members pay fees to the cooperative for access to television programmes and the cooperative pays fees to the television networks.

1 What benefits are there likely to be for cable companies that are part of a cooperative?

2 Why might television networks prefer to deal with a cooperative rather than individual locally licensed cable companies?

Farming cooperatives

Groups of small farmers often join together to form a farming cooperative. The cooperative may provide farmers with tools and equipment, seeds and stock, and shared marketing of products. Farmers can deliver their produce to the cooperative, which sells it on behalf of the farmers. The cooperative may strike deals with bulk purchasers, such as food-processing companies.

Workers' cooperatives

A workers' cooperative employs its members. The members:
■ share responsibility for the success (or failure) of the enterprise
■ work together
■ take decisions together
■ share profits (and losses).

Examples of workers' cooperatives include a carpentry cooperative making furniture and a child-minding cooperative. Shares in the cooperative are owned by the workers. The benefit of such a cooperative is that the group shares responsibility. The drawback is that there can be disagreements between members.

Retail cooperatives

Members of a retail cooperative work together to purchase items that they then sell. The cooperators share in the profits of the business, often in the form of a dividend. Cooperatives often have strong social principles, which means that they seek to give fair prices to suppliers and growers of products. Most cooperatives believe in the principles of **fair trade**. The Winward Islands Farmers' Association (WINFA) brings together banana farmers across Dominica, St Lucia and St Vincent in order to support banana growers and the national economies of the area.

Credit unions and cooperative banks

Credit unions and cooperative banks are fairly common in the Caribbean (see 3.5). Credit unions are usually not-for-profit organisations that are owned by their members. They encourage members to save and in return provide them with credit at relatively low rates of interest. Cooperatives use a one person, one vote system to elect a board of directors, making them potentially more democratic than other types of business organisation.

Table 1.4.1 shows the advantages and disadvantages of being a member of a cooperative enterprise.

Table 1.4.1 Advantages and disadvantages of cooperative enterprises

Advantages	Disadvantages
▦ Cooperators share knowledge, skills and efforts ▦ Cooperators share the rewards more equitably than in other forms of enterprise	▦ Weaker members (e.g. producers of lower quality products) may damage the reputation of others ▦ Can lower the spur to individual initiative and enterprise ▦ Disagreements can arise between cooperators

Summary table

Producer/worker cooperative	Retail cooperative	Credit union
■ Set up by cooperators to produce goods cooperatively ■ Members own the business and work together to produce goods and services	■ Cooperators combine resources to purchase goods collectively to resell ■ Cooperators share profits ■ Profit is dependent on how much they have purchased	■ Cooperators combine their savings into a joint fund ■ The credit union provides credit to members at favourable rates of interest

Summary question

1 Which type of cooperative would provide the following?

  a Loans at low rates of interest

  b Joint marketing of crops

  c Collaboration in the production of goods

  d Discounts on purchases of goods

  e Help to purchase equipment, seeds and livestock

  f A safe way of saving small sums of money

  g Consumer goods for purchase at affordable prices

On completion of this section, you should be able to:

- compare different types of business organisation based on economic sectors and legal structures – franchises and joint ventures.

Franchise: a business that operates under the name of a well-known business and pays the company a fee or royalty for using its name and branding.

Franchisee: the person who has been granted the franchise. The franchisee usually contributes a sum of capital to take on the franchise and pays regular royalties or fees related to sales.

Franchisor: the company or person granting the franchise.

Figure 1.5.1 *Coffee houses are a good example of a franchise business*

Franchise

A **franchise** is a 'business marriage' between an existing, proven business and a newcomer. The newcomer (known as the **franchisee**) buys a licence to copy the business idea of the established company **franchisor**. In return, the franchisee promises to pay the franchisor a percentage of his or her sales. The franchisee needs to work hard, put in long hours and use a lot of initiative to get the business started and to develop it. Franchising is common in the food and beverage industry – coffee shops are good examples of a franchise business (see the case study).

Burger King outlets are often operated on a franchise arrangement. The franchisee provides the capital and undertakes the day-to-day running of the business. The franchisor (Burger King) provides the trading name and management experience, and also often supplies materials and equipment.

A legal document called a franchise agreement is required to form a franchise. This governs the relationship between the two parties. The franchisor will own the brand and intellectual property rights, including operating procedures such as the processes involved in preparing fast food.

CASE STUDY

Rituals

Rituals Coffee House is one of the best-known franchise operations in the Caribbean with outlets in St Lucia, Barbados, Jamaica, Antigua, St Kitts and Nevis, Dominica, Suriname, Guyana and Curacao. It is a fast-growing franchise business. Rituals provides its franchisees with a successful business opportunity: that is, an instantly recognisable brand and coffee shop operation that has been successful in the Caribbean since 2004. The franchisor (Rituals) provides the marketing know-how, the branding (for example, the look of the shop), the menu, equipment and training. The franchisees put in some of their own capital and time to make the franchise a success. The harder the franchisees work, the greater their share of the rewards.

1   Identify at least one other existing franchise opportunity in your area. Try to find out what support the franchisee receives from the franchisor. How successful does the franchise outlet appear to be and what are the benefits to a business entrepreneur of this type of arrangement?

Table 1.5.1 shows the advantages and disadvantages of being part of a franchise.

Table 1.5.1 *The advantages and disadvantages of franchises*

Advantages to franchisor	Disadvantages to franchisor
▪ Input of enterprise and effort from franchisee ▪ Franchisee contributes own capital to the franchise ▪ Franchisor does not have to commit so much of their own capital	▪ Profits shared with franchisee ▪ Reputation of franchisor can be damaged by partnering with an ineffective franchisee

Advantages to franchisee	Disadvantages to franchisee
■ Able to trade using a well-known name ■ Access to other benefits such as training ■ Being able to use business ideas that are proven to work	■ Hard work and long hours required ■ Profits shared with franchisor ■ Do not have complete control over certain aspects of the business such as store layouts and the type of products you can sell

Joint venture

A **joint venture** is where two companies join together to pursue a common interest. A joint venture often involves working with an overseas partner. It is set up through a joint venture agreement. This legal document establishes the ownership and management of the new joint venture and the distribution of profits. In a joint venture, the companies share both the profits and the risks. There are three different types of joint venture:

- **Licensing:** a company enters into an arrangement with a licensee in a foreign market. For a fee or royalty the licensee produces the company's product or uses the company's manufacturing processes. The danger of this type of arrangement is that the licensee may copy the company's idea.

- **Contract manufacturing:** this type of venture enables a company to contract a manufacturer or service provider in a foreign country to produce a product or provide a service in that country. For example, a soft-drinks company might contract a foreign partner to manufacture the soft-drinks under licence in the foreign country. The company does not have to commit its own resources to the manufacturing operation. However, it must rely on the contractor to maintain the quality of the product (and hence preserve the reputation of the brand).

- **Joint ownership:** this type of venture involves two companies joining forces to set up a completely separate company. Each partner in the joint venture could, for example, own a 50 per cent share in the new company. Disagreements may arise over the amount that each company puts in and takes out of the joint venture. A joint ownership venture is a good way of entering a foreign market by partnering a company in that market. This is particularly beneficial where there may be government resistance to full foreign ownership or where the company can benefit from the local knowledge and connections of the foreign partner.

Table 1.5.2 shows some advantages and disadvantages of being part of a joint venture.

Table 1.5.2 The advantages and disadvantages of joint ventures

Advantages	Disadvantages
■ Brings together the best qualities of two existing businesses ■ The partner brings to the venture particular strengths (e.g. technological expertise, marketing knowledge, capital, local and political connections)	■ Partners in the joint venture have to share profits ■ Disagreements may arise, particularly if one partner feels that the other is not pulling their weight

Summary table

Franchise
■ Agreement between a franchisor and a franchisee ■ Both parties put in capital but the franchisee must work to make the business a success

Joint ownership venture

■ Agreement between joint owners:
  □ licensing
  □ contract manufacture
  □ joint ownership
■ A new business is created, bringing together benefits from each of the two ventures
■ Both parties put in capital and share the rewards in proportion to what is set out in the agreement

Summary questions

1 List five advantages and five disadvantages of franchising for a franchisee. What are the main advantages and disadvantages to the franchisor compared with operating the business themselves?

2 What are the main benefits to a Caribbean company of setting up a joint venture in the US with an American partner? Use an example of your choice to illustrate your answer.

Types of business organisation: public sector organisations

Specific objective

On completion of this section, you should be able to:

- compare different types of business organisation based on economic sectors and legal structures – public corporations and statutory boards.

KEY TERMS

Mixed economy: an economy comprising a combination of public sector and private sector enterprises.

Public corporation: a state-owned business or industry that is set up for a specific purpose (e.g. to run the telecommunications service or to provide utility services such as water or gas).

Statutory board: an organisation set up by the government, through legislation, with the aim of performing certain functions, such as managing a port or providing clean and regular water supplies. It reports to a specific government minister.

Did you know?

An executive is a director of a business who is involved in the day-to-day running of a company in a management capacity. A non-executive helps to shape the strategy of the company at board meetings but is not involved in the day-to-day running of the business.

The economies in the Caribbean are **mixed economies**. This means that in addition to privately owned business organisations, there are others that are run by the state. There are also private–public partnerships where the government provides some of the funding to an enterprise or activity and the remainder is provided by the private sector.

Public corporations and statutory boards

Public corporations and **statutory boards** are set up by the government. They are given authority by the government (through legislation) to perform certain activities. The board of these organisations reports directly to a government ministry. For example, Barbados has a range of statutory boards including the Barbados Museum & Historical Society and the Barbados Water Authority. It makes sense to have a single water authority to treat water and ensure that its purity and quality meet the required standards.

Public corporations are accountable to the government and to the wider community. Table 1.6.1 sets out the differences between a public corporation and a public limited company.

Table 1.6.1 *The differences between public corporations and public limited companies*

Public corporation	Public limited company
Set up by legislature (for example, by Act of Parliament)	Set up by issuing a prospectus and inviting public to buy shares
Owned by the government	Owned by shareholders
Run by chairperson/board appointed by government	Run by executive directors appointed by the board on behalf of shareholders
Aims to provide public service as well as having some commercial goals	Commercial goals

The benefits of public corporations

- They avoid wasteful duplication. For example, if a country allowed competition between private providers of railway tracks, there might be more than one track between some cities. If there were several electricity and gas companies, each company might run cables across the same land.

- They run key services. For example, public service broadcasting is accessible to everyone and caters for minority as well as majority interests.

- They prevent exploitation of consumers. The government can restrict prices charged by public corporations and statutory boards where they are the sole operator.

- Jobs and key industries are protected. The government can protect workers' jobs by guaranteeing employment in the public sector.

CASE STUDY

Public service broadcasting in Guyana

Broadcasting in Guyana is dominated by the National Communications Network Incorporated (NCN Inc.), which was formed from the merger of the Guyana Broadcasting Corporation and Guyana Television Broadcasting Company Limited. Radio broadcasting in Guyana goes back to the mid-1920s. For many years the radio services were provided by the private sector in the form of Radio Demerara. However, in the late 1960s the government of Guyana invested a lot of capital in this sector to create a modern broadcasting service. By 1979 the government had taken over broadcasting completely. Broadcasting is a good example of how government ownership can provide a public service that:

■ is accessible to everyone in a geographic area

■ is designed to appeal to everyone

■ helps to shape national identity and community – for example, by broadcasting major national occasions such as election news, key sporting events and cultural festivals

■ caters for both majority and minority listeners and viewers

■ establishes and maintains good programming guidelines in line with the government's or regulator's requirements

■ everyone pays for (for example, by a licence fee or other form of tax).

A public service is one that provides for the interests of everyone rather than specific interests.

1 The list above shows the benefits of public service broadcasting. What are the benefits of a statutory water board? Make a similar list of benefits.

2 Identify some of the possible drawbacks of government involvement in public service broadcasting.

Summary table

What is a public corporation/ statutory board?	An organisation set up by the government to take responsibility for an industry or activity
Who appoints the board?	The government
What are the main benefits?	A public service for everybody Government regulates to ensure minimum standards Minorities benefit as well as majorities
What are the main drawbacks?	May be managed inefficiently as no competition Government may interfere to achieve its own ends and thus reduce real public service benefits

Summary questions

1 Who are the owners of public corporations and who are the consumers of the products of these organisations? Illustrate your answer with examples of three public corporations/statutory boards that are familiar to you.

2 In what situations might the benefits of public services outweigh the costs to the community of running such services?

Types of business organisation: not-for-profit organisations

Specific objective

On completion of this section, you should be able to:

■ compare different types of business organisation based on economic sectors and legal structures – charities and non-governmental organisations.

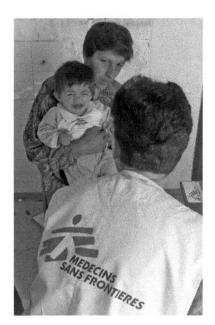

Figure 1.7.1 *Médecins Sans Frontières is a charity that helps civilians in danger from crises such as wars and famine*

Many organisations exist to achieve goals other than making a profit. For example, the main purpose of a **charity** is to help others rather than to make a profit for a business owner. Médecins Sans Frontières is a charity that helps civilians in crises such as wars and famine, regardless of their background. The organisation's purpose is to respond quickly by providing doctors, nurses and medical supplies. The charity runs over 500 projects in half of the world's countries. Most of its funds come from fundraising, with the remainder coming from government and business donations.

There are thousands of other non-profit-making organisations working across the Caribbean in community work, education, medical projects and sporting activities. Examples of voluntary organisations in the Caribbean include:

■ Red Thread: a voluntary organisation set up in Guyana in 2003 to combat violence against women. It was originally set up by women to raise funds, provide women's refuges and protest against violence against women and girls.

■ Food For The Poor: a charity with its headquarters in Florida but which is active throughout the Caribbean, providing help for the poor through building houses, planting fruit-bearing trees and giving aid.

Charities and voluntary organisations

A distinction is sometimes made between charities, which have a community service focus but typically employ salaried staff, and voluntary organisations, which are staffed by voluntary workers who are not paid. However, voluntary organisations share the same features as charities, as listed below.

Features of a charity

There are a number of key features of a charity organisation:

■ It needs to be registered as a charity with the relevant charity commissioners or other officials in a given territory in order to benefit from tax relief (for example, on property taxes) and to be recognised as a reputable charity.

■ The constitution of a charity and any registration documents need to set out clearly the purpose of the charity (for example, a charity to house the homeless).

■ The work, administration and honesty (probity) of a charity is overseen by a group of trustees, who may then appoint managers to supervise specific aspects of the work of the charity.

■ A charity needs to be set up to benefit the wider public (or a specified segment of the wider public) rather than a specific individual.

Charities as business organisations

Although charities are set up on a not-for-profit basis, they are often highly organised businesses with:

■ a clear mission (purpose) for the organisation

■ clear objectives

■ targets and plans

■ accountability for money that is spent.

The reputation of a charity rests on exemplary organisation and the credibility of its trustees, managers and workers.

Whereas a **for-profit organisation** seeks to make a profit, a charity's main focus is on providing a public service. When a charity's income is greater than its expenditure, this is referred to as having a surplus. Any surplus is retained by the charity and reinvested so that it can provide better services. The main difference between a charity and a company seeking to make a profit is that the profit-making business needs to use some of the profit to reward shareholders. It could be argued that some charities may be less efficient because they do not need to make a profit.

Not-for-profit organisations are entitled to a range of tax concessions from the government, which reduce their costs of operation.

Non-governmental organisations

In the modern world, the term **non-governmental organisation** (NGO) is widely used. This is because of the important influence of non-governmental organisations such as Greenpeace (an environmental charity), the Salvation Army (an international Christian church that works with the homeless and poor) and Médecins Sans Frontières. An NGO is:

- made up of individuals with a common purpose, such as disaster relief
- self-governing
- non-governmental
- made up of volunteers.

The World Bank defines NGOs as 'groups and institutions that are entirely or largely independent of government and are characterized primarily by humanitarian or cooperative, rather than commercial, objectives'.

Did you know?

The term NGO covers a range of organisations, including charities. NGOs are organisations with a humanitarian purpose, including **pressure groups** that seek to influence the political decision-making processes.

Summary table

	For-profit organisation	**Not-for-profit organisation (e.g. charity)**
Aim	To run a successful enterprise with a business purpose and to make a profit	To provide a public service – making a surplus is a secondary concern
Ownership	Typically owned by a small number of owners or a larger number of shareholders	Registered as a charity or other form of non-profit organisation to provide a service for society at large or for a significant group
Trustees run the affairs of a charity in the interests of those providing donations and on behalf of recipients
The community is the real owner
Outputs	Goods and services, profits and employment	Public benefits (sometimes in the form of goods and services), surplus and employment

Summary questions

1 What are the purposes of charities and voluntary organisations? Is it possible to distinguish between the two types of organisation?

2 A director of a company might state: 'This year my company has made a profit!' In contrast, a trustee of a charity might state: 'This year we made a surplus!' What is the distinction that is being made here? To whom is this distinction of importance?

3 Why is it important for the trustees of a charity to run the charity in a business like way?

On completion of this section, you should be able to:

- compare different types of business organisation based on economic sectors and legal structures – privatisation and nationalisation.

> **KEY TERMS**
>
> **Nationalisation:** the taking over and running of a business or industry by the government.
>
> **Privatisation:** the transfer of businesses from government ownership to private ownership.

Figure 1.8.1 shows the different types of private and public enterprise. The private sector consists of business organisations and activities that are owned and run by private individuals. The public sector consists of businesses owned and run by the government. The arrows in Figure 1.8.1 illustrate the processes of nationalisation and privatisation.

Nationalisation occurs when the government of a country takes over the ownership and running of industries that were previously in the private sector.

Privatisation is the reverse process and involves the government selling off industries and activities that were previously run by public corporations and statutory boards to private entrepreneurs and companies.

Private sector (individuals and organisations)	**Public sector** (state ownership)
	Government takes ownership of private companies
Government sells off public corporations	**NATIONALISATION**
PRIVATISATION	
Sole traders	Public corporations
Partnerships	Statutory boards
Private limited companies	
Public limited companies	
Cooperatives	
Franchises	
Charities/voluntary organisations	

Figure 1.8.1 *The processes of nationalisation and privatisation*

Nationalisation and privatisation in the Caribbean

The changing landscape of nationalisation and privatisation of industry in the Caribbean is the result of history and politics (Figure 1.8.2). In the post-war period, Caribbean economies found it difficult to compete on a world scale in terms of the products that they produced and exported, such as cane sugar and bananas. As they were relatively small economies, it became increasingly difficult for them to get good prices for their products as supply from larger South American plantations increased. Caribbean countries were exporting low-value agricultural commodities while importing relatively high-priced manufacturing goods.

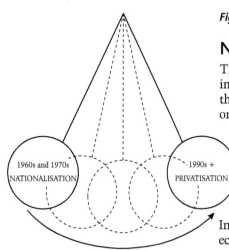

Figure 1.8.2 *The emphasis on nationalisation and privatisation can change in different periods of history, depending on the political influences in a country*

In response, during the 1960s and 1970s, the governments in some economies tried to build up manufacturing in the Caribbean by nationalising many industries, such as cement manufacture and sugar production. The banking sector was also substantially nationalised in some countries. Today there is still quite a strong public sector in some economies, such as Trinidad and Guyana.

However, since the 1990s the pendulum has swung in the direction of privatisation, particularly in Barbados and Jamaica. Barbados has sought to develop a broad entrepreneurial base, encouraging businesses including start-up in fields such as hotels and tourism (for example, Sandals), fishing and agriculture (Cannon Charters), music (Ice Records), film (Film Barbados Inc.), and the rapidly growing information technology sector.

Privatisation versus nationalisation

There are valid political and commercial arguments for both privatisation and nationalisation (see Table 1.8.1).

Table 1.8.1 Arguments for and against privatisation and nationalisation

Supporters of privatisation argue that:	Opponents of privatisation argue that:
▪ commercial incentives lead to the most efficient use of resources ▪ individual entrepreneurs are more likely to take risks and seek new and developing opportunities ▪ the incentives of running your own business are likely to encourage hard work and dedication.	▪ it is a threat to a public service ideal ▪ it creates a divide between successful enterprises and those that get left behind because they lack resources, drive or know-how.
Supporters of nationalisation argue that:	**Opponents of nationalisation argue that:**
▪ taking businesses and industries into government control means that there will be more emphasis on achieving benefits for society rather than for private individuals alone ▪ it enables greater simplification of production and distribution by having one provider rather than many.	▪ nationalised businesses have less incentive to be efficient because the government will usually cover any losses made ▪ nationalised businesses tend to focus on what their managers think should be produced rather than on what the market requires.

In the Caribbean there is a divide between those economies that have sought to follow the private sector model (such as Barbados and Trinidad, which have adopted a free enterprise model similar to the US and Canada), and those that have preferred to follow nationalised models more typical of neighbouring Cuba and Venezuela.

Summary table

	Nationalisation	Privatisation
Sector	Government sector	Private sector
Ownership	Public corporations (businesses owned by the government)	Companies (businesses owned by shareholders)
Political justification	To secure public production and service for all	To secure freedom of choice and enhance enterprise
Commercial justification	To secure benefits of regulated large-scale enterprise	To create greater efficiency resulting from self-interest

Summary questions

1 What are the main types of business in the private sector and who owns them? What are the main types of business in the public sector and who owns them?

2 What are the main benefits to be gained from privatisation of a business or industry? What are the main benefits to be gained from the nationalisation of a business or industry?

3 In your country, is the current emphasis more towards privatisation or nationalisation? Why do you think this is the case?

KEY TERMS

Physical capital: goods that are used to make other goods (e.g. machinery and equipment). Another type of capital, financial capital, will be discussed in 3.1.

Did you know?

The A in SMART can also stand for Assignable. This means tasking someone to take responsibility for achieving an objective.

Did you know?

Businesses often make the mistake of setting unrealistic objectives that are either too difficult or too easy to achieve.

Objectives are specific outcomes that a business is trying to achieve. They provide a business with a sense of direction. Managers and other people working in the organisation need to know what the business's objectives are and how they can help the business to achieve them. Objectives can be short-term, medium-term or long-term. In the short term, a business seeks to establish itself, to win loyal customers and to survive. In the medium and long term it seeks to expand and grow. This involves investing in **physical capital** and developing new products and markets.

Objectives should be SMART, as shown in Table 1.9.1.

Table 1.9.1 *SMART objectives*

	Definition	Explanation
S	Specific	They must be clear and not confusing.
M	Measurable	They can be quantified using numbers (including percentages).
A	Agreed	They can be shared among the people who are working together and accepted by them.
R	Realistic	They are achievable given the resources (including people) and capabilities within an organisation.
T	Time-related	A time period needs to be set for achieving the objectives (for example, during the next year).

Goals and objectives

An important distinction can be made between goals and objectives. Goals are more general and relate to the end result that needs to be achieved, whereas objectives are more precise outlines of steps that need to be taken to secure a goal.

Goal

For example, a Caribbean company selling jet skis might have the general goal of becoming the market leader: that is, the company selling the most products.

Objective

SMART objectives for achieving this goal might include:

■ increasing sales from $100 million to $105 million by 31 December this year (Figure 1.9.1)

■ increasing the effectiveness of advertising so that the brand is recognised by over 50 per cent of potential customers by 31 January next year.

You can assess whether the above objectives are 'SMART' by using the checklist in Table 1.9.2.

Figure 1.9.1 *A specific objective might be to increase sales by a given amount*

Table 1.9.2 Checklist for assessing whether objectives are SMART

Is the objective specific?	▨ What are we selling?
	  ☐ Jet skis.
	▨ Where are we selling them?
	  ☐ In the Caribbean.
	▨ By how much do we want to increase sales?
	  ☐ From $100 million to $105 million.

Is the objective measurable?	▨ How can we quantify the objective?
	  ☐ By demonstrating that sales have increased from $100 million to $105 million by 31 December.
	  ☐ By demonstrating that the brand is recognised by over 50 per cent of potential customers by 31 January.

Is the objective assignable? Is the objective agreed?	▨ We can give responsibility for achieving the objective to the sales and marketing director, who can then assign responsibility for making given levels of sales to the sales staff and responsibility for improving brand recognition to the marketing team. ▨ These assignments must be agreed with the sales and marketing staff.
Is the objective realistic?	▨ Yes, provided we have the resources in place (for example, sales and marketing staff, sales information, compelling offers, etc.).
Is the objective time-related?	▨ Yes, the sales increase needs to be achieved by 31 December and brand awareness needs to be achieved by 31 January.

Did you know?

Organisations like to set objectives in the form of key performance indicators (KPIs). These measure specific aspects of performance, such as performance in reducing waste, improving the level of sales and reducing staff absences. See p30 for more detail.

Summary table

What are goals?	■ The end result that an organisation is working towards
What are objectives?	■ More precise ways of identifying what an organisation needs to do in order to achieve goals ■ Give managers and members of an organisation something more specific to strive towards ■ Need to be specific, measurable, agreed (or assignable), realistic and time-related
What are KPIs?	■ Key performance indicators ■ Sets of metrics related to each of the areas that a company considers to be important

Summary questions

1 Identify likely goals, objectives and KPIs for a company seeking to reduce the amount of waste and packaging that it creates.

2 Identify some SMART objectives that will help you to achieve a high grade in your CAPE Management of Business examinations.

3 What issues might arise if objectives are not specific, measurable, agreed, realistic or time-related?

4 Research online to find a Caribbean company's objectives. Assess to what extent they are SMART and if any improvements could be made.

On completion of this section, you should be able to:

- explain the importance of setting business objectives with regard to the hierarchy of objectives.

As we have seen, objectives are specific outcomes that a business is trying to achieve and which give it a sense of direction. Businesses usually look at objectives in a hierarchical way as shown in Table 1.10.1.

Table 1.10.1 *Hierarchy of business objectives*

Level of objective	Description	Who is responsible for creating them and delivering them?
Top-level objectives ▪ Vision ▪ Mission	Objectives related to the vision and mission of the organisation	Board of directors and the chair/chief executive
Strategic-level objectives	Objectives related to the organisation's key plans	Board and senior executives
Tactical-level objectives	Intermediate objectives that enable an organisation to achieve its strategic objectives	Middle management with senior management input
Operational objectives	Objectives that enable effective day-to-day operational activity	Those responsible for delivery of day-to-day targets

KEY TERMS

Vision: an aspirational picture of what an organisation would like to become in the future. A company's vision is often set out in a vision statement.

Mission: the purpose of an organisation. An organisation's mission is often set out in a mission statement.

Vision and mission

The **vision** of an organisation is a forward-looking projection of what an organisation can become. It should be designed to be inspirational. It should be easy to communicate and simple for the key stakeholders in an organisation to understand.

The **mission** of an organisation sets out the key purpose of an organisation. It is thus more focused on the present than a vision. The case study below outlines the Caribbean Examinations Council's top-level and strategic-level objectives.

CASE STUDY

The Caribbean Examinations Council (CXC)

CXC is an international organisation with a key role in delivering an internationally recognised examining system throughout the Caribbean. Its vision is to 'take examining to the next level'. Its mission is 'to provide the region with:

- syllabuses of the highest quality;
- valid and reliable examinations and certificates of international repute for students of all ages, abilities and interests;
- services to educational institutions in the development of syllabuses, examinations and examination administration in the most cost-effective way.'

The strategic objective of CXC is to create a world-class brand by becoming the main quality assurance and certification body in the region.

Figure 1.10.1 *The Caribbean Examination Council's vision is to 'take examining to the next level'*

The strategic plan to achieve this goal has three main components:
'staff development and engagement
organisational development
[the development of high-quality] products and services.'

1 How is CXC's vision forward looking?

2 What are CXC's strategic objectives?

3 What operational objectives could be set to help staff to work in an efficient way?

Strategic, tactical and operational objectives

Strategies are the ways in which an organisation achieves its mission. For example, CXC seeks to be a world-class brand and to be the main provider of examinations in the Caribbean through staff development, organisational development and the development of high-quality products and services. For business organisations, strategic objectives often relate to market position (for example, market leadership) and profitability.

Tactical objectives set out more clearly the **tactics** (means) required for meeting strategic objectives. CXC has tactical objectives related to the training of examiners and the development of world-class information technology systems for processing results. These tactical objectives help to secure the strategic objective of taking education through curriculum, syllabus and infrastructure development.

Operational objectives relate to the **operations** (day-to-day activities) of the organisation. In the case of CXC, operational objectives include checking that exam papers have been marked accurately and publishing examination results on time.

KEY TERMS

Strategies: plans that an organisation puts in place to meet objectives. Strategies have major resource implications for the organisation as a whole.

Tactics: broad approaches that an organisation takes to deliver strategies.

Operations: the grass-roots activities put in place to ensure that tactics and strategies are implemented.

Summary table

Type of objective	Features	
1 Vision	■ Top-level objectives ■ Relate to organisation	■ Broad in scope ■ Focused on the future
2 Mission	■ Top-level objectives ■ Set out purpose of organisation	■ Organisation-wide objectives
3 Strategic	■ Relate to key plans within the organisation ■ Focus on how the organisation will use major resources	
4 Tactical	■ Focus on intermediate steps to the delivery of strategies	
5 Operational	■ Relate to day-to-day activities	

Summary questions

1 What are objectives and why are they set at different levels within an organisation?

2 How do operational and tactical objectives help an organisation to achieve its mission?

3 Who is responsible for the following?

   a Establishing the mission of an organisation

   b Setting the strategic objectives within an organisation

   c Setting the operational objectives

1.11 Business ethics and corporate social responsibility

Specific objective

On completion of this section, you should be able to:

- explain the importance of ethics and corporate social responsibility in setting business objectives.

Did you know?

Most large companies set out a code of ethics. This is a written set of guidelines issued to help members of an organisation to act in ways which follow the ethical values of the organisation (e.g. to refuse bribes and to be fair and honest in business dealings).

Business ethics

Ethics are moral principles or a set of moral values held by an individual or a group that influence how individuals, groups and society behave. Ethical behaviour is behaviour that is considered to be correct and moral.

Business ethics are therefore moral values and principles applied in the world of business. Whether business owners and managers recognise it or not, all business decisions have an ethical dimension. Here are some of the ethical questions that a business might have to face:

- Should products that potentially damage the health of consumers, such as cigarettes, be withdrawn from the market?
- Should an organisation make sure that its business activities do not damage the environment?
- Should money be spent on providing wheelchair access to workplaces and retail outlets?
- Should an organisation reject a bribe given to secure an overseas contract?
- Should part-time staff be offered the same rights as full-time staff?
- Should a workplace crèche be provided for working parents?

An organisation that answers 'yes' to these questions may be described as operating in an ethical way.

A business should develop SMART ethical objectives, such as:

- '100 per cent of the products we supply will be sourced from ethical suppliers'
- 'we will pay employees above average market wages'
- 'we will recover 100 per cent of the waste we produce'.

Corporate social responsibility

Corporate social responsibility (CSR) is a term used to describe the social, charitable and community-focused responsibilities of business. The people who direct and manage the organisation are mainly responsible for its level of CSR.

Figure 1.11.1 shows the four levels of CSR to which an organisation can commit.

KEY TERMS

Corporate social responsibility: the responsibility of a company to society and the environment.

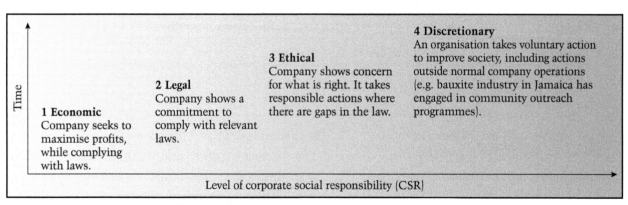

Figure 1.11.1 Levels of corporate social responsibility shown by a company may change over time

Figure 1.11.2 Earth Mother Botanicals is a skincare product company with ethical principles

CASE STUDY

Earth Mother Botanicals

Earth Mother Botanicals is a Barbadian company that manufactures 'green' products. Organic and natural materials are sourced locally with minimal environment impact. The company grows and harvests most of the herbs, fruits and flowers used to manufacture soaps and chemical-free, natural skin care products. It sources its handmade packaging from craftspeople and uses organic techniques to maintain a chemical-free environment and minimise water use. Its environmental goals are to have zero waste and to sell products that sustain resources and the environment. A percentage of its sales revenue is donated to the University Sea Turtle Research Project.

1 What evidence is there to show that Earth Mother Botanicals is committed to CSR?

2 What questions would you want to ask the owners to test their CSR credentials?

3 Where would you place Earth Mother Botanicals in Figure 1.11.1 in terms of its level of CSR? Justify your decision.

Summary table

Term	Definition	Example
Business ethics	Doing the 'right thing' morally in terms of business decisions	Using local solutions to problems rather than foreign ones
Corporate social responsibility (CSR)	Charitable and social support of communities and society by business	Minimising waste and pollution and supporting good causes

Summary questions

1 Provide three examples of business decisions that involve CSR.

2 Compare and contrast two different approaches to CSR.

3 How might an ethical approach support business success?

On completion of this section, you should be able to:

■ explain the importance of ethics and social responsibility in setting business objectives with regard to stakeholder obligations and good corporate governance.

Stakeholder: an individual, organisation or government with an interest in the decisions that a company makes.

Stakeholders

Stakeholders are individuals or groups who have an interest in a business and the decisions that it makes. The stakeholder map in Figure 1.12.1 shows key individuals and groups with an interest in Earth Mother Botanicals (see the case study in 1.11).

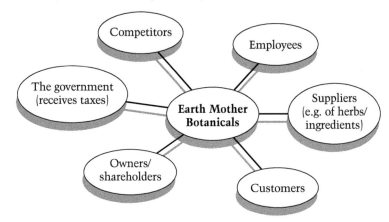

Figure 1.12.1 *Stakeholders with an interest in Earth Mother Botanicals*

You can see that there is a range of stakeholders that the company must consider:

■ Suppliers expect to receive fair prices from Earth Mother Botanicals.

■ Customers want high-quality products that meet their needs.

■ The owners/shareholders want to receive a share of the profits.

■ The government expects to receive taxes on profits paid on time.

■ Employees expect job security, good pay and conditions, and training and development opportunities.

■ Competitors expect a business to compete with them in a fair and lawful way.

With so many different stakeholders involved in a business, there can sometimes be conflicts of interest between them. For example, increased wages for employees will result in reduced profitability for the owners of the company.

Corporate governance: the processes by which the board of directors ensures accountability, fairness and transparency in an organisation. Good corporate governance involves directing a business in an efficient and responsible way.

Corporate governance

Corporate governance is the system of rules and practices by which companies are directed and controlled to ensure accountability, fairness and transparency. The board of directors is responsible for the corporate governance of a company. The board and the auditors (who check the financial reporting and internal controls of a company) are appointed by the shareholders. This gives shareholders the opportunity to ensure that the board introduces a good governance structure.

Often, the interests of those controlling a company (the directors and the company's management) differ significantly from those providing the company's capital (the shareholders). Generally, shareholders are not involved in running a business. Instead they appoint the board and rely on the directors they have appointed and the company's managers to run it for them.

Good governance means making sure that a company not only complies with legal requirements but also balances the expectations of all stakeholders in an appropriate way. Good governance and corporate social responsibility (see 1.11) go hand in hand. Good governance involves:

- complying with the legal requirements associated with running a company
- only taking risks that are acceptable to key stakeholders
- focusing on giving customers what they want
- paying attention to the needs of employees, suppliers and the communities in which the company operates
- respecting society and the environment.

In some smaller Caribbean companies there is often concern that the board of directors, selected by a majority of shareholders, may ignore the wishes of minority shareholders. As a result, decisions and power may be concentrated in the hands of a relatively small number of individuals.

An ethical company takes into account not only the interests of majority and minority shareholders but also the interests of a range of other important stakeholders, including employees, customers and the community.

Effective corporate governance can be achieved by:

- having independent non-executive directors on the boards of companies. These are individuals who are not concerned with day-to-day management and who are therefore independent (rather than being appointed, for example, by a majority shareholder)
- ensuring that directors consider the interests of all stakeholders rather than a specific stakeholder. Many countries have voluntary codes of corporate governance to ensure this happens.

Figure 1.12.2 *The board of directors is responsible for the corporate governance of a company*

Did you know?

The World Bank defines corporate governance as being 'concerned with holding the balance between economic and social goals and between individual and communal goals … The aim is to align as nearly as possible the interests of individuals, corporations and society'.

Summary table

Term	Definition	Examples
Stakeholders	Individuals or groups with an interest in a business and the decisions it makes	Shareholders seeking high dividends Employees seeking secure jobs
Good corporate governance	A system for the direction and running of a company that takes into account the interests of all stakeholders rather than just a narrow group	A company that is well run and enables the views of all stakeholders to be considered

Summary questions

1 For a Caribbean company with which you are familiar, identify the different groups of stakeholders with an interest in the company. In each case, identify their stake in the company.

2 Identify a company that you believe demonstrates good corporate governance. Justify your choice by showing how it demonstrates good governance.

3 What is the role of independent non-executive directors within a company?

Business decision making

Decision making is the process of selecting which course of action to take. Every day a business is faced with possible alternative courses of action and therefore decisions that need to be made. There are different types of decisions that a business needs to make:

- **Strategic decisions:** These are major decisions, often long-term, concerning the environment in which the business operates and its resources (for example, whether to invest in Guyana or Jamaica).
- **Tactical decisions:** These are often more short- and medium-term decisions that enable strategic goals to be achieved.
- **Operational decisions:** These are concerned with the day-to-day running of operations.

Before any decision is made, an organisation needs to analyse the various alternatives using a variety of criteria. This is called **multi-criteria decision analysis (MCDA)**. MCDA is part of the larger process of multi-criteria decision making (MCDM). Once the various alternatives have been analysed, a final decision is made based on the alternative that best meets the criteria.

Information for decision making

Information is required in order to make a decision. This information needs to be:

- accurate
- relevant
- timely
- cost effective
- usable.

Accurate

The information provided for decision making needs to reflect reality. For example, it is essential to have accurate costings and projections of revenues when making a financial business decision. Inaccuracy can lead to the wrong decision being made – such as a less profitable option being chosen over a more profitable one because costs have been estimated incorrectly.

Timely

Figures need to be up to date or relevant to the time period to which the decision is related. Using out-of-date figures will result in a decision being made that is relevant to the past but irrelevant to the present or future.

Relevant

Information needs to be appropriate to the current needs and potential needs of users. For example, if costs that are not relevant to a decision are included, this may result in the costs being overestimated.

Cost effective

Information gathering needs to be carried out in a **cost-effective** way. If the cost of collecting information is too high, this could have a negative impact on the decision being made. For example, carrying out detailed market research may be too expensive. Instead, it might be possible to obtain reliable information from published data (provided they are reliable and accurate).

Usable

The information that is collected and presented should be easy to use and communicate, so that it can be understood and accessed easily.

KEY TERMS

Market research: the systematic gathering, recording and analysis of data about the market for a good or service.

CASE STUDY

Information for a seafood restaurant

Michael has been able to acquire a site to develop a new seafood restaurant in St Lucia. He believes that a focus on specialist seafood dishes will enable him to gain a competitive advantage. He wants a **market research** company to carry out some research prior to developing the idea fully. In particular, he wants the research company to identify an attractive menu and suitable price points that will enable the restaurant to be a success. He has received the following quotes from two companies:

- Online Marketing will sample 10,000 regular restaurant goers using its existing online database. The database was constructed two years ago and covers consumer buying patterns at that time, including a survey of restaurant habits of consumers across the Caribbean. The survey was not constructed specifically to test the seafood concept, but there are sufficient data to be able to extract relevant information. It will take Online Marketing three months to carry out the research and analysis, and it will cost $10,000.

- St Lucia Surveys will charge $2,000 for carrying out a survey of 1,000 restaurant users in St Lucia, including a representative number of tourists. It will take the company one month to carry out the survey, and an additional three months to collate and present the results. St Lucia Surveys will focus specifically on the seafood concept, using questions that have been agreed with Michael. It will carry out a pilot survey before testing its findings in the form of a survey of restaurant users.

1 Compare and contrast the two offers and assess each quote on the accuracy, timeliness, relevance, cost effectiveness and usability of the information.

2 Which of the two companies would you use and why?

Figure 1.13.1 *Market research is useful when setting up a new business but it may prove too costly*

Summary table

Information needs to be:	Description
Accurate	How well does the information provided represent reality?
Timely	Is the information current?
Relevant	To what degree does the information meet the needs of users?
Cost effective	Do the benefits of the information outweigh the costs of obtaining it?
Usable	Is the information understandable and accessible?

Summary questions

1 Define the term 'decision making'.

2 What are the essential features of information required for decision making?

On completion of this section, you should be able to:

- discuss the process of decision making in business organisations in terms of quantitative and qualitative decision making.

Figure 1.14.1 *Quantitative information provides 'hard facts' about levels and trends, but it often needs to be backed up by qualitative analysis*

Business decision-makers can use either a quantitative or a qualitative approach to decision making, or a combination of the two. Quantitative decisions are based on factual information and are considered to be more objective, whereas qualitative decisions are based on opinion and are considered to be more subjective.

Quantitative decision making

Quantitative approaches use numerical data that can be quantified. This **quantitative information** includes sales figures, profit calculations, information about costs, information from market research, calculations of the return on investment, and calculations of the time needed to complete a project.

Managers like to work with numbers because they give a clear indication of business performance. As discussed in 1.9, **key performance indicators (KPIs)** are indicators that can be measured to assess business performance. KPIs allow the board and executive managers to assess how well the company is doing. Some KPIs that might be measured in a retailing company are:

- level of sales
- sales growth
- market share of the company – sales of a product made by the company as a percentage of the total market
- profit level
- profit growth
- total amount of retailing space (floor space) the company holds
- number of stores the company has
- number of employees and employee turnover
- level of customer satisfaction (measured through customer satisfaction surveys)
- number of customer returns and customer complaints.

Quantitative information can be used to inform decisions about:

- which product lines and markets to concentrate on
- which products and markets to cut back on
- specific aspects of the business that need particular attention, such as reducing the number of customer complaints.

Qualitative decision making

Qualitative information reflects opinions, thoughts and feelings, rather than involving numbers. Qualitative information is therefore difficult to measure. For example, if a company dismisses some of its workers, how can it measure the impact on those who lose their jobs and the impact on morale of the workers who continue to work in the company? Another important qualitative consideration is public perception. How will a particular decision impact on the perception that the public (and consumers) have of a brand or company?

Market research can be used to collect qualitative information by encouraging participants to talk about their thoughts and feelings. Qualitative research asks questions such as 'what?' and 'why?' to gain more descriptive answers, whereas quantitative research asks questions such as 'how often?' and 'how much?' to establish quantity.

CASE STUDY

The takeover

Villas with Views is a small family-owned hotel chain in Trinidad and Tobago. It employs 300 staff and managers who are all based locally. The company sources all of its materials, equipment and supplies in Trinidad and Tobago. The company is a private company with the majority of shares being owned by the founding family. However, there are three other shareholders. Recently a foreign multinational company, which is expanding in the Caribbean, has made a **takeover** bid with the intention of growing its market share. The multinational company intends to close down some of the smaller hotels and retain the larger ones. This will lead to the loss of up to 75 jobs. The multinational company has offered to buy the shares at double the price they are currently worth. It believes that it can increase the occupancy rates of the hotels from the current figure of about 60 per cent to a figure of nearer 90 per cent. It will source more supplies from the US and will bring in senior managers from the foreign parent company.

1 What quantitative and what qualitative information should be taken into account by the Villas with Views board of directors in deciding whether to accept the takeover bid?

2 Explain how good governance needs to be taken into consideration when making the decision.

3 In making the decision, how much weight should be given to quantitative factors and how much to qualitative factors?

KEY TERMS

Takeover: where a company buys at least 51 per cent of the shares of another business in order to secure a controlling interest.

Summary table

Quantitative decisions	Qualitative decisions
Based on numbers and statistics	Based on thoughts and feelings (non-numerical criteria)
Considered to be more objective	Considered to be more subjective
Based on calculations of the size and growth of KPIs – enabling measurement	Based on the more subjective feelings of decision-makers

☑ *Exam tip*

When writing essays you should write clear, coherent prose and avoid the use of bullets.

Summary questions

1 Which kinds of decision lend themselves more readily to a quantitative approach and which lend themselves to a qualitative approach?

2 What are KPIs and what sorts of things can they measure?

3 What are the benefits of combining a quantitative and qualitative approach to decision making?

On completion of this section, you should be able to:

- discuss the process of decision making in business organisations in terms of the stages of decision making.

There are six stages to decision making that are relevant to most business decisions. This is the case whether the decision is big (for example, decisions involving millions of dollars of investment) or small (for example, a small operational decision), as shown in Table 1.15.1.

Table 1.15.1 *The decision-making process applied to the example of setting up a new hotel*

Stage in the decision-making process	Example
1 Definition of the problem	Is there scope to set up a new hotel in St Vincent?
2 Data collection – primary research (new research) or secondary research (research that has already been published)	Research into: ■ costs of building ■ nature of competition ■ likely revenues ■ prices that could be charged ■ length of season ■ running costs ■ finance ■ risks of hurricanes.
3 Analysis and evaluation of the data	Assessment of: ■ whether revenues outweigh costs ■ how long it will take to make a profit ■ risks and uncertainties.
4 Formulation of alternative strategies	Consider: ■ buying an existing hotel ■ building a new hotel ■ size of the hotel ■ postponing the decision.
5 Implementation	Build a small hotel on a large site with a view to future expansion.
6 Evaluation	Study results for the first five years for: ■ profitability ■ risk ■ popularity ■ occupancy rates.

Did you know?

The six stages of decision making outlined in Table 1.15.1 can be applied to many different types of business decision, from investing in new products or equipment (see the case study) to whether to take over another company. The six basic stages are the same whatever the type of decision to be made.

The case study below illustrates the six stages of the decision-making process in relation to new product development.

CASE STUDY

Developing new products at Crop Chem Ltd

Crop Chem Ltd is a chemical company that uses science to develop useful products, particularly products for increasing crop yields. Any new product developed at Crop Chem Ltd goes through six stages that mirror the six stages of decision making:

1 **Definition of the problem:** The product needs to help farmers in the Caribbean to increase crop yields. Research and development is required to make this possible. It takes the company 5–10 years to research and develop a new product, such as a crop spray, for use by farmers.

2 **Data collection:** Crop Chem Ltd mainly collects primary data from testing chemicals for their biological activity. Each chemical is tested 15 times in the laboratory. The chemicals are then tested in a greenhouse. Once the chemicals pass initial tests they are then tested in the field. They are sprayed on fields of crops for a number of years to discover their impact. An important aspect of data collection is finding out the impact of the formulations on the environment.

3 **Analysis and evaluation:** Using the data collected from all of the testing outlined above, the company is able to evaluate the effectiveness of different formulations on crop yields. A range of criteria are used, such as impact on crop yield, impact on the environment and the cost of the product relative to crop yield. It is then possible to evaluate the likely benefits and returns from using different formulations.

4 **Formulation of alternative strategies:** The company is now in a position to identify alternative markets in which to sell the products that it has developed. Crop Chem's range of products protects a whole range of crops or their seeds, such as cotton, cocoa and sweet peppers. It is important to identify which markets to focus on and how to engage with farmers (consumers) in those markets.

5 **Implementation:** Having developed crop protection treatments, Crop Chem Ltd needs to work with farmers and agricultural advisers in different parts of the Caribbean to promote different types of crop treatment and to provide appropriate technical advice on the use of different products.

6 **Evaluation:** Increasing crop yields as a result of agricultural research involves a continual process of evaluation. It is important to evaluate the effectiveness of crop protection formulations that farmers use over a long period of time. This involves evaluating yields in different climates and soil types to find out the success rate of different formulations. New formulations are constantly being developed, some of which will replace existing formulations.

1 Why are the steps in the decision-making process outlined above so important?

2 What are the most important steps in decision making?

Summary table

Stages of decision making	Description
1 Setting objective and outlining problem	■ Identify the problem to be solved and how it fits with your objectives
2 Data collection	■ Gather primary and secondary data
3 Analysis and evaluation	■ Interpret the data and weigh up the importance of different aspects
4 Formulation of different strategies	■ Identify strategies based on the information collected ■ Weigh up the pros and cons of each to select a strategy
5 Implementation	■ Carry out the chosen decision
6 Evaluation	■ Assess how effective the decision is and what improvements can be made

Summary questions

1 Create a circular diagram to show the six stages of decision making. Make sure that you can explain each stage.

2 Apply the decision-making cycle to a business decision of your choice.

3 What are the main ways of collecting data for decision making?

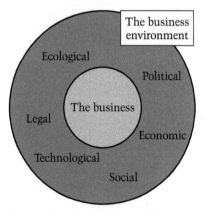

Figure 1.16.1 *Businesses use PESTLE analysis to examine the external environment in which they operate*

Did you know?

Sometimes PESTLE is shortened to PEST (political, economic, social and technological) or SLEPT (social, legal, economic, political and technological). It is a good idea to use PESTLE, as it will remind you of all the factors that should be considered.

PESTLE analysis

There are many outside influences that shape the decisions that a business makes. It is important for a business to analyse the external environment on a regular basis to identify changes that will impact on decision making. Businesses use **PESTLE analysis**, as illustrated in Figure 1.16.1, to do this.

Political, governmental and legal factors

The government and legislature are important influences on business. Governments create the legal framework in which businesses operate, as well as taxing and subsidising some business activities. For this reason, legal factors are often included as a 'political' factor. A change in government (as a result of an election) can lead to different policies for business. Some political parties are more supportive of enterprise (for example, reducing business taxes), while others are less supportive (for example, introducing regulations to limit business activity). Frequent changes in the law, including environmental and health and safety regulations, mean that businesses need to review legislation frequently and ensure that they are operating to the required standards.

Economic factors

The state of the national, Caribbean and global economies has a strong impact on business. Businesses find it more difficult to make sales when the economy is growing slowly (recession) than when the economy is growing quickly (boom). Other economic factors that affect businesses include interest rates (the cost of borrowing money) and the rate of inflation (the rate of increase in prices).

Social, demographic and cultural factors

Society and culture change over time. For example, the structure of the population changes (for example, there may be an ageing population), or society's buying patterns may change (there are more people using the internet for purchases).

Technological factors

The modern world is characterised by rapidly changing technologies, such as:

■ modes of transport (for example, low-cost air transport and the development of electric and solar-powered cars)

■ information technology (for example, laptop computers)

■ methods of production (for example, automatic robotic production lines).

Ecological factors

Humans are part of a fragile ecological system. Business activity can, and often does, impact on the environment and on other species. Increasingly, governments, consumers and pressure groups require businesses to take account of the environment. For example, businesses may be required to pay to dispose of waste and harmful substances, or they may be taxed on the amount of pollution they create.

Human and natural constraints

In addition, it is important to recognise that decision making is limited by the ability of individuals to make decisions. Decision making may be distorted by emotional influences, or a lack of information may result in poor decisions being made.

Using PESTLE analysis

A business should use PESTLE analysis to determine how the external environment will impact on specific decisions. The business should then develop tactics and strategies for coping with, and perhaps taking advantage of, changes in the external environment. For example, if the economy is in recession, the business might be able to produce better-value products that people will still be able to afford. If social and cultural patterns are changing, the firm might be able to produce products that better match its new customers' requirements and tastes, such as tablet computers and mobile devices that allow people to access the internet while on the move. If technology is changing, the business can employ the new technologies to its advantage.

Figure 1.16.2 The development of the cellphone as a means of communication is a key technological and social/cultural change that has impacted on consumer buying patterns and producers' decisions

Summary table

Main influences on business decisions	Description
Political/governmental/legal factors	■ Changes in government policy ■ Changes in the laws that affect business
Economic factors	■ Changes in the economy (for example, recession/slow growth/fast growth) ■ Changes in economic indicators, such as interest and inflation rates
Social, demographic and cultural factors	■ Changes in population and in society (for example, population growth and lifestyle changes)
Technological factors	■ Arrival of new technologies and production methods
Ecological/environmental changes	■ Changes in expectations about a business's responsibility for the environment
Natural and human influences	■ Limitations on decision making resulting from human fallibility and lack of information

Summary questions

1 What is PESTLE analysis and how does it help in business decision making?

2 For a product of your choice, use PESTLE to identify factors that may impact on a decision to expand production of the product within the Caribbean.

CASE STUDY

Carrying out PESTLE analysis

You are a business analyst for a Caribbean marketing cooperative that markets a range of agricultural products. You need to carry out PESTLE analysis for the cooperative. Answer the questions below:

1 Identify at least one legal change that is likely to impact on the marketing of agricultural products in your country.

2 What key economic factors are currently changing that will impact on the sale and marketing of agricultural products?

3 What key social and cultural changes are taking place that are having an impact on the consumption of agricultural products in your country?

4 Which technological factors are changing? How will these changes impact on the marketing and sale of agricultural products?

5 What are the key changes to ecological and environmental considerations? How will these impact on agriculture?

KEY TERMS

Globalisation: the process whereby products, people and capital are highly mobile across the globe.

Multinational: a company that operates in at least two countries and has operating units in other countries.

Did you know?

Economies of scale are the advantages of being a large company which result from being able to produce high volumes of output at low unit cost.

Table 1.17.1 *Ways of creating a foreign subsidiary*

Greenfield investment – parent company sets up a new plant or unit in the overseas country
Example: Foreign hotel chains have built new hotels in the Caribbean
Acquisition of an existing firm
Example: Foreign hotel chains have bought up existing hotels in the Caribbean

Globalisation

In a global economy, goods can be produced in many different places and transported for sale on the other side of the world. **Globalisation** involves the free movement of goods, capital, labour and technology, and results in intense competition because products and resources can be marketed all over the world.

Globalisation presents both an opportunity and a challenge for Caribbean economies. Traditionally, Caribbean economies have relied heavily on the export of agricultural products, particularly to the UK and other European Union countries as well as to the US. Sugar and bananas were key exports for many countries, including Trinidad, the Windward Islands, Guyana and Jamaica. However, competition from larger South American countries has required a reorientation of Caribbean economies from agricultural production towards industrialisation and the development of service industries.

Multinational companies

A **multinational** company is a company that operates in two or more countries. Typically, multinationals operate in many countries. Some multinationals, such as giant car companies, have manufacturing plants in a number of countries, and market and sell their products in over 100 countries. The products of multinationals are globally recognised.

Globalisation offers large companies the opportunity to produce products on a large scale and to exploit vast economies of scale. For example, companies are able to produce vehicles on a huge scale in car plants in Brazil and Mexico, where land and labour are relatively cheap. Advertising and marketing literature, which is standardised to keep costs down, is then used to help market these products through dealerships throughout the Americas and the Caribbean region.

Large-scale production, employed by multinationals, enables:

- low-cost mass production
- low-cost mass marketing
- low-cost mass advertising
- competitive pricing
- global recognition
- mass sales.

Becoming part of a multinational

Subsidiaries

A company can become a multinational by owning a minimum of 50 per cent of the shares in at least one overseas business. The overseas business then becomes a partly owned or fully owned subsidiary. A foreign subsidiary can be created in one of two ways as shown in Table 1.17.1.

Joint ventures

A multinational may also enter into a joint venture to grow its business internationally. In a joint venture, companies based in two countries create and share ownership of a new company. Caribbean entrepreneurs have set up joint ventures with overseas partners. For example, Barbados Port Inc. has set up a joint venture with Royal Caribbean Cruises Ltd and Barbados-based company SMI Infrastructure Solutions Inc. to build a new cruise terminal in Bridgetown, Barbados. The Caribbean entrepreneur brings local knowledge and contacts, while the foreign partner provides additional capital and access to global markets.

Benefits and drawbacks of multinational companies

Table 1.17.2 outlines the benefits and drawbacks of multinationals to the Caribbean.

Table 1.17.2 The benefits and drawbacks of multinationals to the Caribbean

Benefits	Drawbacks
Bring new capital, technologies and ideas to the local economy – new capital is called **inward investment**	Increased competition for small companies from large-scale, cheaper production
Create new job opportunities in the Caribbean	Loss of jobs in the Caribbean
Provide a wider range of products for local consumers	Loss of some local products that are replaced by global brands
Help to modernise the local economy and link it into global developments and trends	Dependency of the local economy on foreign capital
	Government loses some of its powers to control business activity

Figure 1.17.1 Williams Industries constructs hurricane-resistant buildings, such as shopping complexes, throughout the Caribbean

CASE STUDY

Williams Industries, Barbados

Williams Industries is a good example of a multinational based and operating in the Caribbean. The company was set up in Barbados in 1975 with the mission of producing custom designed, high-quality, hurricane-resistant solutions for metal buildings. Since that time, Williams Industries has shipped prefabricated buildings and components to almost every Caribbean country and provided the technical expertise to construct them. All of these buildings (including churches, schools, retail stores, factories, warehouses, hotels, offices and sports complexes) have proved to be hurricane resistant. Williams Industries therefore provides a multinational solution to a specific problem – providing great buildings that can withstand hurricanes. Williams Industries has joint ventures and subsidiaries in a number of Caribbean territories.

1 In what ways is Williams Industries a multinational company?

2 What benefits does Williams Industries provide for territories in the Caribbean?

Summary table

Opportunities for the Caribbean business community resulting from globalisation	■ Access for Caribbean organisations to wider markets and new technologies ■ Access to more capital ■ Opportunity to partner with established foreign enterprises
Threats for the Caribbean business community resulting from globalisation	■ Increased competition from overseas multinationals ■ Dependency on foreign capital

Summary questions

1 Identify at least three multinational companies that operate in your country. Where else do they operate? Why should they be classified as multinational organisations?

2 What are the key benefits and drawbacks of having a specific multinational company operating in your country?

On completion of this section, you should be able to:

■ evaluate the role of the government in globalisation and its impact on Caribbean business organisations.

Figure 1.18.1 *CARICOM encourages the development of Caribbean-based multinationals whilst also trying to attract foreign multinationals*

Did you know?

By 2013, China had become the third-largest investor in the Caribbean (after the US and the Netherlands). Most of the investment has been in industries associated with the extraction of natural resources, such as bauxite in Guyana, and aluminium in Trinidad and Tobago. Other Chinese investment has included the development of a beachfront resort in the Dominican Republic and the building of a cricket stadium in Dominica.

KEY TERMS

CARICOM: the Caribbean Community and Common Market is an organisation made up of 15 Caribbean nations and dependencies that promotes economic integration and operates as a free trade area/single market.

Government plays two main roles in globalisation:

■ facilitator and enabler
■ creator of legal frameworks.

Government: facilitator and enabler of globalisation

As part of a major strategy for the development of the Caribbean, governments have opened up their economies and invited (or allowed) overseas companies to invest in plants and facilities. Historically, the Caribbean has been linked through trade to the UK and North and South America, but in recent years governments have tried to establish other global links to bring in capital and create jobs. There has, for example, been a substantial increase in foreign direct investment from China, particularly in those Caribbean countries that are rich in natural resources. Individual Caribbean governments have also developed stronger international relationships with partners such as the US, the European Union and China. At the same time, governments in the region have developed CARICOM (see below), which has promoted greater cooperation and created a stronger regional trading bloc.

The Caribbean Community (CARICOM)

CARICOM is an organisation of 15 Caribbean nations and dependencies with the purpose of promoting regional economic integration and cooperation. In 2001, the signing of the revised Treaty of Chaguaramas was a step towards the creation of a single market and economy in the region to encourage prosperity in a globalised world. CARICOM enables Caribbean economies to integrate their production systems and markets to make best use of existing resources.

Access to larger regional markets enables producers in member countries to benefit from economies of scale – for example, St Vincent and Trinidad are able to export bottled water on a large scale to tourist islands, as well as selling it on cruise ships. Companies that previously saw themselves as being Trinidadian, Guyanese or Jamaican may now see themselves as Caribbean, competing in a single marketplace. The creation of CARICOM has therefore not only helped to promote the development of Caribbean-based multinationals such as Williams Industries (building construction) and Sandals (hotels and resorts), it has also helped to modernise Caribbean economies in such a way as to attract overseas multinationals. Overseas multinationals that set up in the Caribbean are able to export freely within the single CARICOM market.

The development of the Caribbean Single Market and Economy (CSME) (see 1.21) is a key purpose of CARICOM. It will allow the increased circulation of:

■ goods
■ services
■ agreed categories of people
■ capital.

Government: creator of necessary legal frameworks to support globalisation

Governments also play a key role in encouraging foreign multinationals to invest in the Caribbean. Foreign companies assess the regulatory environment to ensure that it provides conditions within which they can operate. Laws that reduce the amount of paperwork required to set up a business, laws that enforce contracts through the courts, and laws that allow international trading and flows of foreign exchange make the economy more attractive.

CASE STUDY

Ease of Doing Business Index

The World Bank has created an **Ease of Doing Business Index** that ranks countries from 1 to 185. A high ranking means that regulations for businesses are simpler and they have more protection. This ranking provides a good indicator for international companies. On an international scale, Singapore and Hong Kong are at the top of the table and Haiti is near the bottom. Ten factors are used to create the index:

1 ease of starting a business
2 dealing with construction permits
3 paying taxes
4 enforcing contracts
5 registering property
6 protecting investors
7 getting electricity
8 getting credit
9 trading across borders
10 resolving insolvency.

In 2012 St Lucia came 53rd in the index and Antigua and Barbuda came 63rd.

1 Search for the Ease of Doing Business Index online and find out where other Caribbean economies rank.

2 Which of the criteria used for ranking relate to things that are under government control?

Summary table

Role of government	Examples
Facilitating/enabling globalisation	■ Opening up the economy to foreign investment ■ Creating pan-Caribbean organisations such as CARICOM
Creating legal frameworks to support globalisation	■ Creating laws that reduce the paperwork in setting up a business ■ Provision of legally enforceable business contracts

KEY TERMS

Ease of Doing Business Index: an index created by the World Bank to show the ease of doing business in particular countries.

Summary questions

1 How can the government help to encourage foreign investment in a specific economy?

2 How can Caribbean governments work together to encourage greater integration into a global economy?

3 What are the key criteria used in the Ease of Doing Business Index? Why might a foreign multinational company study this index before deciding where to locate one of its operations?

The impact of globalisation: consumer behaviour

On completion of this section, you should be able to:

■ evaluate the impact of globalisation on Caribbean business organisations in terms of the impact on consumer behaviour.

Figure 1.19.1 *Consumers can choose to drink water that is sourced locally or imported from thousands of miles away*

Today, Caribbean consumers have acccss to a great variety of goods and services – some are sourced from local producers, some from producers elsewhere in the Caribbean and others from around the globe. Consumers can therefore make a choice not only about which goods to buy, but also about the origin of the goods: that is, where they come from. For example, you can choose to drink water from the tap, you can purchase bottled water produced from fresh springs in the Caribbean, or you may choose to purchase water that has been bottled in France, the US, Canada or another country.

Benefits of globalisation to consumers

More choice

Many of the products that we consume come in different varieties and brands. Globalisation provides us with more varieties and brands from which to choose. For example, you might buy a shampoo or haircare product produced a few miles away or one produced in another region of the world. The car market is a good example of the choices provided as a result of globalisation, with many international manufacturers (such as Peugeot and Renault from France, Mercedes and Volkswagen from Germany, General Motors from the US, Tata from India, and Honda and Toyota from Japan) offering a range of cars of different sizes and shapes, and with a variety of engine capacities. Global markets allow consumers to benefit from greater choice and higher standards of living.

Competitive pricing

Globalisation introduces more companies to the market and, because both international and national companies are competing for your dollars, it brings down the price of many products. Multinational companies also benefit from global economies of scale, enabling them to produce in bulk at a lower cost. Some of these cost savings are passed on to the consumer because the companies are in competition with each other. Consumers are looking for good value for money, so producers are forced into providing global products at affordable prices.

Improved quality

Being able to access a wide range of products sourced from across the globe enables consumers to select those brands and varieties that they perceive as being of better 'quality'. In business, the term 'quality' refers to fitness for purpose. A 'quality' product meets or surpasses the needs of consumers. Global competition forces domestic producers to increase the quality of their products. Raising quality involves listening to consumers (for example, through market research) and delivering products in line with their requirements.

Disadvantages of globalisation to consumers

Reduction in choice

In markets that are dominated by one or more multinationals there can be a reduction in choice. For example, foreign-owned banks may dominate the financial sector of a Caribbean economy, thereby reducing the choice to customers. Similarly, a foreign hotel chain may buy up local hotels and focus on international tourists at the expense of local holidaymakers.

Higher prices

If there is a reduction in competition, international products with higher prices may become more established in a market, making it more expensive for local consumers. Also, because many Caribbean economies have high levels of tourism, the tourist dollar may push up prices, making many goods more expensive for local consumers.

Reduced quality

Having defined quality as 'fitness for purpose', it should be clear that if choice is reduced through the monopolisation of a market then the overall effect might be a reduction in quality of some goods and services, as businesses have no incentive to improve the quality of their output.

Responsibility

Globalisation gives customers greater responsibility. They have the opportunity and the ability to make choices about which products to buy or not to buy. By opting for international brands, consumers are to a certain extent choosing 'globalisation'. Although global markets bring disadvantages, they also provide the opportunity for consumers to benefit from greater choice and higher living standards.

Governments and consumer groups have a responsibility to protect consumers. For example, governments can, and often do, place restrictions on foreign entry into Caribbean markets to protect jobs and prevent poor-quality products being sold. They can also use import taxes to favour domestic products and to ensure that prices and trading practices are fair. A key organisation in the Caribbean is the Caribbean Consumer Council, a group set up to promote the interests of consumers and protect them from malpractices of producers, including unsafe products and inflated pricing.

Summary table

Advantages of globalisation	Disadvantages of globalisation
■ Greater choice	■ Restricted choice
■ Lower prices	■ Higher prices
■ Better quality	■ Reduced quality

Summary questions

1 How does globalisation give Caribbean consumers greater choice?

2 What are the benefits of globalisation for Caribbean consumers?

3 What are the disadvantages of globalisation for Caribbean consumers?

CASE STUDY

Choice of commercial banks in Trinidad

In Trinidad the three largest banks manage over 70 per cent of bank assets. Of the eight banks operating in Trinidad, six of them are foreign owned. The banks engage in a range of activities from handling customer accounts to providing business loans and even managing pension arrangements for customers.

1 To what extent is a Trinidadian provided with choice when deciding with whom to bank?

2 What sorts of considerations might customers need to bear in mind when choosing a particular bank?

3 What are the likely advantages and disadvantages to customers of having foreign-owned banks operating in Trinidad?

On completion of this section, you should be able to:

- evaluate the impact of globalisation on Caribbean business organisations in terms of opportunities and threats for domestic business.

Did you know?

The pricing policies of domestic businesses have to take into account prices offered by international competitors. Local prices need to be broadly in line with the price of imported items. Prices should be lower if their quality is inferior or higher if their quality is superior.

Globalisation presents both an opportunity and a threat to domestic business.

Globalisation: opportunities for domestic business

Globalisation promotes:

- opportunities for domestic business to sell to a wider market, for example:
  - products such as Jamaican Blue Mountain coffee are sold in many countries across the globe
  - many national and international artists come to recording studios in the Caribbean, such as Geejam recording studios in Jamaica, to record music
  - the internet provides many opportunities for smaller Caribbean businesses to communicate with and sell to global customers
- specialisation – access to wider markets enables businesses to specialise and to develop a steady flow of revenue that makes them sustainable
- opportunities for international collaboration through setting up joint ventures with foreign companies: for example, a number of joint ventures have been set up between Trinidadian and Chinese companies for the extraction of energy reserves in the seas around Trinidad
- increased competition for local businesses, which can act as a spur for business improvement
- business opportunities for local subsidiaries and suppliers: for example, construction projects operated by foreign companies provide building projects for local contractors
- the provision of quality-assured supplies to local businesses. International companies usually need to gain international quality assurance certification for their products. For example, imported electrical equipment from the US, Japan, Korea and Europe meets rigorous international safety standards. As a result Caribbean businesses have the assurance of high-quality imported goods.

Figure 1.20.1 *Three-quarters of a million cruise ship passengers visit Barbados each year, which benefits the Barbados economy*

Globalisation: threats to domestic business

- Local businesses often suffer when foreign companies, building on international economies of scale and brand recognition, are able to offer better-quality products and products that are better value for money as a result of greater opportunities for market research.

- Using mass production, mass marketing and larger advertising budgets, foreign companies have considerable marketing advantages over domestic companies: for example, global brands can use advertising to win market share.

- International companies may be able to win favour with national governments by offering 'sweeteners' (for example by funding infrastructure programmes such as building roads that benefit local communities as well as the commercial operations of the multinational) and by providing employment: for example, global companies may attract skilled labour away from local companies by offering higher rewards.

Exam tip

Globalisation is an important concept so make sure that you can define it. When discussing the benefits and drawbacks ensure that you relate these to specific groups. For example, does the examiner want you to talk about the impact of globalisation on multinational companies, on the host country, on consumers, etc.? Typically the examiner will want you to discuss the impact on Caribbean companies, Caribbean governments and Caribbean consumers.

CASE STUDY

Cruise terminal in Barbados

Barbados has benefited economically from the development of the international cruise industry – with about three-quarters of a million passengers visiting Barbados each year. In 2012 a new joint venture was created between Barbados Port Inc., a Barbadian company called SMI Infrastructure Solutions Inc. and Royal Caribbean Cruises Ltd (the world's second-largest cruise line) to build a new cruise terminal. The terminal will be built on 15 acres of land reclaimed from the sea. The government has encouraged the development.

1 What are the benefits to Barbados and the Barbados-based companies involved in the joint venture from the development of the cruise facility?

2 Are there any potential drawbacks from the development?

Summary table

Opportunities for domestic business	Threats to domestic business
■ Wider markets – more customers and opportunities to source from different suppliers with high quality standards ■ Competition – spurs on local businesses ■ Opportunities to benefit from lower prices for supplies and to be able to charge higher prices on sales	■ Better-quality products – global organisations can undertake more research and development to improve the quality of their products ■ More intense competition – competition with easily recognised global brands (benefiting from advertising, marketing and production economies of scale) ■ Possible governmental favour for overseas companies

Summary questions

1 Why might domestic producers in your country welcome globalisation?

2 Why might they see globalisation as a threat?

3 Do you think that the opportunities for local businesses provided by globalisation are greater than the threats posed?

KEY TERMS

Trade liberalisation: the removal or reduction of trade barriers or restrictions (e.g. import and export taxes) to make it easier for countries and firms to trade across international frontiers.

Figure 1.21.1 *The World Trade Organization was set up in 1995 to encourage free trade through collaboration on the reduction of import tariffs*

Did you know?

The World Trade Organization is made up of over 150 countries. It negotiates trade deals aimed at progressively liberalising trade.

What is trade liberalisation?

Trade liberalisation is the process of opening up trade between nations through the removal of restrictions. The World Trade Organization (WTO) encourages the liberalisation of trade. The aim of trade liberalisation is to encourage countries to specialise in areas where they have the greatest advantage and then trade with other countries to buy what they need for less than the cost of making the products themselves.

The argument in favour of trade liberalisation is that, if countries specialise in their best products and services, global output is increased. This combined with economies of scale means that more is produced of a better quality and at lower unit costs, resulting in greater prosperity.

The argument against trade liberalisation is that it principally benefits rich countries that produce branded and high-technology products and services. Less-developed economies are unable to compete. It results in greater dependency and debt.

Trade liberalisation and the Caribbean

Until the 1980s many Caribbean economies benefited from being able to sell agricultural products to the UK (and later into the European Union) with few or no import taxes. Rival producers from non-Commonwealth countries were not given this advantage and therefore found it difficult to compete. However, during the late 1980s and 1990s the European Union gradually reduced this 'favoured nations' policy. As a result Caribbean countries have had to restructure their economies substantially by reducing sugar and banana production, for example, and diversifying into new industries such as information technology, music and tourism.

The problem for Caribbean economies is that they are relatively small. Opening up Caribbean markets to foreign imports, through trade liberalisation, can disadvantage smaller domestic companies such as banks, food processors, and hotel and resort chains.

To facilitate trade liberalisation in the Caribbean, through economic integration and increased trade links with other countries, the members of CARICOM (see also 1.18) have created a free trade area – the Caribbean Single Market and Economy (CSME).

Key elements of the CSME include:

■ free movement of goods and services

■ the right of establishment, which allows CARICOM-owned businesses to set up in other member states without restrictions

■ a common external tariff – that is, a common import tax for products imported from non-member states

■ free movement of capital from one country to another and convertibility of one currency into another

■ a common trade policy relating to internal and international trade

- free movement of agreed categories of people
- harmonisation of business laws (for example, those relating to intellectual property rights).

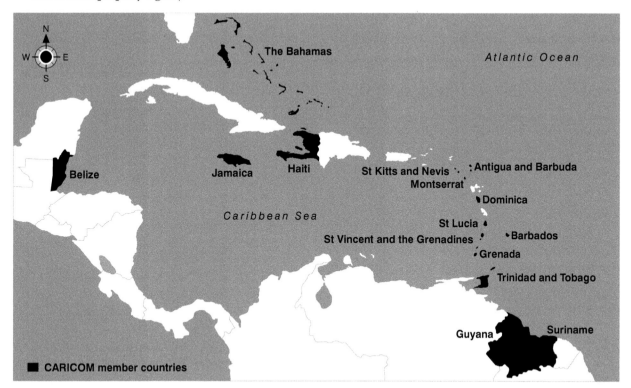

Figure 1.21.2 *CARICOM member states*

Summary table

Trade liberalisation	The removal of barriers to trade – encouraging trade and specialisation
CARICOM	A community of 15 Caribbean member states and associates that enables trade liberalisation within the Caribbean area
The World Trade Organization	An international organisation seeking to open up trade by setting rules and overseeing agreements between countries that encourage trade liberalisation. As of March 2013 the WTO includes 159 countries
CSME	A strategy with the aim of deepening the economic integration of CARICOM members. It is currently being implemented, so far a free-trade agreement has been made

Did you know?

CARICOM comprises 15 Caribbean nations (Figure 1.21.2), plus some additional states with associate member status.

The current full members of CARICOM are Antigua and Barbuda, Bahamas (not part of customs union), Barbados, Belize, Dominica, Grenada, Guyana, Haiti, Jamaica, Montserrat, St Kitts and Nevis, St Lucia, St Vincent and the Grenadines, Suriname, and Trinidad and Tobago.

Summary questions

1 Why might a country want to join CARICOM? How would it help that country in a global international economy?

2 Why might a country choose not to join CARICOM?

3 How has the World Trade Organization sought to liberalise world trade and why?

Answers to all exam-style questions can be found on the accompanying CD.

Section 1: Multiple-choice questions

1 Which of the following activities is an example of a tertiary industry?
   A Drilling for oil off the coast of Trinidad
   B Processing food in Antigua
   C Building roads in Barbados
   D Insuring businesses in the Windward Islands

2 Which of the following is a key feature of a company rather than a sole trader or partnership?
   A It has limited access to funds.
   B The owner's capital is provided by family and friends.
   C The shareholders have limited liability.
   D The number of owners is limited to two.

3 What is the benefit to a company of offering a franchise as compared to owning the business itself?
   A The franchisor takes all the profit.
   B The franchisee takes a greater business risk.
   C The franchisor benefits from a fresh injection of capital into the business.
   D The franchisor has greater control over how business is conducted.

4 A statutory board is created when:
   A a company receives a Certificate of Incorporation
   B legislation is passed in parliament to create the statutory board
   C a business changes from being a partnership to a company
   D a company's Articles of Association are deposited with the registrar of companies.

5 Which of the following illustrates the process of privatisation?
   A A service is transferred from the public sector to the private sector.
   B Investors increase their shareholding in domestic public companies.
   C A sole trader's business expands by introducing two new partners as joint owners.
   D The government takes over a number of foreign-owned oil companies.

6 Which of the following attributes would you most typically associate with a vision statement?
   A It provides a forward-looking picture of what an organisation can become.
   B It focuses on the present and current achievements of a business.
   C It is backward looking and focuses on targets that have been achieved.
   D It does not have a time dimension but simply sets out operational decisions.

7 Which of the following statements shows the highest level of commitment to corporate social responsibility (CSR) by a company?
   A The company is committed to securing high rates of return for shareholders.
   B The company shows a commitment to complying with relevant laws.
   C The company takes some appropriate actions where there are gaps in the law.
   D The company takes voluntary action to improve society.

8 Which of the following is not likely to be considered an important criterion of information used in decision making?
   A The information should be accurate.
   B The information should be historic.
   C The information should be relevant.
   D The information should be cost effective.

9 Which of the following stages in the decision-making cycle would you want to engage with first?
   A Analysis of data
   B Implementation
   C Definition of the problem
   D Formulation of strategies

10 Which of the following may be construed as a criticism of the activities of multinational corporations operating in the Caribbean?
   A They have introduced complex new technologies.
   B They have engaged in foreign direct investment.
   C They repatriate the majority of profits made in the area.
   D They support new training initiatives.

Section 2: Structured questions

11 a State the THREE main types of economic activity that you would expect to find in a Caribbean economy, providing one example of an industry to represent each type of activity. [3]

b State the THREE main benefits for an accountancy business of setting up as a partnership rather than as a sole trader. [6]

c A Caribbean entrepreneur has saved a considerable sum of money from profits from previous business ventures. He would now like to open a new hotel complex in a development area in Barbados. Explain TWO advantages and TWO disadvantages of setting up the business as a public company. [12]

d Outline FOUR distinctive features of a marketing cooperative. [4]

12 a i Outline THREE advantages of running the oil industry in Trinidad as a public corporation. [6]

ii Outline TWO advantages of running the oil industry in Trinidad as private companies with shareholders as compared to running it as a state-owned business. [4]

b Discuss ways in which a privately owned oil company based in Trinidad may benefit from developing a joint venture with an overseas partner. [6]

c State TWO disadvantages to the Trinidadian company of forming a joint venture. [4]

d Some activities in the Caribbean are run by statutory boards. Explain the term 'statutory board' and how they benefit consumers. [5]

13 a Explain the difference between the vision of an organisation and the organisation's objectives. [4]

b Using the example of a company that manufactures sun shades which it exports throughout the Caribbean, explain the benefits of having SMART objectives. [12]

c i Explain the term 'key performance indicators'. [2]

ii Explain how KPIs could help a food-processing company to be effective. [4]

d State THREE actions that a company might take to make sure that it meets its objectives. [3]

14 a i Explain the term 'corporate social responsibility'. [3]

ii Using the example of a textile company, evaluate FOUR actions that it could take to ensure that it is operating in a socially responsible way. [8]

b Explain the relationship between business ethics and corporate social responsibility. [4]

c Who are the stakeholders in a business? How can a business balance the contrasting expectations of its stakeholders? [10]

15 A large business, Fresh Juice Bottlers, is considering a takeover of a smaller company, Innovation Bottlers. Innovation Bottlers has been growing rapidly in recent years, while the sales and profits of Fresh Juice Bottlers have been static. The two companies operate in similar fields, but Innovation Bottlers is exploiting new technologies that Fresh Juice Bottlers has not so far been able to capitalise on. For example, Innovation Bottlers is using computer-aided manufacturing to a much greater degree and is using computer-controlled equipment that enables much higher levels of quality control and waste elimination.

a Outline FIVE key criteria that Fresh Juice Bottlers should take into consideration when deciding whether to take over Innovation Bottlers. Relate your answers to the information given about the two companies. [10]

b Outline the decision-making process that Fresh Juice Bottlers should follow to enable it to make an effective and informed decision. [6]

c Fresh Juice Bottlers is also considering using PESTLE analysis to see if the time is right to take over Innovation Bottlers. Explain what is involved in PESTLE analysis and how it could enable Fresh Juice to make a decision. [9]

> Further exam questions and examples can be found on the accompanying CD.

2   The management of people

General objectives

On completion of this module, you should be able to:

- appreciate the importance of the application of management theories in the operation of business organisations

- understand the roles and responsibilities of employers and employees within an organisation

- develop an awareness of the effects of human motivation on organisational effectiveness

- appreciate the broad formal framework of human resource management.

People are the most valuable resource in any organisation. People come up with the new ideas that take the organisation forward and carry out the essential tasks and processes that enable the organisation to meet its objectives. The management of people is thus one of the most important management functions.

Management theories

Since the early 20th century, management theories have shaped and influenced management styles. This module begins by examining some of the management theories from the early 20th century and explains how they sought to identify a scientific way to organise hierarchical organisations using a top-down management approach.

Since the mid-1920s in management theory there has been an increasing emphasis on giving attention and value to people in the workplace. Theories and management styles have focused more on the individual needs of employees and on the value of developing teamwork structures. The human relations school of people management, developed in the 1920s and 1930s, has strongly influenced modern approaches to human resource management (HRM), in which the needs and aspirations of employees are recognised.

Organisational structures

There are many ways to structure organisations – for example, organisations can be structured according to markets and geographical territories, or along functional lines (marketing, production, sales, etc.). Virtual organisational structures, in which individuals, who are often geographically dispersed, communicate with each other in real time using electronic means, are becoming more common.

Motivation theory

Financial rewards are one way of motivating employees. However, as you will see, key theorists, including the American Frederick Herzberg, showed that real motivation is intrinsic (that is, it comes from inside an individual) and results from carrying out meaningful tasks and activities that give employees personal fulfilment.

Leadership theories

Good managers are able to lead others

Good managers know how to lead others. Leaders are people who can develop a vision to take an organisation or group forward. To be a successful leader you need to have followers. Research has identified a number of different types of leadership styles and approaches. For example, there are autocratic leaders (who tell others what to do) and there are participatory leaders (who employ a more democratic approach). Transformational leaders are leaders who build a vision that they share with followers and who enable others to become leaders.

The importance of teams

Teamwork is a key way of empowering an organisation and the people who make up the organisation. A team is a group of people with a shared sense of purpose and who feel jointly accountable for the outcomes that the team produces. The different stages in building a high-performance team and the characteristics of an effective team are considered in 2.19 and 2.20.

Conflict in organisations

Conflict occurs in all organisations. It can be both negative (for example, where individuals clash for personal reasons) and positive (for example, the healthy discussion of important issues in order to explore multiple options). A good leader is able to manage conflict in a productive way using a number of different strategies (see 2.22 and 2.23).

Managing change

Organisations need to undertake change for internal reasons (for example, to develop new products) and for external reasons (for example, as a result of a change in the law that impacts on the business, or a change in social consumption patterns as consumers switch to new buying conventions). The organisation is likely to need to make changes to its processes (the way in which things are organised and done) and this will result in changes to the way people do things and interact with each other. Change needs to be managed effectively using a variety of strategies.

Communication

Effective communication is essential in managing people. Messages need to be communicated clearly to the target audience using appropriate media. Organisations can employ a number of different approaches to communication (for example, a top-down approach, or a more participative approach where there is a free flow of communications between members of an organisation). Information technology enables more participative communication of information.

Human resource management

Human resource management is the management of an organisation's human resources (that is, its workforce). The main roles of the human resource department are to attract new employees (recruitment), to develop employees (through helping them become more effective) and to enable the high-level performance of employees (through incentives).

Good communication is essential in all parts of business

Evolution of management theories: the classical model

On completion of this section, you should be able to:

■ evaluate the contribution of the classical model of management to present-day organisations.

KEY TERMS

Scientific management: a classical approach to management based on using scientific methods to identify the 'one best way' of doing a job.

Did you know?

F.W. Taylor was given the nickname 'Speedy Taylor' because the emphasis of his work was on speeding up the production process by identifying ways in which labour could be organised more efficiently.

F.W. Taylor is also known as the Father of Scientific Management.

Did you know?

Two criticisms of scientific management theory are that:

■ the approach assumes that people can be treated as a mere extension of the machinery, rather than taking into account human emotions

■ not all activities are easy to measure (e.g. those involving critical thinking or personal relations are more difficult to measure than those associated with mechanical action).

Early management theories in the late 19th and early 20th centuries were based on disciplined ways of controlling organisations. The emphasis was on being organised and organising others. Taylor's scientific management theory, Fayol's principles of organisation and Weber's bureaucracy are all part of the classical model. Some important aspects of these theories are still relevant today.

Scientific management theory

The ideas of **scientific management** are associated with Frederick Winslow Taylor and the automobile manufacturer Henry Ford (see the case study on p51).

F.W. Taylor drew on his experience of working in engineering to develop a theory of efficiency. He used the term 'scientific management' to describe this approach. In 1911 he published the book *Principles of Scientific Management*, in which he focused on the design and analysis of individual tasks. He believed that scientific principles could be applied to identify the best way of carrying out any job. Taylor believed that employees are inclined to seek maximum reward for minimum effort. To overcome this, managers should give detailed instructions for each task and manage employees closely to ensure that tasks are completed. Pay should be linked to performance in order to motivate employees.

Taylor's theory has three implications for working practices:

■ Managers collect knowledge about work processes systematically.

■ Workers' discretion and control over what they do is removed.

■ Managers enforce standard procedures and times for carrying out each job.

Knowledge of how to work therefore becomes the possession of managers. Taylor believed that 'all possible brain work should be removed from the shop and centred in the planning ... department' (Taylor: 1911, pp98–9).

Henri Fayol's principles of organisation

At the same time (that is, in the early 20th century) in France, Henry Fayol was developing other theories of management. Fayol believed that there were sets of principles that applied to any organisation, including:

■ the division of work so that people can concentrate on specialist activities rather than general activities

■ authority and responsibility – those with authority in an organisation should impose sanctions to encourage useful actions

■ discipline – which he believed was essential for the effective running of organisations

■ unity of command – employees should receive orders from one superior only

■ unity of direction – there should be one leader and one plan

■ remuneration – employees should be rewarded fairly for well-directed effort.

Based on these principles, he set out the following management duties:

- **planning** – examining the future, deciding what needs to be done and developing a plan of action
- **organising** – to carry out the organisation's activities
- **command** – ensuring that all employees perform their jobs well and in the interests of the organisation
- **coordination** – verifying that the activities of the organisation work together harmoniously to achieve its goals
- **control** – ensuring that plans, instructions and commands are correctly carried out.

Max Weber and bureaucracy

During the same period, the German sociologist Max Weber identified 'bureaucracy' as an efficient and rational way to organise large organisations, such as government departments, the army and industry. In a bureaucracy the emphasis should be on clear objectives and the organisation of work to achieve those objectives. The features of a bureaucracy include:

- a hierarchical system of authority
- written rules
- a specialised division of labour
- promotion based on individual achievement
- clear patterns of working.

Contribution to present-day organisations

Many modern organisations still contain elements of classical management theory. For example, a fast-food restaurant has standardised systems and processes for ordering food, while a modern canning factory has clear lines of command and systematic production lines. You should remember, however, that many modern service jobs are dependent on personal relations and individual treatment of customers. These activities are more difficult to standardise.

Summary table

Theory	Principles
Scientific management – F.W. Taylor	Careful study of work processes leads to a single best way of organising and managing work.
Principles of organisation – Henry Fayol	Management duties are based on planning, organising, controlling, coordinating and commanding.
Bureaucracy – Max Weber	This is an efficient way to organise an organisation based on clear objectives and rational organisation to achieve its objectives.

CASE STUDY

Fordism

Fordism is a good example of scientific management theory being put into practice. In the 1920s, Henry Ford organised his car company as a giant system to turn inputs efficiently into finished motor vehicles. He created a technical system for producing millions of vehicles using standard repetitive operating procedures and production lines. Workers tended the machines, using systems created by organisation planners and directed by production managers. The weakness of the system was that the aspirations and needs of individual employees were secondary to the industrial system. Labourers were often doing repetitive tasks and did not develop broad skills.

1 What industries today use Fordist production techniques?

2 What are the main advantages of Fordist methods to businesses, managers and consumers?

Summary questions

1 Explain how a modern fast-food restaurant or car factory applies scientific management principles.

2 What similarities are there between the ideas of Fayol, Taylor and Weber?

3 Which aspects of classical management theory do you think are helpful to modern managers?

Specific objective

On completion of this section, you should be able to:

■ evaluate the contribution of the human relations model to present-day organisations.

Did you know?

The term **'Hawthorne effect'** is widely used in research. It refers to any situation where the subjects being researched respond by changing their behaviour – usually in a positive way.

During the late 19th and early 20th centuries, classical approaches to management were the norm and were based on a **top-down approach**. For example, sugar plantations in the Caribbean were hierarchical organisations with a very clear chain of control and management, as shown in Figure 2.2.1.

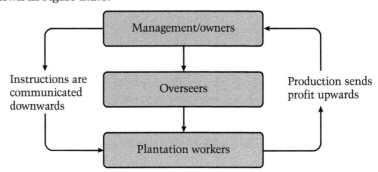

Figure 2.2.1 *The classical model of management as exhibited on a plantation in the Caribbean in the late 19th and early 20th century*

The Hawthorne experiments

In the late 1920s there was a major breakthrough in thinking around employees' motivation. This came about as a result of a series of studies carried out by an Australian researcher, Elton Mayo, between 1927 and 1932 at the Western Electric Hawthorne Works in a suburb of Chicago. These came to be known as the **Hawthorne experiments**.

Initially Mayo and his fellow researchers had sought to identify the impact of changing working conditions on labour productivity. For example, they changed the brightness of the lighting in parts of the workplace, as well as factors such as temperature. They then studied the impact of other variables, such as having breaks and changing working hours.

What quickly emerged from the studies was that, although changing these variables was important, what was more important was the way in which the employees responded to being studied. Mayo identified that the employees were more productive because they knew they were being studied. In other words, employees respond in a positive way when they are singled out and made to feel important.

At the heart of the initial experiments was a small group of women whom Mayo chose to study. Two women were selected, and these two selected another four to form a subgroup in the workplace. Their work involved assembling telephone relays – a component of the telephone system made up of about 40 separate elements. The female workers were required to assemble this component and then drop it into a chute when it was completed. It was therefore easy to measure the output of the employees. The conditions under which these women worked were changed frequently by Mayo and his team. It was then possible to measure changes in productivity resulting from changes in their working conditions. Changes to working conditions were made at regular intervals and then implemented for several weeks. During the period of the experiment, a researcher observed and noted what was taking place and discussed the experiment with the women.

The changes to the working conditions that were made included:

- giving the workers additional breaks
- changing the length of breaks
- providing a meal during a break
- giving the workers more freedom to move around and organise their work
- changing the length of the working day.

Typically, the productivity rate increased when a change was made.

Implications of the Hawthorne experiments

The Hawthorne experiments were seen as ground breaking, in that they provided a rationale for treating employees as human beings rather than just as another workplace resource. The experiments showed that employees:

- respond well to supervisors/managers taking an interest in them
- work well when they have a sense of group identity
- respond well to being given greater freedom to manage their own work routines and schedules
- are likely to take responsibility for their actions if trust is placed in them.

The experiments also showed that employees' self-esteem improves if they feel that they are special.

The **human relations approach**, which was developed in the 1920s, provided the initial stimulus to modern approaches to **human resource management** (HRM). Today, HR managers focus on identifying ways of recognising individuals' needs and aspirations. This might include encouraging the following practices:

- individuals identifying their own work-related aspirations and goals through a personal appraisal process with a line manager
- team working
- taking on more responsibility in the workplace.

> **KEY TERMS**
>
> **Human relations approach:** a management approach that recognises that humans respond to a personal approach. The human relations approach recognises individuals' needs.
>
> **Human resource management:** management of an organisation's workforce. HR managers look for ways of recognising the needs and aspirations of workers.

Summary table

Key features of a human resources model	
Focus	On people and their needs
Recognition	That individuals like to feel part of a group
Management implications	
That employees are more likely to be motivated when managers show an interest in them	

Summary questions

1 The Hawthorne experiments found that a key feature of the workplace is the relationships between people in the workplace (a social system). How can managers build on this social system to encourage and motivate employees?

2 What do you see as being the main differences between a scientific management approach and a human relations approach to managing employees at work?

Specific objective

On completion of this section, you should be able to:

■ evaluate the contribution of a systems approach and contingency approach to management in present-day organisations.

Did you know?

Many managers find this **systems approach** helpful in understanding what needs to be managed within an organisation (i.e. the inputs, processes and outputs).

KEY TERMS

Systems approach: a management approach that looks at organisations and parts of an organisation as systems in which inputs are processed into more desirable outputs. In particular, it focuses on identifying more effective systems and processes.

Primary inputs: settings that control the operation of the system (e.g. the speed of a production line, the temperature at which processes take place, and the amount of time for which the line runs).

Secondary inputs: resources (e.g. the raw materials and ingredients that are processed).

Closed system: a system whose operations are not impacted by the external environment.

Open system: a system that is impacted by the external environment.

A systems approach

An organisational system includes three key elements, as shown in Figure 2.3.1. These are inputs, processes and outputs.

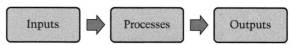

Figure 2.3.1 *The three elements of an organisational system*

For example, a manufacturing company uses inputs of raw materials, components and labour. It then puts these through a number of different manufacturing processes. The outputs are the final products, and the waste that leaves the system.

The challenge for managers is to select the most effective inputs and to use the most efficient and effective processes in order to produce the best possible outputs, while minimising or eliminating waste. Managers need to create systems that enable more valuable outputs to be created by adding value to the inputs (see 1.1).

Open and closed systems

There are two types of production system – a closed system and an open system. Both types require inputs from a user (for example, a production manager who puts in the **primary inputs** and the **secondary inputs**).

Closed systems do not interact with other systems or with the wider environment. As a result they are easier to manage because managers do not have to consider the impact of changes that are outside of their control. They are able to manage the inputs and processes, and as a result have a lot of control over outputs. A production department that produces standardised products in a continual process (for example, a production line producing biscuits) is an example of a closed system.

In contrast, an **open system** is one that interacts with other systems and with the environment. Changes that are external to the system thus impact on it, so that managers have less control and outputs are less predictable. A marketing department that is responding constantly to changes in customers' needs is an example of an open system. As an open system interacts with its environment, understanding the relationship between an open system and its environment (for example, through changing regulations and changing costs of inputs) is essential. For instance, in the example of Caribbean Flavours, changes to government food safety regulations may affect the business.

CASE STUDY

Caribbean Flavours

Caribbean Flavours and Fragrances Ltd, based in Jamaica, supplies flavours and aromas to the flavours and fragrances industry. The company sources essential oils and natural extracts from all over the globe. It then creates unique and delicious products for a range of manufacturing companies. For example, it provides coconut, vanilla, pineapple, strawberry, butter, orange, banana, ginger, almond, bunspice and guava flavourings to the baking and ice cream industries. It provides rose, lemon, lime, mint, jasmine, lavender, peach, floral and gardenia flavourings to the fragrances industry (for example, cosmetics and perfume). Its customers include J Wray and Nephew, Grace Canning, Pepsi Cola, Jamaica Bottling, Banks Barbados and St Kitts Distillers. Using knowledge of chemistry and physics, the company is able to blend and modify flavours and aromas in order to create flavours for the food, beverage, baking, confectionary and pharmaceutical industries, as well as colours to enhance the visual appearance of products.

1 Identify some of the inputs, processes and outputs of Caribbean Flavours.

2 In what way does Caribbean Flavours add value to products?

3 What external factors may impact on the inputs, processes and outputs of Caribbean Flavours?

Entropy and synergy

Over time, systems tend to decline (**entropy**). This is obvious in relation to systems such as the human body and plants. Similarly, organisations and production systems are subject to entropy if they are not carefully managed. From a systems perspective, one of the primary objectives of management is to avoid entropy.

The concept of **synergy** is also important to managers. Synergies are the relationships between the parts of a system that collectively make it more effective than if the individual parts were working alone. Sometimes this is described as $2 + 2 = 5$. Another objective of management is to develop the synergies between the components of the systems they manage.

Contingency approaches

The **contingency approach** to management recognises that there is no single approach that is suitable for all situations. Contingency theories are most closely associated with Fred Fiedler (see 2.15). His work showed that the type of management or leadership approach that works best depends on the situation. The intelligent manager therefore weighs up the situation before deciding on the best way to manage.

> **KEY TERMS**
>
> **Entropy:** the natural tendency for a system to decline.
>
> **Synergy:** the relationships between the parts of a system that collectively make it more effective than if the individual parts were working alone.
>
> **Contingency approach:** an approach to management based on the idea that there is no one best way to manage and that the approach needs to vary according to the context or situation.

Summary table

Systems approach	Shows managers how to focus on what can be managed: that is, inputs, processes and outputs (the production cycle)
Contingency approach	Shows managers the importance of identifying specific variances in the situation they are managing rather than attempting a 'one size fits all' solution

Summary questions

1 Define the following terms: value added, input, output, process, synergy.

2 Which type of system – an open system or closed system – gives managers a greater level of control over systems?

3 What are the benefits of a systems approach?

2.4 Functions of management

Specific objective

On completion of this section, you should be able to:

- evaluate the functions of management in present-day organisations.

Did you know?

Two well-known sayings about planning are: 'Planning is bringing the future into the present so that you can do something about it now' (Alan Lakein) and 'Those that fail to plan, plan to fail'.

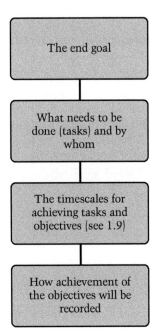

Figure 2.4.1 Points of a managerial plan

A number of different definitions of managers and management are used. We will define them as follows:

- Managers are the people who get things done by using other people. They need to:
  - plan
  - organise
  - lead
  - control
  - ensure that staffing is sufficient and the correct resources are employed.
- Organisational management involves deciding on how agreed objectives can be met, by using people and other resources.

Planning

Managers need to create clear plans for others to follow. These plans are converted into general aims, more specific objectives and tasks to be completed. Organisational objectives need to be allocated to appropriate divisions, teams and individuals within the organisation.

Figure 2.4.1 shows the points that a managerial plan should define.

Different types of plan are established at different levels within an organisation (see 1.10). For example, a strategic plan is a top-level plan that covers the whole, or a significant part, of the organisation. It sets out how the organisation will achieve its objectives. A tactical plan typically involves middle management and is shorter term than a strategic plan. It sets out the means through which particular objectives will be met, for example at departmental level. An operational plan is concerned with how specific operations and processes are carried out.

As an example, a strategic plan for a hotel chain in the Caribbean may be concerned with the development of new hotels across the Caribbean over a 10-year period. This would be made by the board of directors and senior executives. The tactical plan will focus on ensuring hotels are built in the short to medium term and organising the resources and marketing activities to secure this development. This would be made by middle management. An operational plan may relate specifically to the marketing activities associated with the development of a new hotel in Antigua this year. This might be developed by a combination of middle and junior management.

Organising

Managers are expected to organise themselves, their work and their workers by setting up systems, procedures and structures in a logical and efficient way. To do this, managers need to make the most of the resources available. An organised manager gives priority to the most important tasks and ensures that these are completed on time. Organisation involves:

- prioritising and selecting tasks
- deciding who will undertake the tasks
- assigning the tasks
- delegating authority and responsibility to ensure the tasks are achieved
- coordinating different activities and individuals
- making sure that things are done on time in an ordered way.

Leading

Leaders give direction and through their leadership ensure that directions are followed. Traditionally, 'heroic leaders' (that is, managers who are able to lead others by example) were seen as being the most effective. However, today management theorists often place more importance on transformational leadership (see 2.17). Transformational leaders enable others to make important decisions rather than making the decisions themselves.

Controlling

Managers need to create an effective **control system** to make sure that plans are kept on track (for example, that targets and deadlines are met), and that resources are used in an appropriate way. A control system includes targets and performance indicators, so that performance can be measured and managers can track performance against the set targets. When the organisation is falling short of its targets, appropriate control actions can be taken (for example, allocating more resources to tasks).

KEY TERMS

Control system: methods, such as target and performance indicators, used to identify whether a business is on track to achieve its objectives and, where it is not, taking actions to put it back on track.

Staffing

Finally, managers need to have the right people in the right places at the right times. This involves:

- human resource planning – that is, identifying what staff the organisation needs today and in the future, and what skills are required
- training, developing and recruiting the right staff to meet organisational objectives (strategic-level planning)
- making sure that the company plans who is required from day to day to meet company orders (operational-level planning).

Summary table

Functions of management	What this means
Planning	Setting out the plans and targets that will help the organisation to achieve its targets
Organising	Making sure that people and other resources carry out the required tasks in an efficient way
Leading	Making sure that other people in the organisation are working to achieve targets
Controlling	Ensuring that plans are being met by setting performance targets and measuring performance to make sure the company is on track
Staffing	Ensuring that there are sufficient people doing the right things

Summary questions

1 What is the relationship between planning, organising and controlling?

2 Which good leadership skills are required to ensure that a plan is executed?

3 How can managers benefit from measuring performance?

Figure 2.5.1 *Managers are responsible for managing all resources, including people and equipment, within their area of responsibility*

Did you know?

In 1973, in his work entitled *The Nature of Managerial Work*, Henry Mintzberg identified three key management roles:

■ interpersonal roles – the manager leads a team and interacts with others

■ informational roles – the manager collects and disseminates information to his or her team

■ decisional roles – the manager develops enterprising new ideas and makes decisions on how to use resources.

You can find out more about Mintzberg's management roles by searching for 'Mintzberg's 10 management roles' on the internet.

Management responsibilities

At the most senior levels, managers have responsibility for the whole organisation. The chief executive officer and other senior executives are responsible for making sure that effective corporate plans are made for the whole organisation.

Other managers within the organisation are then responsible for putting these plans into action. Each manager is responsible for carrying out the plans for their area of responsibility. Management of the following resources is essential in achieving the organisation's objectives:

■ **people** – directing their activities and looking after their morale and welfare

■ **finance** – making decisions about how to acquire and use finance to drive sales and profits

■ **materials** – using materials in the most efficient way

■ **machinery and equipment** – using the most efficient machinery and making sure that it is in place and maintained in order to meet production targets

■ **time** – ensuring the best use of time

■ **information** – making sure that users have access to up-to-date information and that the right people receive this information in a clear way.

Efficient management versus effective management

In business there is an important distinction between being *efficient* and being *effective*.

An efficient manager does things right, such as using existing resources in the best possible way to achieve the highest levels of output. In other words, the manager achieves the highest levels of output from the existing inputs. Efficiency therefore measures the relationship between inputs and outputs.

An effective manager does the right things. Rather than thinking about how things are done now, an effective manager thinks about new ways of doing things that may achieve better results. For example, instead of just carrying on producing a tried-and-tested product, an effective manager may identify a great opportunity to channel some resources into producing a different product. An effective manager is able to think creatively to come up with new ideas.

Did you know?

People sometimes refer to the 'three Rs' of management:

The three 'Rs' of management	Examples
Resources	Time, finance, people
Responsibilities	Planning, organising, leading, controlling, decision making
Roles	Interpersonal, informational, decisional

Effective management

An effective manager is someone who gets things done through working with others. An effective manager creates plans, organises others, ensures that the right people are doing the right jobs and shows leadership. Simon Williams, the human resource manager for a leading retailing outlet in Trinidad, demonstrates qualities associated with an effective manager. Simon describes his workload and responsibilities:

We are currently developing a human resource plan to take us through a period of strategic growth in which we want to expand our presence into three other major Caribbean territories. Part of this will involve the takeover of existing retail outlets. This will involve looking at what staff they have currently, and any new posts for which we need to recruit. This is a long-term initiative so I need to be looking at who we employ not just this year but over the next five years. This involves interacting with other senior staff at the company who have responsibility for overseeing the expansion process.

On a more week-by-week basis we need to look at which job vacancies we need to fill in the short term. This involves making sure that job advertisements are placed in appropriate media outlets, that job specifications for the new jobs we are advertising are created, and that we have the right people in place to make up the interview panels. I am currently exploring new ways of attracting applicants. Rather than just using traditional newspaper adverts and radio broadcasting, I am exploring new online methods of recruitment which I think will enable us to attract potential candidates from a wider pool. In particular, this is likely to be helpful in the recruitment of managers for our new retail outlets.

Each year there is a set budget allocated by the company for human resource activities including recruitment and training. I have set out a month-by-month outline of how much we should be spending on it and I am able to check that we are keeping within the allocated budget. Where we go into an overspend position, it is important to identify how we can pull this back, perhaps by adjusting some of our existing activities.

I am responsible for a small human resources team within the company that oversees a range of staff-related issues, such as training, recruitment, talking to the relevant trade union officials, and developing policies to retain and motivate staff. It is important that I am up to date with all of the relevant legislation and that I play an active part in making sure that all of the correct processes are in place to run an effective HR team. However, I don't believe in doing everything myself. Yes, it is important to be seen to be running important initiatives, but I also rely on my team to take responsibility for certain areas (for example, taking responsibility for some training initiatives or handling specific aspects of recruitment).

1 In what ways is Simon Williams demonstrating the following aspects of management?

   a Planning   d Controlling

   b Organising   e Staffing

   c Leading

2 In what ways is Simon being both an effective manager and an efficient manager?

Summary table

Efficient management	'Doing the right things' – ensuring that maximum outputs are achieved from your inputs
Effective management	'Doing things right' – identifying even better ways of achieving outcomes

Summary questions

1 How can a manager be both efficient and effective?

2 What sorts of interpersonal behaviour should a manager to be able to carry out well?

3 What are the principal responsibilities of senior managers in an organisation?

On completion of this section, you should be able to:

- explain the features of organisational structures that are classified by function, product and geographical market.

Line of control: the reporting and responsibility structure within an organisation. For example, individuals report to a line manager or supervisor who is responsible for them. The higher up the line an individual is, the greater their seniority and responsibility.

Functions: specialist parts of an organisation (e.g. marketing, finance and human resource management).

An organisation's structure should allow:

- work to be divided up according to what needs to be done
- **lines of control** and communication to be established.

The structure of an organisation can be classified in a number of ways, as explained below and in 2.7 and 2.8.

Function

A **function** is a specific part of an organisation with a defined purpose (such as production, marketing or accounts). An organisation can be structured so that groups of specialists (for example, marketing specialists) work together. This allows specialisation, which enables efficiency (because individuals concentrate on their roles and become good at them, for example). It also provides a simple and easily understood structure with clear lines of command within functions. However, it may result in teams of specialists who operate in isolation within the organisation and who are not familiar with the work of other functions. It can make decision making slow and there may be restricted career opportunities for individuals outside of their specialism. Figure 2.6.1 shows the hierarchical structure of a company organised by function.

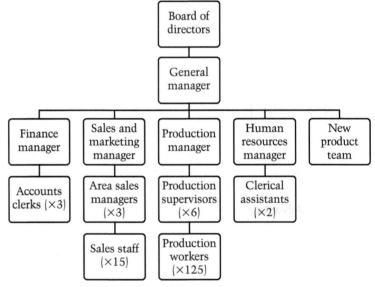

Figure 2.6.1 A company organised by function

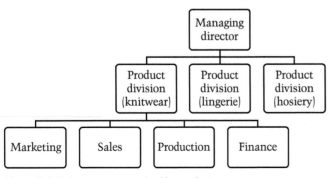

Figure 2.6.2 A company organised by product

Product

As output increases and more products or services are introduced, a functional structure may become less appropriate. Instead, specialist teams may be set up to manage each product area. For example, a textiles company producing knitwear, hosiery and lingerie may be organised into specialist teams for each of these product areas. Each division would be responsible for marketing, production and finance within their product area, as shown in Figure 2.6.2.

On the one hand, this type of organisation allows greater focus on product specialisms and better coordination across functions. On the other hand, there is duplication of functions and competition between the divisions.

Geography

Organisation by geographical region allows an organisation to target its resources and activities to meet the needs and characteristics of customers and suppliers in a particular country or territory. Within each territory (or geographical division), staff can be organised either by product or by function. As a result of meeting the needs of particular territories, an organisation's customer base may increase and the business may grow. However, the organisational structure that was appropriate for serving customers locally may no longer be efficient to satisfy the needs of national or international customers. Operations may become dispersed, resulting in a lack of control and conflict between the regions and the head office.

Organisations in the retail sector are often structured by geographical regions (see Figure 2.6.3). Regions (such as the Eastern Caribbean, consisting of a number of territories) may then be split up further to respond to the needs of their local customers.

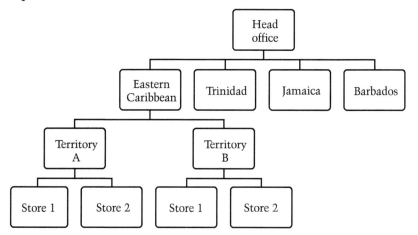

Figure 2.6.3 *A retail company organised by geography*

Summary table

Type of structure	Advantages	Disadvantages
Functional	■ Allows specialisation ■ Efficient use of resources ■ Simple structure	■ Lack of overall organisational awareness within individual functions ■ Restricted career opportunities outside individual functions ■ Centralised decision making may be slow
Product/ geographical division	■ Closer to the customer ■ Enables coordination across functions ■ Flexible	■ Duplication of resources ■ Communication problems across divisions ■ Competition among divisions

Summary questions

1 What form of organisational structure would be most suitable for a business organisation that has manufacturing outlets spread widely across the Caribbean? Justify your answer.

2 In what situations is a company most likely to benefit from employing a geographical organisational structure rather than a functional structure?

2.7 Organisational structure: the matrix structure and team working

Organisational structure: the matrix structure and team working

Specific objective

On completion of this section, you should be able to:

- explain the features of matrix organisational structures.

Did you know?

A flat organisation is one where there is a short chain of command (see 2.9).

Did you know?

A matrix is a structure of management within an organisation in which employees work across functions and report to more than one manager. As a result, employees may be part of a 'cross-functional team'.

Characteristics of a matrix organisation

A **matrix structure** combines the traditional vertical functional structure with a horizontal structure in which people work in project teams across different business functions (Figure 2.7.1). It enables employees from different backgrounds (for example, sales or finance) or from different countries (such as Guyana or Trinidad) to contribute specialist skills and knowledge to the team, and it brings diversity to the team. A matrix structure can be temporary or permanent. A temporary matrix structure can be set up to achieve a short-term target. A permanent matrix structure is a long-term organisational structure with more than one chain of command. Within a matrix structure:

- there is a two-way (vertical and horizontal) flow of information, authority and responsibility
- employees have two or more bosses.

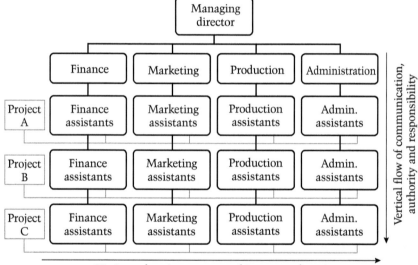

Figure 2.7.1 A matrix structure

Table 2.7.1 shows the advantages and disadvantages of the matrix structure.

Table 2.7.1 Advantages and disadvantages of the matrix structure

Advantages	Disadvantages
- It allows an organisation to respond rapidly to change – as the structure is flatter, decisions can be made more quickly - It enables greater learning opportunities through cooperation and sharing information - As information and resources can be shared across the organisation more easily, this can result in reduced costs - It encourages more new ideas - Cooperation enables people to learn new skills, which encourages staff development	- Potential conflicts of authority may arise and there may be conflicts of loyalty as employees have more than one boss - Multiple chains of command may cause confusion and lead to difficulties in coordinating resources across the functions and the project teams. This may slow down decision making - The initial implementation of the structure may be costly

Development of a matrix structure in New Town University

The following illustration shows how the Dean of New Town University reorganised courses offered by three faculties in his university into a matrix structure. The project identified a number of synergies across the faculty specialisms, meaning that it was possible to set up new courses involving input from each of the three departments. The new permanent matrix structure is shown in Figure 2.7.2.

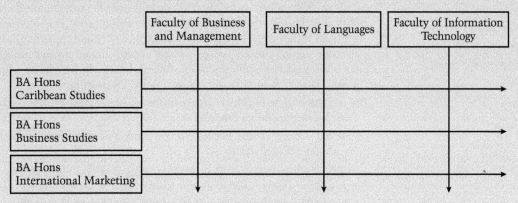

Figure 2.7.2 *Permanent matrix structure at New Town University*

1 What benefits are likely to arise from the matrix structures outlined in this case study?

2 What potential drawbacks might arise from working in such a matrix structure?

The importance of team working

Team working is integral to a matrix structure. A matrix structure brings together groups of people with different skills and capabilities to work as part of a team and seek to achieve shared objectives. A formal team is one that has been set up by the organisation itself with the purpose of achieving specific objectives (see 2.19). There are usually rules and guidelines about how and when the team should meet and some form of leadership structure.

Many modern organisations, such as information technology companies, employ knowledge workers who focus on assembling and analysing information. Knowledge workers often collaborate in virtual teams (online).

Summary questions

1 In what situations might a matrix structure be more effective than a structure based purely on functional organisation?

2 Why might a matrix structure not be appropriate in a small organisation?

3 In a large organisation, what problems might result from having a matrix structure?

Summary table

Type of organisation	Description	Benefits	Drawbacks
Matrix	■ Organisational structure combining the traditional vertical functional structure with horizontal project teams working across the functions ■ Has more than one line of command	■ Flexibility ■ Greater learning opportunities ■ Greater sharing of skills, resources, information and ideas	■ Conflict of authority ■ Difficulties in coordinating ■ Costly to implement

Network structures

A network structure is a collection of autonomous organisations that work together as one entity to achieve common goals. It is based on informal rather than formal relationships. Coordination is facilitated through regular contact using modern communications technologies (such as video conferencing and a shared database). There are a number of different types of network arrangement, for example:

■ an internal network structure made up of separate profit-making units of the same company

■ a network structure between a company and suppliers to which it has outsourced activities.

An illustration of very informal networking is where independent companies or units simply network with each other for specific activities (for example, the joint running of a large music festival or conference).

The network structure described in the case study below illustrates a permanent network of separate units with a shared interest in the collection of regional statistics.

CASE STUDY

The Caribbean Regional Statistics Department

The Caribbean Regional Statistics Department is a network organisation bringing together the statistical offices of the Caribbean Community (CARICOM) so that statisticians can share data, working methods and approaches. Caribbean Community Statistics links statisticians in Antigua and Barbuda with those in other Caribbean countries such as the Bahamas, Barbados, Belize, Dominica, Grenada, Guyana, Haiti and Jamaica.

Collectively this group of statisticians can build up a large-scale picture of what is happening in terms of the Caribbean economy – for example, who is trading with whom, how trade figures are changing and what is happening to population in the various territories. Not only does this provide a picture of differences and similarities between the various members of the Caribbean Community, but it also provides a total picture of changes in the Gross Domestic Product (GDP) and other key indicators of CARICOM as a whole.

The principal links between statisticians are neither phone communications nor face-to-face meetings (although these are important), but instead regular interrogation of shared databases of statistics and electronic communications. Electronic communication links bring together teams of statisticians working in the various CARICOM member states.

1 How can statisticians working for the Caribbean Regional Statistics Department be described as knowledge workers?

2 What is the process for linking Caribbean statisticians into a network?

Whereas the classical model of organisation outlined by Fayol, Taylor and Weber (see 2.1) has a hierarchical structure, a network structure allows individuals and groups to take far more responsibility for decision making. Networking allows much more opportunity for innovation because the teams and individuals who make up the network are enabled to come up with new ideas facilitated by changing electronic technologies.

Online discussion is an important means of communication within a network community. Just as individuals can share ideas and experiences through social media sites, such as Facebook and Twitter, work-related issues can be discussed through networked business connections. Enterprise 2.0 is freeform social network software that can be used within an organisation for the networking of ideas.

Key features of a network structure

- There are multiple links between individuals, groups and projects.
- The key links are based on information and communications technology.
- Teams work independently from formal management lines and structures.
- Teams share information.
- All parties in the network input and access information.
- There is a greater equality of power in terms of decision making than in traditional organisational structures.

Virtual organisations

A **virtual organisation** is an extreme form of networked organisational structure. As with all organisations, a virtual organisation is made up of a group of individuals and business partners working together to achieve shared objectives. However, in this case no physical office or place of work exists. The organisation simply consists of the individuals and the network of links that they create with each other. Electronic technology is used to link people together.

Virtual organisations foster creativity and are highly flexible. They may consist of virtual sellers (for example, providers of information) and virtual buyers (those willing to pay for information). For a virtual organisation to be successful, there needs to be collaboration between the participants in the organisation. As with network structures, potential weaknesses include the lack of direct contact (distance) between individuals and potential lack of clarity about accountability and responsibility.

A good example of a virtual organisation is the Open Campus of the University of the West Indies. Students pay to study courses online and are brought together with online tutors within a virtual organisation.

Did you know?

The following terminology is associated with network organisations:

- Telecommuting – where employees work at locations away from the usual workplace site.
- Mobile workers – those working away from the workplace site, using technology such as cellphones, pagers and laptops.
- Hot desks – desks equipped with electronic links that can be used by many different network workers when visiting business locations.
- Hoteling – when a client provides a hot desk from which suppliers' knowledge workers can work.

KEY TERMS

Virtual organisation: a network organisation in which the components of the organisational structure (including people) are linked electronically so that they can operate from different physical locations.

Summary table

Type of organisation	Description	Benefits	Drawbacks
Network organisations	■ Individuals and groups that are linked through electronic communications	■ They enable greater sharing of information, and encourage flexibility and innovation ■ They allow greater autonomy and equality of decision making	■ There can be great distances between the participants ■ They may suffer from a lack of clarity and accountability/ responsibility in decision making
Virtual organisations	■ Organisations that have no set physical locations ■ Communication between stakeholders with a shared purpose is through electronic communications (e.g. buying and selling specific aspects of knowledge)		

Summary questions

1 Why have network and virtual organisations become particularly important in the 21st century?

2 How are networked organisations particularly relevant in a Caribbean context?

3 What difficulties may arise in the establishment of a virtual organisation?

Specific objective

On completion of this section, you should be able to:

- explain the features of formal organisational structure.

KEY TERMS

Hierarchy: the different levels within an organisation representing the degree of authority and responsibility.

Chain of command: successive links from top to bottom in a hierarchy showing lines of responsibility.

Span of control: number of employees accountable to a manager.

Line manager: a manager directly responsible for someone else.

Organisational charts

Organisational charts display important characteristics of formal organisational structures. These include:

- the organisation's **hierarchy** – the different levels within the organisation, representing the degree of authority and responsibility
- the **chain of command** – the reporting system within the organisation, from operators at the lowest level of the hierarchy up to the managing director
- the **span of control** – the number of employees who are accountable to each individual manager, which varies depending on the type of product or service being produced and the nature of the work involved, but is narrower towards the top of the organisation
- formal relationships within an organisation show how the work within the organisation is structured – by function, product or geography.

Tall organisations

Organisations can be tall or flat. A tall organisation (Figure 2.9.1) has:

- many hierarchical levels
- a long chain of command
- a small span of control.

Flat organisations

A flat organisation (Figure 2.9.2) has:

- few hierarchical levels
- a short chain of command
- a large span of control.

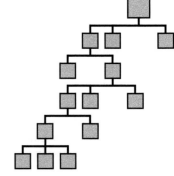

Figure 2.9.1 A tall organisation

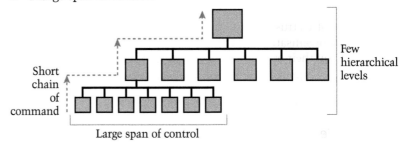

Figure 2.9.2 A flat organisation

In today's competitive business environment there has been a shift towards flatter organisational structures. These are characterised by fewer levels in the hierarchy and a shorter chain of command to enable clearer communication and speedier decision making.

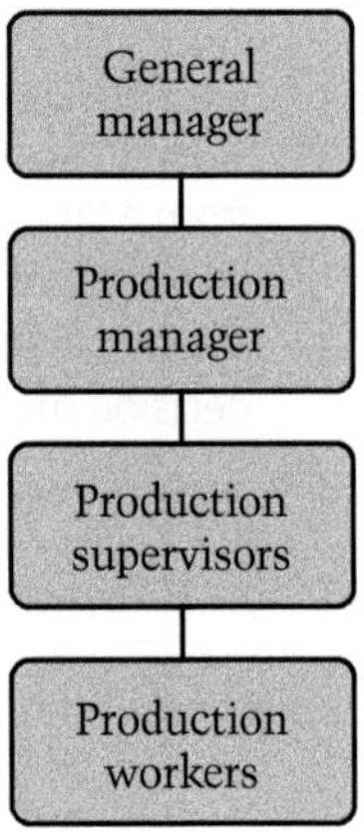

Line management and staff relationships

A **line manager** is a person who is directly responsible for a subordinate. For example, in Figure 2.9.3 the general manager has line management responsibility for the production manager, who in turn has line

General manager

Production manager

Production supervisors

Production workers

Figure 2.9.3 The line management structure within a production department

management responsibility for the production supervisors, who in turn manage the production workers.

Members of staff not involved directly in operational functions provide valuable support services. They may have technical expertise (for example, a legal adviser) that can assist personnel involved in production and top-level management in various business activities. Managers within these support functions are not part of the chain of command that relates directly to production of the products or services, but instead have authority over other individuals within the chain of command.

Within a chain of command, managers need to:

- delegate
- be responsible
- understand their levels of authority
- be accountable.

Responsibility

Responsibility is the duty of an individual to carry out tasks that are expected of him or her. Levels of responsibility flow from the bottom of an organisation to the top, meaning that subordinates have less responsibility than their managers or supervisors.

Authority

Authority is the right of an individual to carry out well-defined tasks and to give commands and orders for things to be done. A person's authority usually results from the position that they hold within an organisation (for example, the production manager has the authority to create production schedules for production-line workers). Authority flows from superiors to their subordinates. It is through authority that a manager exercises control. Authority can be delegated by a senior to a subordinate within an organisational structure.

Accountability

When someone has **accountability**, they are required to justify their actions and decisions. Individuals with responsibilities are accountable for those responsibilities – in other words, they need to be able to justify their actions or decisions in relation to their responsibilities.

Delegation

Delegation involves trusting someone else to carry out some of your duties. In large organisations, managers are unable to complete all of the tasks required on their own. They therefore need to:

- assign tasks and duties
- assign responsibility and accountability
- grant authority.

Did you know?

There are different types of authority: line authority, staff authority and functional authority. Use the internet to find out about each type.

KEY TERMS

Responsibility: duty to carry out tasks according to the level expected.

Authority: legitimate rights associated with a specific role.

Accountability: being answerable for actions taken and tasks performed.

Delegation: trusting someone (usually a subordinate) to carry out duties.

Summary questions

1 Explain the relationship between responsibility and accountability of managers in an organisation.

2 How is managers' span of control likely to vary according to their position in the hierarchy?

3 Explain what the line management structure might look like within a large insurance office or bank and its effect on staff relationships.

Summary table

Tall organisations	■ Many layers ■ Small span of control	■ Hierarchical with clear chain of command
Flat organisations	■ Few layers ■ Larger span of control	■ Short chain of command
Characteristics of formal organisations	■ Hierarchy ■ Chain of command ■ Span of control ■ Line and staff relationships	■ Responsibility ■ Authority ■ Accountability ■ Delegation

2.10 The characteristics of formal organisational structure: centralisation and decentralisation

Specific objective

On completion of this section, you should be able to:

- explain the features of centralised and decentralised organisational structures.

 Exam tip

When asked to distinguish between two features you should not just define them. You need to indicate what makes them different. Words and phrases such as 'while' or 'on the other hand' can be used to show that a distinction is being made.

Centralisation and decentralisation are terms used to describe the relationship between a company's corporate centre (head office) and its organisational divisions (branches).

Centralisation

Centralisation exists where the main responsibilities and running of the business are carried out within departments at a central headquarters. It can:

- strengthen management control – management at the central headquarters has more control
- improve coordination through centralised planning
- reduce costs – as costs are not duplicated
- help in monitoring quality – through reports provided to central managers.

Organisations may want a centralised structure to maintain control through standardisation of methods and management systems, and to reduce the risk of mistakes resulting from poor control of geographically dispersed units.

Decentralisation

In a decentralised organisation, certain responsibilities are delegated to branches or regional headquarters. Decentralisation occurs mainly in larger organisations. In many organisations, some degree of decentralisation is necessary to extend the availability of goods and services to a larger area or to obtain raw materials from other locations. When considering decentralisation, an organisation should take into account:

- the day-to-day management of the company (that is, whether there is sufficient management experience across the whole organisation or whether the experience is concentrated in the head office)
- the need for standardisation or specialisation of products (that is, does the product need to be produced in a standardised way or can it be produced in different ways in different parts of the organisation?).

CASE STUDY

FirstCaribbean International Bank

FirstCaribbean International Bank is one of the major commercial banks in the Caribbean. Its vision is to become the leading financial services provider in the region. FirstCaribbean operates in 17 Caribbean countries, including large countries like Trinidad and Jamaica and smaller ones such as the Turks and Caicos. The head office for the company is based in Toronto, Canada, but the regional head office is based in Barbados.

FirstCaribbean has 69 branches in the Caribbean and employs over 3,400 people. The executive

team of the company is representative of the major countries and sub-regions: for example, there are managing directors for the Dutch Caribbean, Jamaica, Barbados, Trinidad and Tobago, and the Cayman Islands. As well as providing financial services for Caribbean nationals, it also offers offshore financial services for overseas nationals.

1 To what extent does FirstCaribbean International Bank operate both a centralised and a decentralised structure?

2 What are the benefits to FirstCaribbean of centralising some of its activities and decentralising others?

Table 2.10.1 outlines the advantages and disadvantages of centralisation and decentralisation.

Table 2.10.1 The advantages and disadvantages of centralisation and decentralisation

Centralisation		Decentralisation	
Advantages	**Disadvantages**	**Advantages**	**Disadvantages**
A single management structure results in: ▪ quick decision making ▪ consistent plans throughout the organisation	Organisation may not be responsive to local conditions and needs	Flexibility	May lead to costly duplication of processes carried out at the centre
Easy to control and monitor operations	May lead to duplication of tasks at the centre and in the local regions	Allows a swift response to local needs and conditions	May lead to poor coordination and loss of control
Departments/teams do not become isolated	Centre may be seen as distant and conflicts may arise between the centre and local units	Local staff feel involved in decisions	May result in cultural clashes between local units and centre
Easy to coordinate functions		Allows local initiative	
One location results in reduced overheads		Supervision carried out locally	
Opportunities for economies of scale		Staff may feel they can express views more openly to local managers	

Summary table

Centralisation	The main responsibilities in an organisation rest with head office, which issues commands and creates policies.
Decentralisation	Branches and local areas are able to make substantial decisions for themselves.

Summary questions

1 How might a Caribbean-wide hotel chain benefit from adopting a centralised structure?

2 How might a Caribbean-wide hotel chain benefit from adopting a decentralised structure?

3 Which type of organisation – a decentralised organisation or a centralised organisation – is likely to be more expensive to run?

On completion of this section, you should be able to:

■ explain the factors that influence motivation.

KEY TERMS

Expectancy theory: the belief that rewards can be achieved for working hard (high expectations).

Did you know?

The valence expectancy theory can be summarised as:

1 I value a particular reward.

2 I believe that I can earn this reward by working hard.

3 I am motivated to work hard in order to achieve the reward.

What is motivation?

Motivation is:

■ the reason why people act or behave in a particular way

■ a desire or willingness to do something.

What motivates people? Does the drive to work hard come from an inner need within the individual or some external motivator such as reward or punishment?

The study of motivation investigates all the factors – biological, social and psychological – that encourage us to work hard. There are several theoretical approaches to motivation:

■ **Intrinsic theories** (for example, Maslow – see 2.12): these theories suggest that self-satisfaction and belief in one's own worth are the greatest motivators.

■ **Satisfaction theories** (for example, Herzberg – see 2.12): these theories suggest that if workers are satisfied, they will stick with one employer for longer. Happy workers also have higher morale, better mental health and higher levels of self-motivation, and as a result, they are more productive.

■ **Expectancy theories** (for example, Vroom's valence **expectancy theory**): these theories suggest that rewards and incentives are the greatest motivators. Rewards are given to an employee for hard work or effort. The employee needs to believe that he or she can achieve the standard required to receive the reward and that the reward is worth striving for. The greater the reward, the more the employee wants it. As a result, the employee is more likely to be motivated to achieve it.

■ **Incentive theories**: these maintain that higher production is brought about through higher rewards, using the psychological principle of reinforcement (in other words, employees receive rewards each time they achieve the desired standards). Incentive theories do not always take into account whether the person being incentivised believes that they can achieve the target or whether they place a high enough value on the incentive.

In 2.2 you looked at Mayo's human relations approach to work. Mayo's research concluded that the desire to be regarded highly by colleagues is a greater motivator than self-fulfilment and self-achievement.

Individual needs

What motivates us varies from one person to another. However, research shows that all individuals have three key psychological needs in relation to the workplace:

■ the need to feel part of a group – hence the importance of teamwork (as outlined by Mayo)

■ the need to feel that we are good at something – to have a sense of competence and to feel valued because we do things well

■ the need to feel that what we are doing is worthwhile – that it has meaning and purpose.

Every organisation should ensure that these fundamental needs are satisfied.

CASE STUDY

McClelland's motivational needs theory

McClelland's **motivational needs** theory identifies four main types of emotional need that motivate people.

1 Achievement

Achievement is seen as a worthwhile goal and individuals motivated by achievement work hard to demonstrate that they are high achievers. Managers motivated by achievement expect their subordinates to be motivated in a similar way.

2 Affiliation

An individual motivated by affiliation seeks to be accepted and valued by the group to which they belong. They may not be very good at taking tough decisions.

3 Competence

An individual motivated by competence needs to be good at something. A job well done is a reward in itself.

4 Power

Individuals motivated by power want to influence and motivate others. They like to control people and events, and do not mind taking risks to do so.

1 Which of the motivational needs outlined above do you recognise as being most significant in motivating you?

2 What are the benefits and drawbacks of this theory?

Self-motivation (intrinsic motivation)

Managers can create conditions that encourage motivation but they cannot directly make individuals motivated. Individual employees need to find their own **intrinsic motivation**.

The researchers in the Hawthorne experiments (see 2.2) helped to create the conditions that motivated the production-line workers. However, it was the employees themselves who chose to be motivated.

Ability to make choices

Choice can encourage motivation. Where individuals can choose which tasks to perform, they are most likely to choose the tasks that provide them with the greatest motivation.

Environmental opportunities (extrinsic motivation)

Extrinsic motivation comes from outside of an individual. Examples of external motivating factors are promotion or financial reward for working hard. These external motivators may provide more satisfaction than the satisfaction of completing the task itself.

KEY TERMS

Motivational needs: internal psychological motivators, such as the need for power or the need to be accepted (affiliation).

Intrinsic motivation: motivation that comes from within an individual (self-motivation).

Extrinsic motivation: factors in the external environment that encourage motivation, such as pay and other rewards (external motivation).

Summary table

Motivation theory	Summary
Intrinsic motivation	Motivation results from internal drivers.
Extrinsic motivation	Motivation that results from factors external to the individual, e.g. by providing better conditions at work.
Satisfaction theories	Satisfied workers are more motivated.
Incentive theories	Establishing rewards that employees value is most likely to result in motivation.

Summary questions

1 What is the difference between extrinsic and intrinsic motivation?

2 How do motivational needs influence motivation?

3 What are the key factors that are likely to lead to higher levels of motivation?

Maslow's theory of motivation

Abraham Maslow's theory of motivation is based on meeting individual needs. Maslow identified a hierarchy of needs containing five levels (Figure 2.12.1).

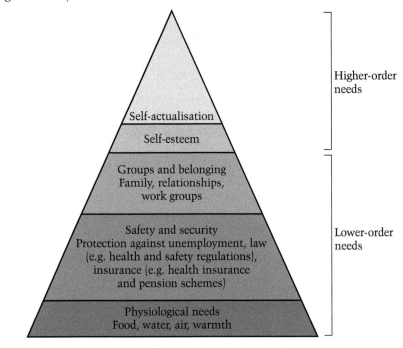

Figure 2.12.1 *Maslow's hierarchy of needs*

■ At the bottom level an individual's motivation to work comes from his or her need to survive (for example, obtain food and shelter). Once these basic needs have been met, employees are motivated by higher-order needs.

■ At the next level, safety and security needs (including protection against unemployment, safe working practices, health and safety regulations and pension schemes) provide motivation.

■ A sense of belonging to a group is important to most people. Organising employees into team structures can encourage a sense of belonging and encourage teamwork and communication.

■ At the next level, individuals need recognition of their accomplishments and to utilise their creative talents and initiatives to the full to satisfy their self-esteem needs.

■ At the top level, employees' psychological needs for personal growth and development – for example, through experiencing challenge within their jobs – need to be met to fulfil their self-actualisation needs.

Figure 2.12.2 *Employment enables people to meet a range of human needs, ranging from basic needs to be able to pay for food and shelter, to higher order needs such as having a sense of worth and pride*

Needs must be satisfied at all levels to motivate employees. Managers within an organisation can apply Maslow's hierarchy in a number of ways: for example, satisfying lower-level needs through a safe and pleasant working environment and satisfying higher-level needs by providing opportunities for employee development.

Herzberg's hygiene theory

Frederick Herzberg's theory, like Maslow's, is based on needs that have to be satisfied. Herzberg developed his theory by asking samples of engineers and accountants to identify occasions when they had felt motivated at work and occasions when they had felt unmotivated at work.

Herzberg believed that some factors – **motivators** – spur people to action, whereas other factors – **hygiene factors** – have the opposite effect and can lead to dissatisfaction if they are not met.

Motivators

Motivators ('satisfiers') are factors relating to an employee's personal development, achievement, recognition, promotion and responsibility, and the actual nature of the work itself. These satisfy and motivate people to work.

Hygiene factors

Hygiene factors ('dissatisfiers') are factors that relate to the working environment, such as effective company policy and management practices, good working conditions and relationships, and salary. If these factors are not met then employees become dissatisfied. This dissatisfaction is often a temporary state until employees 'accept' the hygiene factors.

Herzberg concluded that financial rewards are not long-term motivators. Of course, people are happy to receive a pay rise or financial incentive, but the impact of this extrinsic reward soon wears off. More recent research, however, indicates that money can act as a motivator, if the person receiving the pay increase associates this reward with recognition of his or her efforts and competence.

Herzberg's work suggests that managers need to consider both motivators and hygiene factors to improve performance and ensure that there is no dissatisfaction.

> **KEY TERMS**
>
> **Motivators:** the reasons why an individual takes certain actions.
>
> **Hygiene factors:** factors that need to be present in the workplace to ensure basic satisfaction (e.g. safe and clean working conditions and reasonable pay). Without these factors employees would be unmotivated.

Did you know?

Herzberg's theory is often referred to as the 'two factor' theory – differentiating hygiene factors from satisfiers.

Summary table

Needs	Examples
Maslow's lower-order needs	Physiological, security, being a member of and belonging to a group
Maslow's higher-order needs	Self-esteem, self-actualisation
Herzberg's motivators (satisfiers)	Personal development, achievement, recognition, promotion, responsibility, the work itself
Herzberg's hygiene factors (dissatisfiers)	Company policy and management practice, good levels of pay and reward

Summary questions

1 For each level of Maslow's hierarchy, what can be provided in the workplace to meet an employee's needs (for example, a wage to meet biological and physical needs)?

2 Why are Herzberg's hygiene factors not seen as being motivators?

3 What similarities can you identify between Herzberg's and Maslow's theories?

Figure 2.13.1 *Job enrichment is key to keeping employees motivated*

Both Maslow's and Herzberg's theories are founded on observations and research of real-world situations. Herzberg's research was based on interviews with 200 engineers and accountants, in which he asked them to identify occasions when they had felt motivated at work. Herzberg found that managers could motivate employees through:

- job enrichment
- job enlargement
- job rotation.

Job enrichment

Job enrichment involves increasing the range of tasks and challenges for an employee, providing more stimulating work with varying degrees of difficulty.

Enriched jobs should include:

- a range of tasks
- meaningful tasks – for example, where an employee carries out a complete task as part of a larger project (such as painting a whole room as part of a larger-scale construction project)
- opportunities for employees to use the full range of their abilities and skills.

Job enrichment builds increased levels of complexity and variety (known as 'vertical loading'). It can meet some of the higher-order needs of an employee, thereby facilitating psychological growth. Variety increases the level of interest and gives the employee a sense of responsibility and the feeling that they are progressing. Job enrichment can also improve employee loyalty, which in turn reduces the turnover of the labour force.

Job enlargement

Job enlargement is where a worker is given more tasks to do at the same level of challenge. This is sometimes known as 'horizontal loading'. Job enlargement allows employees to do new tasks, which may reduce the repetitive nature of their role. However, they may feel put upon if they are given more tasks to do for the same amount of money.

Job rotation

Job rotation involves giving employees a variety of tasks. Often when an employee joins a company in a management position, he or she starts out by spending time in the various functions of the company to get an overview of how the business fits together. Similarly, job rotation can be used at other levels and in other roles. For example, job rotation on a production line (moving from one task to another at the same level on a regular basis) would give production-line workers a better understanding of how the various processes fit together.

Once employees are trained to carry out new roles, they may be more productive because they are inspired by the variety of their work. They are less likely to take days off sick or turn up late. The cost of training is repaid through better output from employees in the medium and long term. Where employees rotate to a new job, they may work harder and more diligently, reducing errors and accidents at work.

As a result of job rotation, employees may find themselves working at a different site. The novelty of working in a new situation may provide motivation. However, employees may not be keen to travel to a new location or to work alongside new workmates. Another disadvantage of job rotation is that it can disrupt existing schedules and patterns of work. It can also lead to inefficiency during the early days when a worker starts to learn a new task.

Job satisfaction

Satisfying employees is an important objective for managers in present-day organisations. Typically, job satisfaction can be measured through employee satisfaction surveys, which ask employees what aspects of their work they enjoy. Managers can improve job satisfaction by incorporating more of these factors.

Job satisfaction results in benefits for the employee, the employer and the organisation, as shown in Table 2.13.1.

Table 2.13.1 The benefits of job satisfaction

Employee's benefits	Employer's benefits	Organisational benefits
More interesting work	Better staff motivation	People used to their full potential
Less stress	Fewer staff absences	Higher levels of productivity and quality
Higher self-esteem	Improved productivity	Improved customer satisfaction
Potential for promotion	More flexible staff	Company growth and profits
Enjoying work		

Summary table

Job enrichment	Motivating employees by providing them with more stretching tasks and involving them more in decision making
Job enlargement	Motivating employees through providing a wider variety of tasks
Job rotation	Motivating employees by enabling them to work in new roles

Summary questions

1 Identify a job role with which you are familiar. How could this job role be improved through job rotation, job enlargement or job enrichment?

2 Compare the benefits of horizontal loading with those of vertical loading.

3 What is the relationship between job enrichment and the ideas of Maslow and Herzberg?

CASE STUDY

Applying motivational theory in a bank

A large Caribbean-wide bank is looking at ways of motivating existing employees. One way is to give managers and trainee managers assignments in other banks elsewhere in the Caribbean that are part of the same banking group. A six-month management placement in another bank gives the managers wider experience, prepares them for promotion, and opens their eyes to best practice in other parts of the same group.

Another approach is to increase the number of tasks that new employees (who are also new to management) carry out as they become more experienced. For example, they could take responsibility for dealing with a greater number of small business accounts as they grow in competence and confidence.

More experienced employees could be encouraged to take on new roles. For example, an employee with good customer-facing skills could become a personal financial adviser, working with customers to advise them about a range of additional financial services that are available (for example, home insurance, mortgages and new types of savings account).

Another approach that has proved particularly motivating in the past is to change the tasks that the more experienced staff do on a week-by-week basis.

1 Identify the motivational techniques described in the case study.

2 What are the benefits and drawbacks of each of the techniques for the bank's employees?

2.14 Financial and non-financial motivational strategies

Specific objective

On completion of this section, you should be able to:

- explain the theories and practices of motivation in relation to financial and non-financial incentives.

Did you know?

Share options are another type of financial incentive. Employees are offered shares in a company as part of their reward package. This encourages the employees to work hard for themselves and for the company to increase profits and therefore their share in the profits.

KEY TERMS

Performance appraisal: a method by which the job performance of an employee is evaluated.

An incentive encourages us to carry out a desired action. Incentives can be positive or negative. For example, you can offer a dog a reward (positive incentive), such as a dog biscuit, for being good. Alternatively, you might punish it (negative incentive) for being disobedient.

Financial incentives

A financial incentive is a tangible monetary reward for employees who work hard and achieve. The harder they work, the more likely they are to receive a bonus, better rates of pay and a share of the company profits. Of course, if the rewards are tied to the company's performance and the company is not doing very well, this might have a negative effect on effort. The main types of financial incentive are outlined below.

- **Variable pay:** pay is tied to levels of individual, group or company performance. The better the performance, the higher the pay. An organisation needs to ensure that the cost to the organisation of performance-related pay is more than matched by the increased profits resulting from improved performance.
- **Bonuses:** these are frequently used in sales organisations, where bonuses are tied to the achievement of specified sales targets.
- **Profit sharing:** rewards are linked to the level of profits that a business makes.

Appraisal

Performance-related incentive schemes depend on being able to measure performance against targets. **Performance appraisal** is a useful technique for setting targets and monitoring whether they are achieved. An individual employee sits down with their line manager (typically at six-monthly intervals or annually) to establish targets for the coming year and to review performance from the previous year. Work targets are established which then feed into performance-related pay or bonuses. The appraisal at the end of the period can be used to check whether the employee's targets have been achieved.

Job evaluation

Job evaluation is a way of determining the value of a job, which can then be linked to rewards. There are four main methods of job evaluation.

Job ranking

Jobs are ranked from highest to lowest in terms of their relative importance to the company: that is, in terms of how valuable they are in helping the company to meet its objectives. These factors are then weighted in terms of their importance within a particular job role. If the job includes several highly weighted factors then it is likely to be rewarded more highly. It may prove difficult to rank jobs in large organisations and, because of the subjectivity involved in the method, it may act as a disincentive to employees who feel that their job has been given a lower ranking.

Job classification

Jobs are assigned to particular predetermined classes (for example, Class 1 Executives; Class 2 Skilled workers; Class 3 Semi-skilled workers and Class 4 Unskilled workers). This method is relatively easy to understand and less subjective than ranking, but there may be disagreements about the class into which a particular job falls.

Factor comparison method

This is the most complex method of job evaluation. A specific job is ranked against a number of factors, such as skill required, responsibility and supervisory responsibility. These factors are then weighted in terms of their importance within a particular job. If a particular factor receives a high weighting and it is part of a certain job, that job will be rewarded more highly. If a job includes several factors with a high weighting, the job will be particularly well rewarded. This method is quite complex to calculate but is more sophisticated in terms of assigning values to specific components of a job.

Work study

This approach is used to identify the components of jobs and work tasks. For example, in the case of a production-line job, a work analyst would identify the movements and activities carried out by a production worker to identify the components of the job. Scientific analysis of the results can then be used to identify appropriate rewards for the job. A key benefit of this approach is that managers have a better understanding of how to restructure jobs to improve efficiency.

Non-financial incentives

Herzberg showed that non-financial incentives – the satisfiers/motivators – are perhaps more important than financial reward. There are many ways of using non-financial techniques to incentivise employees. Non-monetary rewards might include compliments, a personal 'thank you', training programmes, flexible work schedules, job enrichment or the granting of unpaid leave.

They may also come in the form of an achievement certificate or a career development opportunity, or a gift such as a mug, T-shirt or a company umbrella. All of these can reinforce good performance, provide recognition to a particular employee and encourage everyone to strive to produce their best performance. These types of reward are often described as intrinsic rewards because they meet the employee's internal needs, such as self-esteem, recognition and personal fulfilment. Non-monetary rewards can be used frequently, and often have a longer-lasting effect than financial rewards.

Summary table

Type of benefit	Advantages
Financial benefits	■ Provide a clear reward that can be linked to performance (and calculated easily) ■ Incentive can be linked to performance through appraisal and work study
Non-financial benefits	■ Aligned with intrinsic motivation ■ Have a longer-term impact on motivation

Did you know?

Jobs can also be evaluated using a points system. This is similar to the factor comparison method. Again, a job is broken down into key factors. Points are associated with each key factor of the job: for example, skill level and hours worked. The points are then added up to identify the value of the job. Jobs with a similar total of points receive similar rewards.

Did you know?

Four major advantages of non-monetary rewards are:

- **Memory value:** Money gets spent and is gone. Other forms of recognition are remembered for longer.
- **Trophy value:** Non-monetary rewards can be shown to friends.
- **Flexibility:** There are many different ways a company can provide non-financial rewards.
- **Cost:** Non-monetary rewards cost a company less money.

Summary questions

1 Compare and contrast the benefits of giving praise and giving performance-related pay as ways of incentivising employees.

2 How can work performance be measured in order to link performance to pay?

3 What would be the best methods for incentivising employees working in customer-facing roles in a bank?

Specific objective

On completion of this section, you should be able to:

■ differentiate between types of leadership skills and styles by understanding leadership theories.

According to the *Oxford English Dictionary*, leadership is 'the action of leading a group of people or organization, or the ability to do this'. A leader establishes a clear vision that he or she encourages others to follow.

Management versus leadership

Leadership is an important quality associated with most managers. However, leadership and management are different. Table 2.15.1 explains the difference between management and leadership.

Table 2.15.1 Management versus leadership

Management	Leadership
Management is concerned with coping with complexity.	Leadership is concerned with coping with change.
Managers manage people (i.e. they organise and direct them).	Leaders lead people – to be a leader, you need to have followers.

Leadership theories

Leadership theories fall into three main categories: trait theories, style theories and contingency theories.

Trait theories

Trait theories assume that leaders have certain personal and physical characteristics called **traits** that enable them to lead other people and get them to perform. Typical traits associated with good leadership include judgement, integrity, energy, decisiveness, dependability, fairness, dedication, cooperation, initiative, foresight, drive, people skills, emotional stability, ambition and objectivity.

Style theories

Style theories focus on a predominant approach (that is, what the leader does and the way in which he or she treats and directs employees, handles problems and makes decisions) rather than on individual traits.

KEY TERMS

Traits: personal and psychological characteristics of individuals. Trait theories of management assume that leaders possess one or more specific traits (e.g. above average intelligence) that make them more suited to leadership.

Style theories: theories that state that leaders have a preferred style of management (e.g. autocratic or democratic), which they apply in a range of situations.

CASE STUDY

McGregor's Theory X and Theory Y managers

In the 1960s Douglas McGregor, an American psychologist, carried out research that identified two main styles of management (Theory X managers and Theory Y managers), as shown in Table 2.15.2.

Table 2.15.2 The two main styles of management as identified by McGregor

Theory X managers believe that employees:	Theory Y managers believe that employees:
■ dislike work and will avoid it if they can	■ want to work
■ prefer to be directed, want to avoid responsibility and have little ambition	■ want responsibility providing they are rewarded for taking it on
■ need to be controlled and coerced	■ are generally quite creative

Typically, managers' thinking falls into either the Theory X or the Theory Y category and this shapes the way that they manage. A Theory X manager is inclined to be autocratic – telling employees what needs to be done, punishing and reprimanding them when they step out of line and giving rewards for conforming to requirements. A Theory Y manager is inclined to be more democratic – giving more responsibility to employees, and trusting them to work independently.

The Theory X manager is most likely to create a climate that simply meets Maslow's lower-order needs and that focuses on Herzberg's hygiene factors. The Theory Y manager seeks to create opportunities for employees so that they are motivated through fulfilment of higher-order needs and genuine 'motivators'.

1 Would you respond more positively to a Theory X or Theory Y manager? Explain your answer.

Contingency theories

As we saw in 2.3, contingency theories of leadership are based on the assumption that no one leadership style is ideal because situations and other factors vary. The style of leadership varies depending on factors such as the situation and the people involved.

Adair's action-centred leadership theory

Adair's research showed that effective leadership involves achieving the right balance between the three sets of needs:

- **task needs:** the requirements of the task
- **group needs:** a sense of group unity
- **individual needs:** so that individuals can meet their own psychological and physical needs.

The circumstances of each situation (danger, time available, etc.) affect the priority given to each set of needs. For example:

- where the project is crucial, the needs of the task may be most important
- where consensus is required, group needs will be most important
- where the project has to meet the needs of all of the stakeholders individually, individual needs will be the most important.

Fiedler's contingency model

Fiedler's theory states that there are three variables that determine the style of a leader.

- **Leader–follower relations:** how much trust, respect and confidence is there between the leader and followers? Do group members want to be told what to do, or do they want to have responsibility to make decisions themselves?
- **The degree and structure of the task:** how much control can be given to the followers? Is it a low-level task that needs to be done in a routine way or is complex, requiring independent judgement and thought?
- **The power and authority of the leader's position:** do the followers accept the leader's power?

Summary table

Trait theories	Leadership is based on personal characteristics.
Style theories	Leadership effectiveness is based on what leaders do and how they do it: e.g. Theory X and Theory Y.
Contingency theories	The style of leadership varies depending on the situation.

Summary questions

1 What is meant by a predominant style of leadership? Why might an individual have a particular leadership style?

2 In the event of an emergency (for example, a hurricane hitting an island), what factors are likely to impact on and influence the style of leadership approach used?

3 What are traits? Why are traits likely to influence the leadership approach employed?

On completion of this section, you should be able to:

- differentiate between types of leadership style, including autocratic, consultative, democratic and laissez-faire.

There are five commonly accepted leadership styles, as set out in Table 2.16.1.

Table 2.16.1 Different leadership styles and their characteristics

Leadership style	Characteristics
Autocratic	■ The leader makes decisions, sets objectives and tells others what to do. ■ There is little or no scope for subordinates to question decisions. ■ Communication is from the top downwards. ■ Tasks are set out and explained by the leader or set out in manuals. ■ Rules and instructions are dictated by the leader.
Consultative	■ The leader makes decisions, sets objectives and consults others about courses of action. ■ Subordinates are given outlines of what needs doing but are allowed to ask questions. ■ Communication is from the top downwards with some feedback. ■ Tasks are set out by the leader but there is some consultation on appropriate steps and actions.
Democratic (also known as participative)	■ Objectives, policies and decisions are created and agreed upon jointly by teams. ■ The leader supports decision making. ■ There is a multi-channel flow of communications. ■ The way in which objectives are achieved is agreed through discussion. ■ The leader and teams jointly praise successful behaviours that meet team requirements.
Laissez-faire	■ The team is free to create its own objectives and policies, and to make its own decisions. ■ The leader has minimal involvement in decision making. ■ The team is free to communicate in whatever way it sees fit. ■ The team is self-managing and decides on its own patterns of working and how things will be done.
Transformational	See 2.17.

Tannenbaum and Schmidt's model of leadership

Robert Tannenbaum and Warren H. Schmidt's 1973 model of leadership suggests a **continuum** in which leadership styles fall between the authoritarian and the democratic. It shows the degree of freedom a manager gives to his or her subordinates, as against the level of authority that the manager exerts. This is easier to understand when looked at in diagrammatic form (see Figure 2.16.1).

Blake and Mouton's managerial grid model

In 1964, Robert R. Blake and Jane Mouton developed a managerial grid model to identify leadership style. Instead of focusing on autocratic versus democratic styles, this model identifies five different leadership styles

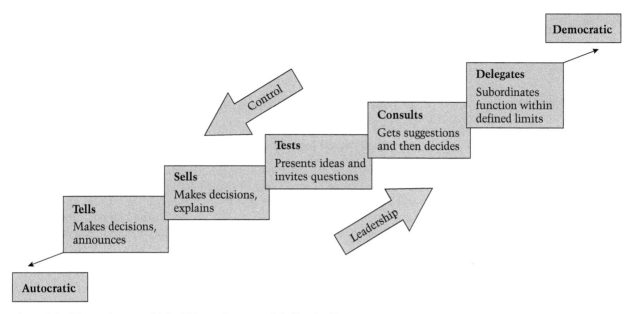

Figure 2.16.1 *Tannenbaum and Schmidt's continuum model of leadership*

based on 'concern for people' and 'concern for production', as shown in Figure 2.16.2. 'Concern for people' is the degree to which a leader considers the needs of people within a team and 'concern for production' is the degree to which a leader considers how best to complete a task. A leader showing:

- 'team leadership' is the ideal, as they consider the needs of both people and production equally
- 'country club leadership' is too concerned with people and gets little done
- 'task leadership' is too concerned with production and creates low morale
- 'impoverished leadership' has no concern for people or output
- 'middle-of-the-road leadership' shows some concern for people and some concern for production.

A manager who is familiar with the grid can assess where his or her leadership style lies, and consider where improvement is possible.

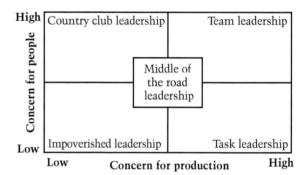

Figure 2.16.2 *Blake and Mouton's continuum of leadership styles*

Summary table

Style of leadership	Chosen style of leading
Autocratic	Top-down approach
Consultative	Takes into consideration the views of others
Democratic (participative)	Joint decision making between the leader and the team
Laissez-faire	Hands-off approach
Team	Combines concern for people and production

Summary questions

1 Compare and contrast the effectiveness of autocratic and democratic styles of leadership in a business context of your choice.

2 What are the weaknesses of the 'country club' and 'impoverished' styles of leadership?

3 Why might a 'team' approach to leadership be more effective than a 'middle-of-the-road' approach?

2.17 Transformational leadership and skills required for effective leadership

Specific objective

On completion of this section, you should be able to:

■ differentiate between types of leadership skills and styles with regard to transformational leadership and the skills required for effective leadership.

KEY TERMS

Transformational leadership: a type of leadership that establishes a clear vision and enables others to share that vision. Transformational leaders encourage followers to behave in a positive way (e.g. working more collaboratively with others to make well-informed decisions).

Did you know?

A key distinction is made between transactional leadership and transformational leadership. Transactional leadership approaches simply involve an exchange of rewards between a leader and followers. In contrast, the transformational leader shows a genuine concern for the well-being of others in the organisation and helps to develop their sense of self-worth.

Transformational leadership

In 1978 James MacGregor Burns introduced the concept of **transformational leadership**, which continues to be influential today.

According to Burns, a transformational leader establishes a clear vision, which he or she is able to get others to share. Followers therefore also become leaders because they share and take responsibility for delivering the vision. Burns believed that transformational leaders could engage with followers to identify and change their motives and needs, and inspire them to become leaders in working towards a common goal. This is particularly important in large, modern organisations.

In 1989 the American business writer Harry Schroder identified specific behaviours associated with transformational leadership.

Schroder identified four clusters of behaviours that a transformational leader needs to learn:

■ **Thinking behaviour:** thinking behaviour brings high-quality information to the decision-making process. Top-quality thinking involves researching information and presenting it in an intelligible way to others. It also involves offering a range of options to be considered when making a decision.

■ **Involving behaviour:** this involves bringing other people and their ideas into the decision-making process. A good way to do this is to listen actively to the ideas of others and to encourage others to speak up and present their ideas. They should also be involved in decision making.

■ **Inspiring behaviour:** inspirational behaviour involves building confidence in others through making effective decisions and communicating in a clear and interesting way.

■ **Performing behaviour:** performing behaviour enables action to take place in an organisation and then creates systems for monitoring and recording progress.

These four clusters of behaviour are very important for any leader. A good leader needs to identify their strengths and weaknesses in relation to each of these behaviours and to improve on any areas of weakness.

A transformational leader is not an autocratic leader – rather he or she is someone with a clear vision of where they want to take an organisation. Transformational leaders recognise that they cannot achieve this vision alone, so it is important to enable others to become leaders and for them to share and build the vision together.

Studies suggest that warmth of personality is a key quality required in an effective transformational leader.

Skills and traits associated with effective leadership

An effective leader requires three main skills:

- **Critical thinking:** this is the ability to think clearly and rationally about a situation and to understand how it may change in the future. The leader needs to employ critical thinking to anticipate the change and decide what needs to be done.
- **Adaptability:** leaders need to be able to change their behaviour and adapt resources in order to manage change.
- **Communication:** it is no good diagnosing a problem and adapting resources to resolve it if the solution is not communicated effectively to those who need to implement it.

Leaders also need to have problem-solving skills. They need to be able to define problems and then to propose solutions for dealing with them. They need to be able to make a well-informed choice from the available options. The leader needs to focus on two key areas in decision-making situations:

- ensuring that the goal or task is achieved
- maintaining good relations within the organisation by building a good leader–follower relationship in order to achieve the goal.

Summary table

Transformational leadership	■ Sharing a vision and then enabling followers to take on some leadership responsibility
Leadership behaviours	■ Thinking behaviour ■ Involving behaviour ■ Inspiring behaviour ■ Performing behaviour
Leadership skills	■ Critical thinking ■ Adaptability ■ Communication ■ Problem solving
Leadership roles	■ Setting objectives and getting tasks completed ■ Focusing on the needs of people in the organisation

Figure 2.17.1 *Martin Luther King is often cited as a transformational leader. He created a vision for others to follow and had the ability to encourage others to take on leadership roles in the Civil Rights movement.*

Summary questions

1 What overlap can you identify between effective leadership behaviour and effective leadership skills?

2 What is the relationship between leadership behaviour and the outcomes of such behaviour? How can managers develop better leadership behaviour?

3 What leadership skills are required when considering various options prior to making a decision?

4 What leadership skills are required to resolve disagreements during the decision-making process?

Specific objective

On completion of this section, you should be able to:

- differentiate between types of leadership skills and styles, including informal leadership.

Did you know?

When the nuclear reactors at the Japanese nuclear plant at Fukushima overheated following the tsunami in 2011, the technical experts at the plant took on informal leadership roles and responsibilities to control the situation.

KEY TERMS

Formal leadership: where a person is officially designated as the leader of a group.

Informal leadership: leadership by a person who is not officially recognised as a leader. Members of a group 'appoint' him or her as a leader.

Formal versus informal leadership

Formal leadership

Formal leadership is when an individual is given authority by virtue of their role – for example, as a marketing director or chief executive officer. There are certain leadership powers and responsibilities that come with such roles. The leader has a formal role to play in directing and organising others.

Informal leadership

In contrast, an informal leader is a person who does not have official authority to direct a group. In certain situations, a person who has power may be accepted by his or her peers as an informal leader. **Informal leadership** may arise for a number of reasons:

- An informal leader may have particular expertise in a given situation. For example, an engineer may be able to take the lead in repairing a computer or other piece of machinery.
- An informal leader may assume leadership powers as a result of his or her charisma and personality. Followers look up to leaders with strong characters and personalities.
- An informal leader shares the goals and vision of the followers. For example, a work colleague who voices the views and opinions of the group may assume informal leadership of the group.

The influence of an informal leader is based on his or her ability to gain respect and trust from others. The informal leader may not deliberately set out to perform a leadership role but may grow into this role because of the expectations of others.

Working with informal leaders

It is essential for formal leaders to understand the importance of informal leadership. An informal leader may work collaboratively with the formal leader or may create conflict.

Whereas a formal leader works with and directs others to achieve the targets and objectives of the organisation, the informal leader may be working to his or her own agenda. Typically, the loyalty of the formal leader is to the organisation whereas the informal leader's loyalty may be to a group or groups within the organisation.

There are a number of strategies that a formal leader can employ when working with an informal leader. The formal leader should:

- seek to work collaboratively with the informal leader to exchange ideas, clarify the objectives of the informal leader, identify shared objectives and identify where compromises can be made – by making the informal leader an ally, the formal leader can gain more control of work groups within an organisation
- offer rewards to the followers of the informal leader to persuade them to follow the company line if needed
- make very clear to organisation members the benefits of following company objectives and guidelines.

Table 2.18.1 shows the advantages and disadvantages of informal leadership to an organisation.

Table 2.18.1 *Advantages and disadvantages of informal leadership to an organisation*

Advantages	Disadvantages
■ It creates additional power structures within the organisation, which can be used to help the organisation achieve its objectives. ■ It provides opportunities for new leaders to emerge within an organisation.	■ Alternative sources of power can create conflict within an organisation. ■ Groups within an organisation can lose sight of the overarching objectives of the organisation.

CASE STUDY

Conflict at the bus depot

Kingstown Bus Depot is the island's central bus depot. Portia is the superintendent at the depot and is responsible for making sure that buses leave punctually so that customers can start their bus journey in a regular and ordered way, and get to work and school on time. Drivers are expected to report to the depot at 7am each day so that bus services can commence from 7.30am and so that the superintendent can make sure that there is a regular flow of buses from the depot on to the island's roads at regular intervals.

However, recently there has been an increasing number of complaints from customers about buses falling behind schedule and arriving late, meaning that children are late for school and workers are late getting to work. In addition, the government ministry responsible for road traffic has started to criticise the bus depot because of the large number of buses coming on to the roads at the same time

in the period leading up to 8am and because drivers are taking risks to catch up time on their schedules.

Michael has found himself becoming the unofficial spokesperson for the bus drivers. The drivers argue that it is unrealistic for them to arrive punctually at 7am every morning and that there is congestion on the roads which slows down their journey to work. They believe that the time at which buses start should be put back to 7.45am or even 8 o'clock to give them time to get to work. Michael has worked as a driver for many years and is a strong character who is also regarded as the best driver.

1 Identify the formal and informal leaders in this context.

2 What actions might the formal leaders take to resolve this dispute? What case would the formal leaders put forward and what tactics could they employ to secure an effective leadership structure?

Summary table

Skills and styles of formal leaders	An officially designated leader uses authority and formal channels to direct and lead others.
Skills and styles of informal leaders	Informal leaders are more likely to use personal influence over groups in which they work.

Summary questions

1 What strategies can a formal leader use to encourage informal leaders to collaborate in meeting organisational objectives?

2 How can transformational leaders (see 2.17) work with informal leaders?

Specific objective

On completion of this section, you should be able to:

■ describe the group (team) formation process.

Groups

A **group** is a collection of people who come together for a specific purpose. As part of a group, individuals usually have to adjust to the expectations of others. When people feel part of a group, they share some of the characteristics of the group (for example, a shared way of dressing or the values and language of the group).

Formal groups are groups that are set up by an organisation to achieve specific purposes whereas informal groups arise through chance or spontaneous interactions.

A team

A **team** is much more than just a group. A team shares a sense of common purpose and a goal.

CASE STUDY

Katzenbach and Smith's high-performance team

In the early 1990s, Jon Katzenbach and Douglas Smith carried out some research to identify what makes a successful team. They stated that a group becomes a team when it consists of 'a small number of people with complementary skills who are committed to a common purpose, performance goals and an approach for which they feel mutually accountable'.

Their researched identified four different types of team within the workplace and determined which groups/teams were the most effective, and therefore the most successful (Figure 2.19.1).

■ **Working groups:** these are the least effective type of team. A working group is essentially a collection of individuals who share information and best practice. The total work of the group is often no more than the individuals could produce on their own.

■ **Pseudo-teams:** a pseudo-team consists of individuals who are notionally part of a team, but who lack clarity and direction, and frequently obstruct one another. People may perform poorly in a pseudo-team because they are obstructing each other.

■ **Potential teams:** a potential team is a collection of individuals who are trying hard to work together. They have not yet succeeded because they lack clarity about what they should be doing or because there is no clear team structure. Katzenbach and Smith feel that most

organisations have lots of potential teams that could be turned into **high-performance teams** – for example, through giving them:

□ clarity of direction
□ stimulating and motivating tasks
□ training to form a real team.

■ **High-performance teams:** a high-performance team is a team with a strong sense of shared responsibility and commitment to the team and to team goals. Members of the team are prepared to take on extra responsibilities to ensure the success of the team.

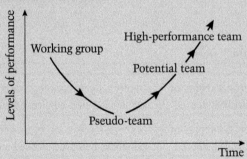

Figure 2.19.1 *The team performance curve*

1 Identify a team to which you have belonged, which has been through a number of the stages outlined in Figure 2.19.1.

2 Explain how the team was able to improve its performance over time.

3 Identify a team to which you have belonged, where performance did not improve over time. Why was this the case?

Stages of team development

Bruce Tuckman and Mary Ann Jensen (1977) published a model of **team development** that explains how small groups and teams develop. There are four stages:

1 **Forming:** a number of individuals come together to form a loose collection with no clear sense of purpose.

2 **Storming:** the group begins to exchange ideas, but as yet there is little structure to the group and there are no clear plans to take the group forward.

3 **Norming:** the group begins to share ideas. A leadership pattern may begin to emerge, and the group starts to conform to a given set of ideas. The group begins to formulate decisions.

4 **Performing:** a clear organised pattern is established. The team enjoys mutual respect, shares ideas and encourages participation from all members of the team. Every member of the team is therefore able to make the best possible contribution to the team process.

Tuckman and Jensen added a fifth stage (**adjourning**) to the group development model. This is when the group breaks up.

A number of issues are worth considering in relation to the stages outlined above:

1 In the early stages of team formation, when there is no appointed leader, the team may be dominated by individuals or small cliques of individuals who are determined to dominate and pull the group towards their thinking. Quieter members of the group may not be heard at this stage.

2 During the storming stage, if the group focuses solely on completing tasks in the short term, the longer-term development needs of the group may be overlooked, resulting in reduced effectiveness in the long term. Social relationships within the group may be poor, so no clear team spirit is created.

3 During the norming stage, if the team focuses on the development of social relationships at the expense of getting tasks completed, relationships may deteriorate due to frustration. People want to see tasks completed in order to do a good job.

4 At the performing stage, a group with established bonds and group members may not be ready to incorporate new members. The group may be reluctant to accept new people with new ideas.

KEY TERMS

High-performance team: an effective team based on collaboration, shared goals, shared accountabilities and shared responsibility. Members of the team are committed to each other and to achieving the team's goals.

Team development: the stages that a team goes through to become an effective, high-performing team.

Did you know?

Sometimes the adjourning stage is referred to as the mourning stage because when groups break up it can be likened to bereavement.

Summary table

Katzenbach and Smith's team formation process	1	Working group	3	Potential team		
	2	Pseudo team	4	High-performance team		
Tuckman and Jensen's team development model	1	Forming	3	Norming	5	Adjourning
	2	Storming	4	Performing		

Summary questions

1 How does the norming stage of team development differ from the performing and adjourning stages?

2 What is a high-performance team? How would team members know that they are part of a high-performance team?

3 What is the difference between a team and the following?

 a A formal group

 b An informal group

2.20 The characteristics and composition of effective teams

Characteristics

There are a number of characteristics of an effective team and effective team members, as outlined below:

- **Commitment:** each member is committed to the team and to its goals. They demonstrate this by working hard for the team and through their pride in being a member of the team.
- **Participation:** each member gets involved in team activities. Rather than standing back and letting others carry out the work, they are willing to get involved so that the team achieves better results.
- **Trust:** members of the team can trust and rely on each other. This means that team members have to be honest, open and reliable in their relationships with each other and in team activities.
- **Decisions are made by consensus:** there may be disagreements between team members about particular decisions. These should be aired openly – but once decisions are agreed on, everyone should accept them as being the best for the team and work together to implement the decision or approach (even though it may not be their preferred solution).
- **Flexibility:** the team needs to learn to adapt over time rather than expecting to do things in the same way every time. Flexibility enables new working practices to be employed (where appropriate) and allows new members to join the team and to suggest new ideas.
- **Encouragement:** team members should encourage each other. In this module, you have already seen how the human relations approach (2.2) demonstrated that workers benefit from recognition. Encouragement is also a great motivator.
- **Support and growth:** a team needs support so that it can improve and grow over time. Team-building activities are helpful in developing the team-working skills of individuals and the team as a whole. For example, organisations may employ team-building experts and use team-building activities, such as collaborative problem-solving activities and challenges that require a team to pull together.

CASE STUDY

A 'sandtastic' team-building exercise

Team-building exercises often involve bringing groups of people who work together into unfamiliar settings (for example, an away-day at a hotel to work on team-building exercises and challenges together). One example of a team-building exercise might involve building a beach sculpture – a 'sandtastic' team-building experience. It enables individuals to see each other in a different light. The team is required to cooperate in order to build the sculpture. There are sometimes a number of teams competing against one another. Team-building exercises often enable team members to appreciate the hidden skills and abilities of those with whom they work. They can be carried out in informal settings in a friendly and encouraging way.

1   How can a team-building exercise, such as building a sand sculpture, help participants develop the characteristics of an effective team? Refer to the characteristics of an effective team listed above.

Figure 2.20.1 Building a sand sculpture is a good example of a team-building exercise

Composition

Raymond Meredith Belbin's *Management Teams: Why They Succeed or Fail*, published in 1981, is one of the most influential pieces of management research. Belbin studied the way people behaved when put into groups or syndicates. His research initially identified eight roles that members could fill and found that winning teams were those containing all of these different roles:

- The coordinator coordinates the team's efforts and ensures that all resources are used effectively in achieving goals.
- Shapers set the team's objectives and priorities, and guide the team towards completion of the task.
- The plant is the creative, 'ideas' person.
- The monitor-evaluator is shrewd and analytical, analysing problems and evaluating progress.
- The resource investigator is extrovert and good at making contacts outside of the team and reporting on developments outside the team.
- The implementer is practical, loyal and task orientated.
- The team worker is caring and highly person orientated. He or she keeps the team together and improves communication within the team.
- The completer-finisher maintains momentum and ensures completion of the task.

More recently, Belbin introduced another important role – the specialist – as many team tasks require specialist knowledge or skills.

These roles do not reflect team members' personality types, but the way they prefer to operate when they are doing a shared task. An individual's role depends on the way they like to work, the group's needs and the demands of the particular project.

Did you know?

Belbin's team roles can be grouped into three main categories:

1 Those that focus on the needs of the team (e.g. the team worker).

2 Those that focus on the task (e.g. the implementer).

3 Those roles that involve more thought than action (e.g. the monitor-evaluator).

Summary table

Characteristics of effective teams	Description
Commitment	Commitment to the team and to getting the task completed
Participation	Participation in team activities by every member
Trust	Trust in each other and in the team
Consensus	Disagreements are aired and decisions are made that are best for the team
Flexibility	Flexibility to allow new ideas and practices to be implemented
Encouragement	Team members encourage one another
Support	Team-building and support activities need to be undertaken to enable the team to grow over time

Summary questions

1 For a team with which you are familiar, identify which of the characteristics of effective teams are shown by the team.

2 Why is it important for teams to be flexible and to facilitate team growth over time?

3 Which of Belbin's team roles have you performed in recent team activities? Do you tend to play the same type of role in different team situations? What problems might arise in teams where some of Belbin's roles are missing?

Group cohesiveness and advantages and disadvantages of teams to an organisation

On completion of this section, you should be able to:

- describe the characteristics of effective teams in terms of factors that influence group cohesiveness
- describe the advantages and disadvantages of teams to an organisation.

KEY TERMS

Group cohesiveness: the level of attachment of members to a group.

Did you know?

It has been suggested that the optimum team size is five people because:

- the odd number prevents a deadlock
- the team is large enough to avoid making mistakes due to insufficient information and to avoid power being concentrated in the hands of one individual with a fixed view
- the team is small enough to involve everyone.

Did you know?

Teams need to do two things well: focus on achieving tasks and build a good teamwork process. Where group goals are clear and there is sufficient time to build team cohesiveness, it is possible to focus on the task and the process at the same time.

Group cohesiveness is the extent to which a group gels together in terms of smooth interactions and willingness to work closely together.

Factors that influence group cohesiveness

There are a number of important factors that influence group cohesiveness, including the size of the group, the goals of the group, and the similarities and diversity within the group.

Size of the group

There are a number of reasons why it is easier to make decisions within small groups (for example, a group of five or six people) than in larger groups. Within a smaller group:

- fewer people are drawn into the decision-making process
- it is easier to involve everyone in the decision-making process
- it is easier to achieve consensus
- there is general satisfaction with the way the group operates
- individuals find it easier to identify with the group, and subgroups are less likely to form.

As the size of the group grows, the leader needs to take centralised control over decision making in order to prevent the group from becoming fragmented.

However, there are also advantages of a larger group:

- a large group can call on a greater pool of skills, energy and resources
- if many members of an organisation are involved in the decision-making process, they may be more willing to implement policies.

Group goals

A sense of shared responsibility for achieving goals creates cohesiveness within a team. If goals are clear then a team is more likely to work as a cohesive unit to achieve them. For example, if a goal relates to being the market leader then a team is likely to work together to make this happen.

Similarities and diversity

Where people are similar, they are often more likely to agree because they have a similar mindset. However, this means that decisions may not take into consideration broader opinions and may be based on a narrow set of information. Diversity within a group ensures that a wider selection of views and opinions are taken into consideration, thereby enabling better decision making.

Attraction

Attraction is the extent to which individuals get along with one another because they feel a sense of affinity and association with other members of the team. Teams in which there is more interpersonal attraction between members are more likely to be committed.

Lack of cohesion

A lack of cohesion is most likely to occur when:

- team goals are poorly defined
- there is a high turnover of team members
- contributions are not recognised or rewarded
- there is either weak or authoritarian team leadership
- team leaders are challenged by members of the team
- members of the team are not able to work in a team-working situation.

Advantages and disadvantages

Table 2.21.1 outlines the advantages and disadvantages of teams to an organisation.

Table 2.21.1 *The advantages and disadvantages of teams to an organisation*

Advantages	Disadvantages
• Hard-working teams help an organisation to achieve its objectives. • Teams work collectively and enable better results than when individuals work on their own. • Targets can be set for teams, including individual targets for team members. • Teams and teamwork encourage motivation and a greater sense of belonging. • Teamwork encourages the development of new ideas and innovation, as all members are encouraged to speak up. • Expertise and skills are shared.	• Teams involve the break-up of the organisation into smaller segments – so the team may become detached from the larger organisation. • Team members may become so committed to the team and to informal leaders that they fail to respond effectively to formal leaders.

Summary table

Factors influencing group cohesiveness	How each factor affects group cohesiveness
The size of the group	Too large a group can lead to differences and disagreements. Too small a group can result in power being concentrated in the hands of one individual with a fixed view.
Group goals	Clear goals create a sense of cohesiveness, as they can be shared by all group members.
Similarities/diversity	Where groups consist of similar individuals, they may share common values and beliefs. However, this may reduce the range and variety of views, thereby reducing the quality of decision making.
Attraction	If there is more interpersonal attraction between members, the team will be more committed to its goals.

Summary questions

1 What is an ideal group size or team size and why?
2 How do clear goals that are shared by team members make it easier to develop a cohesive team?
3 Which factors are most likely to reduce group cohesiveness?

On completion of this section, you should be able to:

■ describe possible causes of conflict in organisations, including management style, competition for scarce resources, lack of communication and clash of personalities

■ understand the advantages and disadvantages of functional and dysfunctional conflict.

Figure 2.22.1 *Causes of conflict*

Conflict arises in the boardroom of a company, in management meetings and in team meetings. It is inevitable in situations where decisions need to be made. **Functional (constructive) conflict** should be welcomed because it enables the sharing of views and ideas. The important thing is to be able to manage conflict effectively (see 2.23). The main causes of conflict are shown below in Figure 2.22.1.

Management styles

A manager's style may be one or more of the following:

■ **Dominant:** dominant managers make things happen by exercising control and influence. They may be forceful and dynamic in pushing their ideas forward and getting others to follow their lead.

■ **Submissive:** submissive managers let things happen rather than taking control of events. They adopt a laid-back attitude and give in easily, preferring to accept the ideas of others rather than standing up for their own ideas.

■ **Warm:** warm managers are sensitive and responsive to the needs of others. They demonstrate open and caring behaviour with a high regard for other people's feelings.

■ **Hostile:** hostile managers place their own needs first and are insensitive to the needs of others, which can result in anger. They are unresponsive to human needs at work.

A manager may exhibit a combination of these styles. Table 2.22.1 shows how these different styles may be combined and how each style may lead to conflict.

KEY TERMS

Functional (constructive) conflict: a moderate level of disagreement that can improve a team's performance and help it to achieve its goals through open discussion.

Table 2.22.1 *How different management styles may lead to conflict*

Management style	Description	How it may cause conflict
Dominant and hostile	■ Tells staff what to do and expects it to be done ■ An old-fashioned approach	This style is likely to cause conflict. Employees feel that their views are not being taken into consideration. They may build up grievances. Conflict may be hidden below the surface in poor performance and lack of motivation.
Dominant and warm	■ Provides clear direction ■ Shows care and concern for people	This is the least likely style to cause conflict. Staff are given clear leadership with a good approach to human relations.
Submissive and hostile	■ Avoids decision making ■ Is negative	This style often leads to conflict. The combination of no clear direction and hostility creates animosity.
Submissive and warm	■ Pacifies ■ Tries to be friendly	This style is likely to lead to conflict. People like a caring approach but also want leadership. As a result of a lack of vision and sense of direction, staff may oppose a manager with this style.

Competition for scarce resources

An organisation has limited resources available to it. Organisations consist of divisions, departments and teams, each of which may feel that they deserve more resources because their work is the most important. Conflicts over resources will thus arise between teams, between departmental managers and between other groups. Creating an organisational budget is a good way of allocating resources across departments and teams. However, the creation of the budget is often a major source of dispute in an organisation.

Lack of communication

Poor communication can lead to conflict. The main causes of a lack of communication are:

- **misunderstandings:** a lack of clarity and explanation is one of the biggest causes of conflict in an organisation
- **lack of information:** if people in an organisation do not receive information, they cannot act on it and cannot make appropriate decisions
- **access to information:** if some people are given information and others are not, it can lead to a feeling of inequality and unfairness (for example, 'Why was I the last one to be told?')
- **poor communication channels:** information may be distributed through inappropriate channels (for example, it may be put on a message board or in a document that people do not read).

Clash of personalities

Human beings often clash with each other. This may be because they have similar personalities (for example, two autocratic individuals) or because they have very different personalities (for example, a dominant and warm person and a hostile and submissive person). This is one of the main issues within boardrooms across the world, where dominant individuals can be aggressive and employ bullying behaviours.

Functional and dysfunctional conflict

Conflict can be healthy and helpful to an organisation if managed properly. Otherwise, it can become dysfunctional and create problems, as shown in Figure 2.22.2.

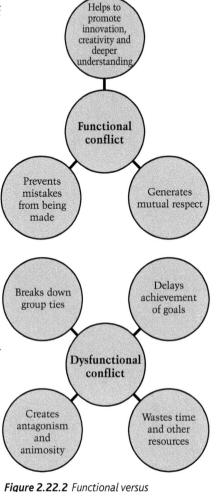

Figure 2.22.2 *Functional versus dysfunctional conflict*

Summary table

Cause of conflict	Reason
Management style	Manager may be too dominant or too weak
Competition for resources	Competing claims for company resources
Lack of communication	Confused messages and/or poor information
Clash of personalities	Personality types that are too similar or very different

Summary questions

1 For a group with which you are familiar, what are likely to be the main causes of conflict?

2 What are likely to be the main causes of conflict in a small start-up business?

3 Is all conflict negative?

2.23 Conflict management strategies

Specific objective

On completion of this section, you should be able to:

- assess the effectiveness of strategies used to manage conflict in organisations.

A model of conflict resolution

There are a number of ways of dealing with conflict, as identified by Kenneth W. Thomas and Ralph H. Kilmann in their 1974 conflict resolution model. Thomas and Kilmann believe that strategies for dealing with conflict need to take into consideration levels of assertiveness and cooperativeness.

Assertiveness

Assertiveness is the ability to stand up for ourselves and to express an opinion. It involves being honest about your feelings and intentions, expressing your own views in a calm and clear way, and often disagreeing with another point of view. An assertive person is prepared to challenge others in a positive (rather than a negative) way.

Cooperativeness

Cooperativeness is the extent to which an individual tries to take into account and, where possible, accommodates the concerns of others.

Approaches to dealing with conflict

Thomas and Kilmann used these factors to identify five possible approaches to dealing with conflict, as shown in Figure 2.23.1.

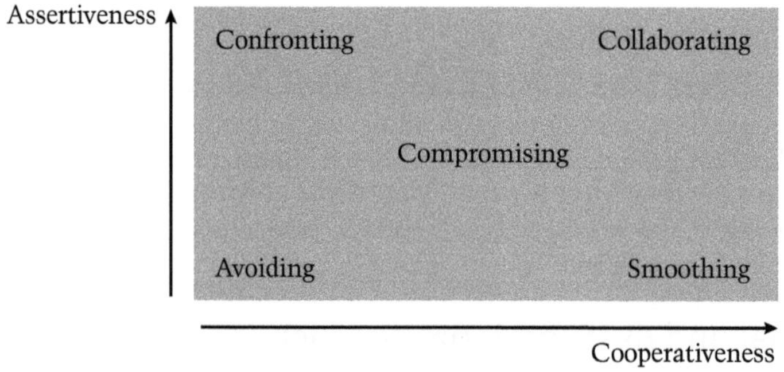

Figure 2.23.1 *A conflict resolution model based on Thomas and Kilmann*

Did you know?

Confronting can be an effective approach when the conflicting parties display a willingness to identify the underlying causes of conflict and share information openly to search for mutually beneficial solutions incorporating everyone's concerns.

Confronting

Individuals may choose a confrontational position in which they take an assertive approach in order to achieve their own goals. They may be standing up for their rights or just trying to win. This can lead to distrust and antagonism. In this situation, the whole group will lose out (although one individual may feel that he or she has won).

Smoothing

Here, an individual is cooperative but not assertive. He or she seeks to minimise differences and emphasise the common interest of the conflicting groups, and may show more concern about the emotional aspects of the conflict rather than dealing with the cause of the conflict. For example, a junior manager may seek to smooth over potential conflict with a senior manager, even when he or she disagrees with the decision that the senior manager is about to impose on the group. The whole team may lose out because the decision taken may not be in the interests of the group.

Avoiding

An individual takes an unassertive and uncooperative approach. He or she may not get involved or may step back from an issue, or may just be disinterested. This is a highly undesirable situation because everyone – both individuals and the group as a whole – will lose out.

Collaborating

In this approach there is a strong emphasis on both collaboration and assertiveness. Those involved in a disagreement are prepared to stand their ground, while at the same time being willing to find a solution. This is the most desirable approach as everyone 'wins'. Collaboration is associated with high-performance teams and is the model used by transformational leaders.

Compromising

Compromise lies at the centre of the diagram, as it is, to some extent, both cooperative and assertive. Both sides achieve certain things but have to concede on other things. The group may be better off, but it will not be as well off as in the collaborative situation.

Effective transformational leaders seek to achieve a collaborative resolution by encouraging the members of the team to engage in a process of constructive challenge. Challenge leads to better outcomes being achieved. Good leaders seek to build a collaborative **organisational culture** in which assertiveness and cooperation are welcomed in equal measure.

> **KEY TERMS**
>
> **Organisational culture**: the accepted way of behaving and interacting in an organisation.

Conflict resolution

Where conflict does occur, it is important to establish a set of ground rules that everyone understands and agrees on for resolving the conflict. Each person should be encouraged to identify what they see as the problem. It is then possible to look at the problem objectively rather than emotionally (that is, ensuring personal issues and loyalties are not involved). Then it is helpful to identify what each of the participants believes would be a good resolution to the conflict. Finally, once the problem has been dealt with, each person should commit to making a change in their behaviour.

Summary table

Conflict resolution strategy	Description
Avoiding	Conflict is ignored. Individuals do not want to get involved.
Confronting	An individual puts his or her own interests above those of the group or team.
Smoothing	An individual puts the group's interests above his or her own.
Compromising	Both sides gain but both sides also concede, so an agreement is made by mutual concession.
Collaborating	Both parties come to an agreement by standing up for what they believe but also cooperating to reach a decision.

Summary questions

1 Explain how collaboration provides a winning position all round and how other positions involve at least one party or the whole group losing out.

2 What is conflict resolution? Why is it so important to an organisation?

3 Why is it important to establish ground rules as part of the conflict resolution process?

Specific objective

On completion of this section, you should be able to:

- justify the need to cope with and manage change in organisations by understanding the nature of change.

Change takes place in businesses because of change in:

- the external environment in which the business operates
- the internal environment – for example, a new managing director is appointed who wants to move the company in a new direction.

The external environment

Businesses and other organisations operate in a dynamic, fast-changing environment. There are many factors outside the organisation's control that impact on it. Managers of the organisation therefore need to scan the external environment to identify changes and then adapt the organisation to the changing environment. Those organisations that stand still (for example, a bank that does not update its technology and processes) will fail.

In order to manage change, organisations need to consider:

- **Changes in competition:** new competitors enter markets and existing competitors get stronger.
- **Changes in the technological environment:** new techniques and processes for producing goods and services are introduced. The biggest change has come from the development of hyper-fast electronic communications and computer-aided production technologies.
- **Changes in the economy:** the Caribbean has increasingly integrated into a global economy as well as into the CARICOM trading area. This gives Caribbean companies more access to regional and global markets, while at the same time exposing Caribbean businesses increasingly to external competition.
- **Social and demographic changes:** over time social attitudes and buying patterns alter. In addition there are changes in the average age of the population which may impact on buying patterns, while emigration may affect the size of a market.
- **Political and legal changes:** these impact on the rules governing how businesses can operate. New governments are likely to change the rules affecting business.
- **Ecological changes:** environmental issues such as recycling and waste disposal can result in pressure from governments and conservation groups to change processes and ethics in an organisation.

Figure 2.24.1 *Increasingly people are using technology to access their bank accounts online*

CASE STUDY

Changing work practices in a bank

The way in which work is organised in a bank is determined just as much by what is happening in the external environment as by what is happening within the bank itself. Today banking is a highly competitive industry, so customers in most Caribbean countries have a choice of which bank to use for banking services. A scanning exercise (a detailed analysis of the external environment) of Caribbean banks shows the following.

Technological change

Today, banks use computer terminals and computer databases to record transactions. Caribbean banks have had to introduce the latest banking technologies to provide a rapid and efficient service to customers.

Economic change

Living standards in the Caribbean are higher than ever before and an increasing proportion of people are using banking services. Many of the major banks operating in the area have at least 1 million Caribbean-based customers each. The creation of CARICOM (see 1.18) means that banks can compete with each other for business within the CARICOM area.

Demographic change

Jamaica, for example, has a very low rate of population growth. According to the 2011 census, population growth was at 0.36 per cent. The median age was 27, which provides a relatively young workforce, although the average age of the population has started to rise, resulting in an increasing number of elderly people. The implications for banking in Jamaica are that:

- a steady number of people are likely to be seeking bank work
- new services may need to be developed for elderly customers
- competition within the country between banks is likely to become more intense because there will be fewer customers as a result of the low rate of population growth.

Social change

Education standards are improving year on year, so more and more young graduates are seeking professional jobs. In addition, the use of information technology has become part of everyday life, so people now expect their banks to provide the same high-tech services that they receive in other areas of their lives.

Increasingly, people want to be able to carry out their banking transactions from the comfort of their own homes using online banking services.

Legal change

Legislation is in place that covers, for example:

- the numbers of hours that people can work
- health and safety
- customer protection against aggressive selling of services by the banks.

1 How may the changes outlined above impact on the services offered by a modern Caribbean bank?

2 How are the changes likely to affect the way in which work is organised in a bank?

3 How are the changes likely to impact on bank employees?

Anticipating and managing external change

Managers therefore need to anticipate changes so that they prepare responses prior to the change occurring rather than being caught unawares. Regular review meetings need to take place to identify the key changes that are likely to impact on a business tomorrow, in the near future, and in the longer-term future. Managing change involves responding to these changes in an appropriate way. As you can see, this is reminiscent of the PESTLE analysis you learned about in 1.16. Businesses frequently carry out PESTLE analysis to study political, economic, social, technological, legal and ecological changes, so that they can anticipate and plan for change.

The internal environment

In addition to managing changes in the external environment, an organisation needs to manage change within its internal environment. Clearly, the organisation has much more control over the internal environment. Internal changes can take place at both a strategic level (major organisation-wide changes) and an operational level (changes in how the organisation organises a specific operation). Managers need to be just as aware of the need for internal change as they are of external change, so that they can respond just as efficiently and effectively.

Summary questions

1 How does PESTLE analysis enable managers to plan appropriate changes?

2 To what extent is an organisation able to control the external environment? Use examples to illustrate your answer.

3 Which of the factors outlined in this section do you see as being the most significant for small Caribbean businesses?

Summary table

Type of change	Example of how it may affect a business
Political and legal	New regulations requiring a change in the way a product is manufactured (e.g. food safety standards)
Economic	Changes in the income per head of members of a country, leading to a general increase in demand for goods
Social and demographic	Changes in fashions and trends, meaning that some new goods become more popular Changes in average age of population
Technological	Changes in manufacturing processes that make it cheaper to produce certain items
Ecological	Changes in opinion on energy use that affect how a product is designed (e.g. electric and hybrid cars)

Specific objective

On completion of this section, you should be able to:

■ justify the need to cope with and manage change in the organisation by understanding resistance to change.

Figure 2.25.1 *Individuals may be resistant to change because of the fear they have about how it will impact on them, their job security and their responsibilities to their families*

People within an organisation can respond to change in three main ways:

■ They may **accept** the necessity for change and comply. For example, people who have been working for a number of years in an oppressive organisation may welcome the **'new broom' approach**.

■ They may **resist** change. This is a common reaction and may be done subtly (for example, employees being slow in carrying out instructions) or there may be open antagonism.

■ A more extreme form of resistance is **open conflict**, which may take the form of flare-ups at staff meetings, deliberate sabotage and wilful destruction.

Individual barriers to change

People may resist change for a number of reasons:

■ **Fear of the unknown:** employees may not know what to expect. Change can threaten or appear to threaten existing ways of working and relationships at work. Individuals may feel that they are being asked to take on responsibilities that they are not qualified to carry out or that they feel unable to carry out. Often employees are resistant to change when they are asked to engage with new technologies or processes.

■ **Disrupted habits:** workers develop routines and habits. Asking them to change may be seen as a threat to a worker's existing patterns.

■ **Loss of control/confidence:** those being asked to change may feel that they will lose control of the work that they are currently doing. For example, asking someone to share responsibility with a second person may result in a feeling of loss of control (for example, they may think that they will not be able to do things their way or to their standards). Often people do not feel confident enough to implement something that is new and unfamiliar.

■ **Poor training:** if employees are not trained appropriately to make a change, they will be unable to carry out new ways of working.

■ **Redistribution of workload and lack of purpose:** employees may be comfortable with their existing workload and be resistant to reorganising their time and efforts. Unless the purpose of what they are doing is clear they may also feel that they have lost some of their original purpose, which can be demotivating.

■ **Loss of power:** over time, individuals (particularly at management level) establish power within an organisation. They may be resistant to a change that they perceive as reducing their power.

■ **Lack of communication:** people may resist change simply because they feel that it has not been communicated effectively.

■ **Different assessments of the situation:** there may be disagreement over the need for change, including disagreement about its benefits and disadvantages.

■ **Economic implications:** employees are likely to resist change that may affect their pay or rewards.

Organisational barriers to change

In addition to individual barriers, there may be organisational barriers, due to:

- structural inertia – existing structures are so deeply ingrained that they are difficult to shift
- resistance from existing power structures – those with power in the organisation may resist change
- resistance from informal work groups
- the fact that previous change initiatives have failed
- a lack of sufficient resources to make the changes effectively.

Recognising resistance

It is important for managers to recognise that resistance is likely to occur whatever the degree of change involved. Managers therefore need to understand the causes of resistance and seek to identify individuals and groups who are most resistant to change, so that they can develop approaches to overcome their resistance.

Resistance can become evident through the conversations that people have in the workplace, demonstrating fear of changes and mis-understandings about their nature. Managers therefore need to pay careful attention to these conversations and use them to think carefully about how they can communicate details of the change (for example, why the change is needed and its implications for people in the organisation).

Did you know?

Key ways to overcome resistance to change from individuals include encouraging them to take ownership for some aspects of the change and making sure that they understand the reasons for the change and how they will benefit.

Summary table

Individual barriers to change	Organisational barriers to change
■ Fear of the unknown ■ Disruption of established routines ■ Fear of loss of control ■ Fear of not being able to carry out new work roles ■ Fear of loss of income and security ■ Fear of loss of power ■ Lack of communication	■ Structural inertia ■ Existing power structures including work groups ■ Experience of previous failures ■ Lack of resources to make the changes work well ■ Lack of experience of existing managers in leading change

Summary questions

1 Which of the barriers to change are likely to result from poor management?

2 Which of the barriers to change are most likely to come from long-established workers in an organisation?

3 How might organisational barriers combine with individual barriers?

2.26　Strategies to manage change

Specific objective

On completion of this section, you should be able to:

■ justify the need to cope with and manage change in the organisation and understand strategies to manage change.

KEY TERMS

Change objectives: what the change will achieve and by when.

Change plan: a plan showing the activities that will enable the organisation to achieve the change.

Managing change is a complex process requiring high-level leadership skills. The change process usually involves three stages:

1 establishing objectives and outcomes
2 planning the change
3 managing people so that they embrace the change.

Establishing objectives and outcomes

If the objectives of the change are not set out clearly then it may fail. Change usually occurs for a reason (that is, something triggers it). For example, an organisation's current performance may be poor because the company is engaging in a new strategy or because the company has identified new opportunities that are worth following up. Once the reason why change is needed has been identified, it is important to establish what sort of change is required and what specific objectives need to be addressed by the change. **Change objectives** help to establish the nature of the change, what needs to be achieved and by when.

Planning the change

Planning involves a number of steps. The organisation needs to:

■ establish the change management team

■ put in place structures for managing the change

■ identify a set of activities, in the form of a **change plan**, that will enable the organisation to achieve the change

■ establish which individuals within the organisation need to be committed to making the change work

■ carry out an ongoing audit and evaluation of the change to monitor progress and make sure that it is being implemented in an appropriate way

■ put in place training and development activities to ensure that people have the right support to make the change work.

Managing people so they embrace the change

People are a key element of the change process. If people are behind the change then it is more likely to be successful. There are four steps that an organisation should take to manage people so that they embrace the change:

■ make people aware of the need for change

■ provide individuals with regular feedback on their performance so that they are aware of the differences between current performance and desired performance, requiring improvements in quality or productivity

■ ensure that managers understand the fears and uncertainties that people may have that can act as barriers to change

■ publicise successful change to show people the benefits resulting from the change.

Figure 2.26.1 *Managers need to make sure that people are aware of the need for change*

Winning support for the change

There are a number of strategies that managers can employ to get support from employees for change.

- **Educating employees about the change:** employees get used to existing patterns and structures, so an education programme is required to clarify what the change involves, why it is being introduced, how it will impact on individuals and groups, what they will need to do differently and what successful change will look like.

- **Participation:** change almost certainly involves people. For the change process to be successful, it is important that managers consult with employees about the change in a democratic way. If employees participate in the change process, they are more likely to take ownership of it and want it to succeed.

- **Change champions/agents: change agents** or champions are people within the organisation who take most responsibility for the change. Usually, an organisation will run initial workshops for the change champions to explain the benefits and the processes associated with the change. The change champions then model new practices and explain the change to other employees. It is helpful to select dynamic and respected employees as change champions.

> **KEY TERMS**
>
> **Change agents:** individuals with a key role in championing the change.

- **Communication:** clear and transparent communication is at the heart of successful change. The degree to which the change needs to be communicated and the type of communication needed depends on the level of involvement of individuals and the impact on them. To explain this it is helpful to consider a 'communications escalator' (see 2.27). At the bottom of the escalator are people who simply need to be informed about the change because it only affects them in minor ways. Higher up the escalator are the people, like the change champions, who need to be committed to the change and therefore need more detailed communication. At the top of the communications escalator are people who are responsible for implementing the change. In their case, communications need to be detailed and two-way.

- **Shared ownership:** where ownership of change is shared by everyone in the organisation, it is likely to succeed. Everyone then feels responsible and accountable for making a change succeed. For change to be successful, it is important to build a sense of togetherness.

Summary table

Strategies to secure change	
Clarify objectives	Establish what the purpose of change is
Build the plan	Who will be involved? What will they do? Put in place the required training
Manage people	Raise understanding, give feedback, deal with fears, celebrate success
Win support	Educate about the change, gain participation, use change champions, communicate, secure shared ownership

Summary questions

1 What is the relationship between change objectives and a plan for change? Illustrate your answer by providing a practical example.

2 Does change need to be communicated to everyone within an organisation to the same degree? Explain your answer.

3 What is meant by 'ownership' of a change initiative? How can this be secured?

Specific objective

On completion of this section, you should be able to:

■ explain the importance of effective communication in organisations with reference to the communication process.

Communication is integral to the day-to-day operations of a business. Business communications can either be internal (for example, a memo or email about the process of change) or external (for example, an advertisement or a press release).

The four stages of communication

The communications process is made up of four key stages, beginning with the sender and ending with the receiver (Figure 2.27.1).

1 The sender (the person initiating the communication) encodes the message – that is, expresses it orally, in writing, visually or through other non-verbal channels.

2 The message is transmitted using a medium (or communication channel), such as the company's website, noticeboards or company briefings for employees.

3 The message is then decoded (or interpreted) by the receiver. If the message is decoded correctly by the receiver, the information has been communicated successfully.

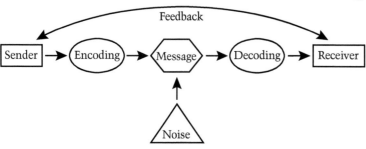

Figure 2.27.1 The communication process

4 Action/feedback is the final stage in the process. After receiving the information, the receiver responds to the sender.

Table 2.27.1 shows how this works in practice using the example of an organisation communicating change in respect of its production methods.

Table 2.27.1 Communicating change in respect of production methods

Stage in the communication process	Example
Sender	Change committee
Message	New more efficient methods of production are being introduced
Transmission medium	Company meetings, website or training sessions
Receiver	Production manager implements change

Noise

Certain barriers can prevent the receiver from receiving the full message or understanding it. Noise is any form of interference that leads to the distortion of the message and affects the flow of the information. Noise may, for example, be the result of linguistic and cultural differences between the sender and the receiver. In the example of communicating changes about the production method, rather than seeing that the change will lead to better pay and conditions and less stressful work, employees may interpret the change negatively because they feel that they might lose their jobs or be asked to do things that they are not trained to do.

One of the most common sources of noise is conversations in informal work groups. If the change has been communicated poorly (for example, through poor messaging or inappropriate media), or if there is resistance to change, then the messages provided by managers can be distorted. The challenge for managers is to steer or manage the conversations that are taking place.

Communication medium

To increase the chances of a message being communicated effectively, an organisation needs to think carefully about the target audience. It is important to channel the message through the 'best' media. For example advertising a new mass market electronic gadget might work best on a widely viewed national television channel. It may also be necessary to repeat the message several times using clear language, so that the objectives and benefits are clearly set out. Change champions can perform a key role in helping to transmit the message when it relates to organisational changes.

KEY TERMS

Communications escalator: a way of illustrating the progressive (rising) intensity of communications required to engage individuals and groups involved in delivering change processes.

CASE STUDY

The communications escalator

In internal communication it is important to consider the level of communication required. Some recipients of corporate communications only need a general awareness of the message, whereas others need a much deeper engagement with it. This is particularly important in communicating messages about change.

Take the example of the introduction of a new product range in the home section of a department store. In the department itself, managers involved in steering the change need to be **committed** to it. Other members of the home department need to be **involved** in learning how to promote new lines. New trainees in the department need **support** to learn how to deliver sales messages. Customers need to **understand** what new alternatives are

available. At the bottom level, sales staff in other departments only need a general **awareness** of the change.

This change requires different types of communication for each level, which can be displayed using a **communications escalator**. For example, the company may place a news feature on its staff website to raise awareness. Advertising may help potential customers to understand the new products on offer. At the top level, the department managers may be involved in face-to-face meetings to secure commitment from senior managers.

1 Illustrate the five steps, **Awareness**, **Understanding**, **Support**, **Involvement** and **Commitment**, on a communications escalator.

Summary table

Stage in the communication process	Description
Encoding	The process of expressing a message so that it can be sent
Medium (or channel)	The means through which the message is sent
Transmission	Sending the message
Noise	Interference that blocks or distorts a message
Decoding	Interpretation of the message by the receiver
Action/feedback	How the receiver responds to the message

Summary questions

1 How does noise arise and how can it be restricted?

2 How can a communications escalator be used to convert awareness into commitment when implementing change?

3 How can change managers ensure that the objectives and planning for a change initiative are very clear?

On completion of this section, you should be able to:

- explain the importance of effective communication in organisations with reference to communication channels and communication methods.

Communication channels

As we have seen, good, clear communication is essential when managing an organisation's day-to-day business. A clear channel of communication is required to ensure that the message is communicated effectively. The main channels of communication are:

- oral
- visual
- written
- other non-verbal forms.

Table 2.28.1 outlines the main channels of communication and their advantages and disadvantages.

Table 2.28.1 The main channels of communication

Channel	Examples	Advantages and disadvantages
Oral	■ Oral briefings by a senior manager ■ One-to-one discussions between individuals ■ Telephone conversations ■ Training sessions ■ Meetings ■ Appraisals	■ Involves face-to-face direct contact and so entails interpersonal relationships ■ If communication is two way, it provides an opportunity to check understanding and ask questions
Written	■ Business letters ■ Reports ■ Emails ■ Employee suggestion schemes ■ In-house magazines	■ Can be carefully scrutinised, analysed and checked for meaning
Visual	■ Illustrations ■ Pictures ■ Diagrams, presentations (e.g. a slideshow) ■ Video	■ Make business messages easy to understand ■ Can oversimplify information ■ Information may be delivered so fast that important details are forgotten quickly
Non-verbal	■ Positive body language (e.g. smiling, nodding in agreement, good eye contact, uncrossed arms) ■ Negative body language (e.g. frowning, tension, no eye contact, crossed arms)	■ You can tell from a person's body language whether they are being defensive, aggressive or passive, or whether they are expressing other emotions. You can then adjust your interaction to build better communication

Communication methods

Modern-day businesses have access to a wide range of communication methods for use both internally and externally.

Business letters

A business letter should contain five main elements:

- salutation – a well-structured business letter should start with a clear salutation (for example, 'Dear Sir/Madam')
- introduction – explanation of what the letter is about and why it is being written
- details – the information to be conveyed to the recipient

- next steps – explanation of how the reader needs to respond to the letter
- sign-off (for example, 'Yours faithfully').

Memorandum

A memorandum (or memo for short) is an internal business communication between different departments within the same organisation.

Fax

A fax (facsimile) is a method of external communication that is now being rapidly replaced by the online transmission of diagrams and documents through email attachments (see below). A fax machine is connected to the telephone network. A fax message can combine written and visual information and is useful for sending contracts, legal documents, diagrams and important letters.

Emails

An email is electronic and provides a quick way of sending a message. One of the problems with email communication is that messages are often sent in haste without due care and attention to how meaning is expressed. The message may sometimes be interpreted by the recipient in a different way to the way in which it was intended, causing misunderstanding or anger.

Internet

The internet provides an excellent way for an organisation to communicate to both its internal and external audience. The internet has enabled many Caribbean businesses to grow from a relatively small base to global businesses, and to manage their relationships with the outside world in a sophisticated way. More and more people are beginning to use mobile devices to access the internet anywhere at any time. Companies are now optimising their websites to work on smartphones.

Cellphones

Cellphones enable people to keep in touch when they are out on business. Smartphones with access to emails and the internet have helped increase companies' productivity, although they have also created a culture in which people are 'always available'. Telephone calls are more personal than email, so there is less scope for misinterpretation and messages can be communicated just as quickly.

Intranet

An intranet is a computer network similar to the internet, but it is accessible only to members of an organisation or other approved users. It provides a repository for invaluable company information (for example, messages) and data (databases and files) for internal users.

Video conferencing

Some companies with more than one office use video conferencing to save travelling time and costs. Video conferencing allows people at two or more different locations to talk to each other by means of a video link. It is a useful method of communication if visual information needs to be shared.

Summary table

Written communication
■ Memos
■ Reports
■ Faxes
■ Suggestion schemes
■ In-house magazine
■ Letters

Oral communication
■ Company meetings
■ Training sessions
■ Appraisals
■ Team briefings
■ Presentations
■ Spoken instructions

Visual communication
■ Diagrams
■ Presentations
■ Illustrations
■ Video

Non-verbal communication
■ Body language

Summary questions

1 Which methods of communication can include both a visual and a written component?

2 Which method of communication may be best for communicating information about change in an organisation?

3 Which methods of communication include an electronic component? How does the electronic component enhance these communication methods?

On completion of this section, you should be able to:

■ explain the importance of effective communication in organisations with reference to formal and informal lines of communication.

Formal communications

Formal communication is written or verbal communication that takes place along well-established channels within an organisation. Formal communications usually flows from the top downwards and follow company procedures. Some examples of formal communication are shown in Table 2.29.1.

Table 2.29.1 Examples of formal communications

Formal written communications	Formal verbal communications
■ Formal reports	■ Company meetings
■ Emails using company guidelines	■ Training sessions
■ Written procedures and policies	■ Appraisal interviews
■ Posters and noticeboard displays	■ Team briefings
■ Suggestion schemes	■ Presentations
■ Company newsletters and other publications	■ Giving feedback
	■ Giving instructions

Did you know?

Horizontal communication takes place in team working and in quality circles. Quality circles are small groups in the same area of work who meet regularly to discuss improvements to working methods.

Vertical and horizontal lines of communication

In 2.9 you learned about the characteristics of formal organisational structures. Vertical communication is when the message is communicated down (and sometimes up) the structure: for example, from manager to supervisor. Horizontal communication occurs between role holders at the same level: for example, from a manager in one department to a manager in another.

Advantages of formal communications

■ Formal communications help to maintain authority and discipline in an organisation.

■ Communication is reliable and accurate, and the message is clear.

Disadvantages of formal communications

■ Formal messages may be ignored because they are seen as company propaganda.

■ They are time consuming and costly – for example, it is costly to set up a company meeting for all employees.

■ Messages can be distorted and create misunderstanding.

 Exam tip

Where appropriate, you should include definitions and diagrams as part of your answers, even if you are not specifically told to provide them.

Informal communications

Informal communications are often seen as unofficial messages that are not formally sent by an organisation. This type of communication does not follow any set structure with relation to the hierarchy of the company. Instead it flows through the network of personal relationships that exist within an organisation. This means that informal communications can flow in all directions.

Advantages of informal communications

- Information can be passed on quickly.
- Informal communications can be used by management to gauge staff feeling about a planned change.

Disadvantages of informal communications

- Messages may be distorted through rumours and gossip.
- As a result of distortion, messages may be contradictory and therefore confusing.
- It is likely that messages have not been approved by managers and therefore may contradict or conflict with management expectations.

Communication networks

There are two main types of communication network along which formal communications can flow, as shown in Figure 2.29.1: centralised or decentralised.

- In a centralised network, information flows through a key person in the group. Decision making is dependent on the key person and decisions may therefore be made quickly.
- In a decentralised network, decision making is shared. As a result, decision making may take longer but there is input from a number of sources.

An intranet or other form of electronic communications (for example, a shared database) enables a completely connected formal flow of information and can aid decision making.

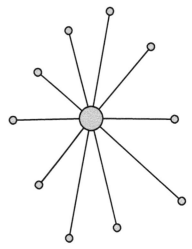

Centralised

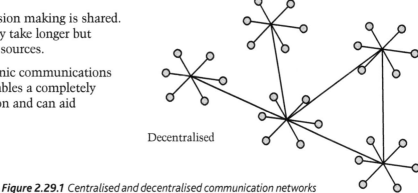

Decentralised

Figure 2.29.1 Centralised and decentralised communication networks

Summary table

Line of communication	Description
Formal communication	Communication that follows company guidelines
Informal communication	Word-of-mouth communication
Vertical communication	Communication down (sometimes up) the hierarchical structures of an organisation
Horizontal communication	Communication between role holders at the same level
Centralised communication	Communication that goes through a key individual
Decentralised communication	An open communication network

Summary questions

1 What are the key differences between formal and informal communications?

2 What are the advantages and disadvantages of centralised and decentralised communication networks?

3 An insurance company based in Trinidad has offices in Barbados, Jamaica and Grenada. What would be the benefits to the organisation of a centralised communication network? How might it benefit from a decentralised network?

Specific objective

On completion of this section, you should be able to:

- explain the importance of effective communication in organisations with reference to barriers to effective communication.

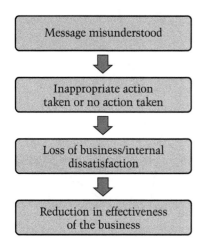

Figure 2.30.1 *Poor communication can reduce the effectiveness of the business*

Did you know?

Sometimes a combination of channels is the best option. For example, training may be more effectively communicated through a combination of written and visual forms rather than just orally.

As shown in Figure 2.30.1, poor communication can lead to a business becoming less effective. Businesses therefore need to deal with any barriers to communication to prevent them from becoming problems.

Barriers to communication

Language

The sender may use jargon or technical language with which the receiver is not familiar. He or she may use abbreviations and shortened versions of words. This can be a particular barrier for new employees who are still familiarising themselves with their surroundings and learning the 'language' of the business. Care must also be taken to pitch the communication at the right level for the receivers. Another obvious barrier is geographical languages – for example, between the French-speaking Caribbean areas, such as Guadeloupe, and the Spanish- and English-speaking areas.

Noise

You have already learned that noise can distort or block the sender's message so that the receiver does not receive it or receives a message that is different from the one sent originally. Noise may be the result of linguistic and cultural differences or may come from informal communication. Review noise in 2.27.

Attitudes

Attitude can affect how a message is communicated or interpreted:

- the sender may be upset or angry and may not put enough thought into sending a clear, rational message – instead the communication may just be an outpouring of the sender's emotion
- the receiver may be anxious or upset and could jump to conclusions, resulting in misinterpretation of the message
- the receiver may have no interest in the message – the message needs to capture the receiver's interest.

Communication channel

Sometimes the wrong communication channel can be a barrier. For example, using a written channel to communicate an important business change that will have an impact on employee working conditions may result in more of a barrier than if it were communicated orally.

Communication method

If the method of communication (for example, the physical conditions such as the venue or location for delivering the message) is inappropriate for the receiver, the message will be distorted. For example:

- If the sales conference of a multimillion-dollar company were to take place in the summer in a hotel with few facilities, no air conditioning and poor food, the level of understanding and participation might be reduced.
- If an employer reprimands an employee on the shop floor, the employee may only receive part of the message because they are worrying about what their colleagues are thinking. It would be much more professional to have the conversation in a quiet office in private.

Line of communication

The line of communication can also be a barrier. For example, if an important change to a process was communicated along an informal line of communication, the message may get distorted and errors in production might occur as a result.

Cultural bias

Cultural bias, due to different cultural experiences, may influence the receiver's interpretation of the message. Managers of businesses operating globally and in other parts of the Caribbean should have an in-depth understanding of cultural differences so as not to offend or give inappropriate messages. In the Caribbean, the most significant religious groups by numbers are Christians, Hindus, Muslims and Rastafarians.

Selective perception of the message

From a sender's point of view, you want recipients to select, understand and act on the messages that you are trying to communicate. However, in some instances, the receiver may interpret the message in the way that suits him or her best. A receiver may hear some parts of the message selectively and ignore other parts. For example, in an advertisement the recipient may choose to focus on visual images and storyline rather than the name of the brand.

Reducing barriers to communication

There are a number of ways to reduce barriers to communication. Organisations need to ensure the following:

- Employees understand the importance of effective communication. In order to do this, employees need to appreciate the consequences of poor communication. They also need to be kept up to date with the latest technology and be introduced to communication methods that will make their job easier.
- Employees are given appropriate training to be effective communicators. Employees need to be effective listeners. They also need to be able to present information clearly – verbally, in writing or visually. Giving and receiving feedback is another area that needs to be developed to ensure effective communication.
- The culture of an organisation and its social climate encourage effective communication, otherwise communication failure will result.
- The choice of channel is right. For example, if the organisation is communicating key changes, a formal company meeting is a more appropriate channel for this information than a newsletter.

Did you know?

Messages can also be lost through using the wrong media: for example, handing out promotional leaflets in the street that are thrown away, or broadcasting television adverts during programmes that very few people watch.

Summary table

Barriers to effective communication	Solution
Language	Use clear language focused on audience needs.
Noise	Identify potential barriers and use appropriate channels and methods to avoid confusion.
Attitude	Check that the receiver is emotionally open to hearing the message and that they are attentive in recording what has been said.
Inappropriate channel, method or line	Choose the best method of communicating the message.
Cultural differences	Be sensitive to cultural differences.
Selective perception	Make it clear which parts of your message are important.

Summary questions

1 What is the main barrier to effective communication? How can this barrier be overcome?

2 Which aspects of poor communication are caused by the sender and which by the recipient?

3 How important is the choice of channel and the way the message is set out in reducing barriers to communication?

Specific objective

On completion of this section, you should be able to:

■ evaluate the importance of human resource management in organisations by understanding the role of human resource management.

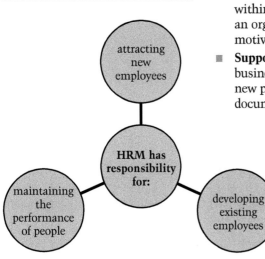

Figure 2.31.1 *The role of human resource management (HRM)*

What is human resource management?

Human resource management (HRM) is the management of an organisation's workforce (or human resources). It deals with new employees, existing employees and performance, as shown in Figure 2.31.1.

Theories and ideas used in modern-day HRM stem from the ideas first set out by the human relations approach (see 2.2).

The human resources (HR) department within an organisation performs a number of important functions that help it to fulfil its role:

■ **Strategy:** it helps to create high-level plans for the use of people within an organisation. People are the most important resource in an organisation, so they need careful attention if they are going to be motivated and committed to the organisation.

■ **Support:** the HR department supports other functions within a business. For example, if the marketing department wants to recruit new people, HR specialists will support marketing to produce the right documents and to set up the right procedures for effective recruitment.

■ **Human resource planning and succession planning:** this involves identifying what people the organisation has now and what skills they possess, and also identifying what people the organisation will need in the future and what skills they will require. The human resource plan identifies where shortages are likely to occur in the future. Plans can then be put in place to recruit new employees and to train existing employees so that they can fill any gaps that might emerge.

In a small company, the HR department may consist of only a few people (for example, the head of HR, a training manager and a payroll manager). In large companies there is far more specialisation, with specialists taking responsibility for a range of areas, such as induction of new employees, appraisal, training, and pay and benefits.

To be successful and effective, HRM must be a two-way process. It has to take account of individual employees' goals as well as the objectives of the organisation. If employees are to show loyalty to the company, they need to feel that they are developing personally as well as producing results for the employer.

Hard and soft HRM

The notions of hard and soft HRM were originally put forward in the late 1980s.

Hard HRM

A hard HRM approach considers employees as just another resource. It considers the needs of the business and then recruits, develops and manages employees accordingly. The needs of the business take priority over the needs of employees.

Soft HRM

A soft HRM approach values employees and puts the employees' interests on an equal basis with the organisation's aims. It encourages motivation by offering rewards. Soft HRM takes a human approach: people are considered to be the most important resource and their development benefits both themselves and the organisation. The company takes into consideration both its own organisational objectives and its employees' visions and goals. Employees are offered the training and development they need to reach their own goals, while at the same time serving the organisation's needs.

A psychological contract

At the heart of soft HRM is the recognition of the importance of the **psychological contract**. A psychological contract is an unwritten agreement between the employer and the employee. It is a two-way process:

- Employees work hard for the organisation because they believe that the organisation has their best interests at heart and will look after them.

- In return, the organisation looks after its employees, and values and trusts them.

In such an organisation there is a shared sense of accountability. However, if any aspects of the psychological contract break down, this can lead to a cycle of negativity.

Table 2.31.1 shows the main features of the hard and soft approaches to HRM.

> **KEY TERMS**
>
> **Psychological contract:** an unwritten, informal agreement between an employer and employees based on mutual commitment

Table 2.31.1 *The main features of the hard and soft approaches to HRM*

Hard approach to HRM	Soft approach to HRM
The focus is on production targets.	The focus is on helping individuals to identify their own targets as well as identifying how they can help the organisation to achieve its targets.
Training is designed to ensure that employees meet targets.	Individual development planning is based on employees' needs.
There is little differentiation between human resources and other resources.	Human resources are considered to be special and unique.
There is little career and development planning for employees.	The emphasis is on career development planning for employees.
Rewards and incentives are likely to be in the form of pay.	It offers a range of non-financial and financial incentives that focus on intrinsic motivation and reward.

Summary table

Concept	Summary
Human resource management (HRM)	The management of an organisation's workforce (or human resources)
Strategic HRM	Ensures people-related issues are at the top of the agenda in business planning
Hard HRM	An approach to HRM where the needs of the organisation take priority
Soft HRM	An approach to HRM that gives employees' needs an equal weighting to the needs of the organisation

Summary questions

1 What are the three core areas of responsibility of the human resources department?

2 In what ways can HRM be seen to flow from the initial ideas of the human relations approach?

3 Are people at work more likely to benefit from a hard HRM approach or a soft HRM approach?

2.32 Functions of the HR department: recruitment and selection

Specific objective

On completion of this section, you should be able to:

■ evaluate the importance of human resource management in organisations by understanding the functions of recruitment and selection.

The main function of the HR department is to recruit and select suitable internal and external candidates to work within the organisation.

Recruitment

Without the right people it is unlikely that the business will make good decisions. There are many different ways in which businesses can attract staff. Traditional methods of making people aware of job vacancies are now being supplemented or replaced by internet-based methods of recruitment. Table 2.32.1 shows the different types of traditional and online methods that can be employed to find the best staff.

Table 2.32.1 *Traditional and online methods of recruitment*

Traditional methods of recruitment	Internet-based methods of recruitment
Newspaper advertisements	Online application forms
Paper-based curriculum vitae	Online curriculum vitae
Letter	Email
Word of mouth	Web advertisements
Paper-based application forms	Webpage containing details of vacancies
Careers fair	Webpage pop-up
Posters	

Online recruitment is not only much faster than traditional paper-based methods, it also has a number of other benefits:

■ It is possible to monitor how many people have visited a website to look at a job advertisement, in order to gauge the level of interest in a vacancy.

■ The business can see how many of those people then go on to apply for the job, so it knows whether or not this method of recruitment is the best way to encourage people to work for the business.

■ By using online application forms, data supplied by applicants can be put straight into computer software.

Organisations use both **internal** and **external recruitment** to obtain employees. Table 2.32.2 outlines the advantages and disadvantages of internal recruitment (from the organisation's perspective).

> **KEY TERMS**
>
> **Internal recruitment:** recruitment from amongst a firm's existing employees.
>
> **External recruitment:** recruitment from candidates who are not currently working for the company.

Table 2.32.2 *The advantages and disadvantages of internal recruitment for an organisation*

Advantages	Disadvantages
■ The organisation knows what it is getting. ■ It saves on recruitment costs. ■ It saves on induction costs. ■ Promotion acts as an incentive for all members of the organisation to work harder.	■ No new ideas are brought into the organisation. ■ There is no 'buzz' of efficiency that follows an external appointment. ■ The person moved to a new position will need to be replaced. ■ Promotion of one person may upset someone else who thinks they have been overlooked.

Selection

Selection is the process of choosing people to work in an organisation. The selection system should attempt to:

- get the best people within existing budgets – that is, those with the most appropriate skills, experience and attitudes
- select people who will stay with the organisation for a reasonable time
- minimise the costs of recruitment and selection by using the most appropriate methods to attract and then select the best possible candidates (for example, an advertisement in a national newspaper is not appropriate when recruiting for a low level administrative position because the costs would be prohibitive compared to using the local press).

A selection panel has the responsibility for carrying out interviews and other tests and then choosing the most suitable candidate.

Applications

1 Before selecting candidates for interview, the organisation should have a clear picture of the ideal candidate. Organisations can obtain this through **job analysis**. It involves examining the job that is to be advertised to identify what skills, tasks and abilities are required.

2 The results of the job analysis are then fed into a job specification. This specifies the details of the job to be carried out and the essential and desirable characteristics that the job applicant needs to have in order to meet the requirements.

3 A job description is created that specifies the tasks that the job holder is required to do.

4 The candidates' application forms and CVs are compared to the **person specification** to identify a shortlist of candidates who best meet the requirements of the post.

Interviews

The person specification should also be used by the selection panel to structure their interview questions. The candidate who most closely meets the specification should be selected. Selection interviews should be organised carefully. They should be arranged at convenient times and at convenient locations. The candidates should be provided with an accurate description of what the job entails.

Testing

As part of the selection process, candidates may be given tasks to complete to test their aptitudes. They may also be asked questions that test their ability to perform the job.

> **KEY TERMS**
>
> **Job analysis**: identifying the requirements of a job.
>
> **Person specification**: document setting out the skills and qualities that a candidate needs to have in order to be selected.

Summary table

Function	Definition	Methods
Recruitment	The process of attracting suitable candidates to apply for job vacancies	■ Traditional methods of advertising (e.g. newspaper advert, careers fair, poster) ■ Online methods (e.g. email and web adverts)
Selection	Choosing the best candidate/s from those who apply	■ Comparison of applications against person specification ■ Interviews ■ Testing

Summary questions

1 What is the relationship between recruitment and selection?

2 What steps can be put in place to make sure that the most suitable candidates are selected?

3 What is the difference between a job analysis and a person specification? When would they be used?

On completion of this section, you should be able to:

- evaluate the importance of human resource management in organisations by understanding the functions of training and development.

The HR function is also responsible for the training and development of staff. These are two distinctly different activities. Training focuses on the needs of the organisation (involving a hard HR approach) whereas development focuses on the needs of employees (a soft HR approach).

Training

The purpose of training is to change behaviour in the workplace in order to increase efficiency and raise performance standards. The vehicle for changing behaviour is **learning**, as this is the process through which those being trained acquire new knowledge, skills and attitudes. Training is a partnership between the trainer and the trainee, so clear targets and objectives must be set and progress must be evaluated.

CASE STUDY

Training in practice

A young apprentice joins an organisation after leaving school. He needs to be able to use the equipment that he will be working with in order to provide useful outputs for the organisation. The organisation therefore provides a series of training courses for the apprentice, where he learns the necessary knowledge, skills and capabilities required for working with the machinery.

The apprentice brings to the training session a range of knowledge, skills and attitudes that he has acquired previously. The organisation must build on these attributes. The attributes will vary from individual to individual, as will motivation and the way the apprentice prefers to learn (for example, some will prefer to be told what to do while others will prefer to experiment for themselves). The training therefore needs to be tailored to each individual's needs. Training is a highly skilled process, requiring a clear understanding not only of the organisation's training needs but also of learning processes and the needs of learners.

1 What are the essential ingredients of training?
2 In what situations is training most likely to be effective?

KEY TERMS

Learning: a relatively permanent change of behaviour that occurs as a result of practice or experience.

Types of training

Induction

This is the process of introducing a new employee to the organisation and their new job or function. An induction includes:

- an introduction to the job, colleagues, workplace and organisation
- rules, regulations and procedures (for example, health and safety)
- terms and conditions of employment (including benefits and facilities).

Understanding job requirements

This type of training ensures that the employee can meet the basic requirements of the job.

Developing job skills

Training to develop an employee's job skills, helping them to become a better worker, is essential in ensuring their effectiveness and continued productivity.

Preparing the employee for greater responsibility

If an organisation wants to retain its staff, it should provide training that develops individuals and prepares them for greater responsibilities. This type of training provides employees with a greater range of knowledge and skills so that they can take on additional responsibilities.

Developing new capabilities

The world of work is continually changing, particularly with regard to new technologies. It is essential that an organisation provides employees with this kind of training to ensure that they are equipped to work with new technologies, so that the business can continue to move forward.

On-the-job training

On-the-job training takes place while employees are working. For example, they may learn by working alongside a more experienced employee. The benefits of on-the-job training are that the employee is:

- working while learning and therefore contributing to output
- learning from practical experience in real situations.

Off-the-job training

Off-the-job training takes place away from the workplace (for example, at college or university or in a training centre). This may allow the employee to experience a wider range of opportunities and to use a wider range of equipment than would typically be available within their workplace.

Development

Development focuses on the needs of employees. The human resources department is responsible for creating a people-centred approach that recognises the importance of motivated employees. Employees are most likely to be motivated if their development needs are recognised.

A regular appraisal interview is important to ensure that an individual's development needs are recognised and addressed. An appraisal is a two-way communication process that enables:

- the appraiser (often the line manager) to communicate organisational requirements to the person being appraised
- the person being appraised to communicate their aspirations, frustrations and other personal concerns to the appraiser.

Appraisal, so long as it is conducted well, is an important vehicle for motivating the workforce.

Training, development and learning needs analysis (TDLNA)

A TDLNA is a systematic process that looks at current practice, skills and knowledge within an organisation and identifies any gaps that need to be addressed through training and development to enable the organisation to operate at the desired level. A TDLNA:

- identifies what is currently being done well by individuals, groups and the organisation as a whole
- identifies any gaps that need to be addressed
- assesses whether the existing training and development provision is effective in meeting organisational and individual needs
- makes recommendations for new training and development requirements that will meet individual, group and organisational needs
- provides a basis from which to plan and implement individual development (for example, by setting up appraisal, training and development programmes).

Summary table

Training
<ul><li>Focuses on the needs of the organisation</li><li>Builds skills and capabilities</li><li>Is concerned with organisational effectiveness</li><li>Is allied to the hard HRM approach</li></ul>

Development
<ul><li>Focuses on the needs of the individual</li><li>Addresses the development needs of the individual</li><li>Is concerned with motivation of individuals</li><li>Is allied to the soft HRM approach</li></ul>

Summary questions

1 Which is more important to an organisation – training or development? Why?

2 Why is motivation important for training to be effective? How can effective training enhance motivation?

3 How can a TDLNA enable an organisation to develop suitable training and development programmes?

Functions of the HR department: compensation and performance management

Specific objective

On completion of this section, you should be able to:

■ evaluate the importance of human resource management in organisations by understanding the functions of compensation and performance management.

HR plays a key role in securing the long-term commitment, motivation and performance of employees. Employees' commitment can be secured by ensuring that the organisation provides for all of their needs (both hygiene and motivator needs), as shown in Figure 2.34.1.

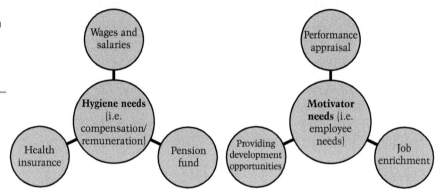

Figure 2.34.1 *Employees' commitment can be secured by ensuring that the organisation provides for all of their needs*

Compensation

One of the main functions of the HR department is to design remuneration and other incentive packages. The term 'wage' implies that the employee is likely to be paid on a weekly basis for the number of hours worked. A 'salary' is paid monthly to a professional worker.

Wages and salaries need to be competitive with similar jobs or similar occupations if a company is to attract good-quality employees who are willing to work hard. In addition, bonuses may be paid out for achieving targets.

CASE STUDY

Remuneration packages for police in Trinidad

In September 2012, *Trinidad Express News* carried the following story about police pay.

Acting CoP wants better pay for police

By Joel Julien, Trinidad Express
Story Created: Sep 6, 2012 at 10:00 PM ECT

ACTING Police Commissioner Stephen Williams is calling for a "reasonable remuneration" package for policemen and policewomen.

Williams made the statement as he addressed the weekly press briefing at the Police Administration building, Sackville Street, Port of Spain on Wednesday.

"On the face of it, if you took a constable receiving a basic salary of $5,123 as the starting point, security guards are

receiving more than that, so it is obvious compared... you are talking at a national level, the unit which is charged with the responsibility of providing this country with quality policing service should be treated in a particular way," Williams said.

"I pledge support to the [Police Service Social and Welfare] Association in its pursuit of a reasonable remuneration package. While we are making a special demand of the officers to perform, there is a need for their salary allowances and other terms and conditions to be revisited and that takes a process."

1 Why is it important in this instance to create an effective and attractive reward package?

2 What factors would HR need to consider in creating an appropriate compensation package for police officers?

Although wages or salaries are often seen as a hygiene factor (see 2.12), they can also serve as a motivator, since higher wages and salaries can be seen as a status symbol, which raises the self-esteem of the employee.

The HR department is also responsible for the other elements of the compensation package, such as the pension fund. Employees make a contribution towards their own pensions which is deducted from their salary. In addition, the employer also often makes a contribution. The company may put regular sums (from profits) into a pension fund to contribute to employees' pensions when they retire. A secure and attractive pension scheme is an incentive that encourages employee loyalty. In addition to the pension fund, a company may provide other benefits, such as a health insurance scheme to provide benefits to employees when they are sick or unable to work.

Performance management

As discussed in 2.33, appraisal is an important way of identifying individual development needs. Appraisal can also be used to assess formally the performance of an employee.

Performance appraisal involves establishing clear, but fair, objectives for each employee and giving a fair evaluation of actual performance against the objectives and achievement of targets. An appraisal is a one-to-one discussion that takes place periodically (either every six months or yearly) between an employee and their line manager. The appraisal:

- assesses performance against expectations or targets
- identifies the individual's strengths and weaknesses in relation to their performance.

The appraisal discussion may consider specific performance measures, such as individual output, or may involve a more general review of the contribution that the employee makes to the smooth running of the business. Appraisal is a two-way discussion in which the employee should be encouraged to participate and take ownership, rather just one-way feedback from the manager.

Appraisal can be used to:

- improve employees' performance
- provide feedback about performance
- identify future training needs
- identify employees who are capable of advancement.

The outcomes of appraisal include:

- greater motivation
- identification of the employee's training and learning needs.

Work performance rating

Performance-related appraisal usually involves some method of rating an individual's work performance. For example, one method is to set out a checklist of **competencies** that need to be achieved and against which the employee is measured.

The rating system often allows one job to be compared with another or one employee's performance to be compared with another's. Alternatively, individual performance may be ranked, with the most successful performance receiving the highest rewards and benefits.

KEY TERMS

Competency: a characteristic or a skill that a person possesses that enables him or her to do something within a job effectively or successfully.

Summary table

The HR function designs compensation packages.
These are the rewards and benefits that are designed to motivate employees at work.
The HR function creates performance management systems.
These are systems such as appraisal which seek to identify and monitor aspects of individual, team and business performance in order to encourage higher levels of performance.

Summary questions

1 How can a list of competencies be used to relate performance to pay?

2 Why might HR managers consider both hygiene and motivator factors in designing a reward system for employees?

3 How can performance appraisal be related to both development needs and to a reward system?

Answers to all exam-style questions can be found on the accompanying CD

Section 1: Multiple-choice questions

1 Scientific management seeks to:

   A find ways of motivating employees through job enrichment

   B identify a single best way of organising work tasks

   C use a human relations approach to securing employee commitment

   D use science and technology to solve production problems.

2 What did the Hawthorne experiments demonstrate?

   A Lower-order needs must be met before moving on to higher-order needs.

   B Some employees respond best when they are given clear instructions.

   C Employees respond well to managers and supervisors who take an interest in them.

   D Employees work harder when financial rewards are greater.

3 Which of the following organisational structures is most likely to enable a two-way flow of information, authority and responsibility?

   A A matrix structure

   B A functional structure

   C A geographical structure

   D A product structure

4 An open campus of a university brings together online tutors and learners. This is an example of:

   A a centralised organisation

   B a bureaucratic organisation

   C a virtual organisation

   D a tall organisation.

5 Which of the following is a characteristic of a tall organisation?

   A Few hierarchical levels

   B Short chain of command

   C Small span of control for each level in the hierarchy

   D Few employees

6 Maslow's concept of self-fulfilment or self-actualisation (as a requirement to meet higher-order psychological needs) fits with Herzberg's concept of:

   A hygiene factors

   B dissatisfiers

   C basic needs

   D motivators.

7 On what do trait theories of leadership focus?

   A The situation in which the leader makes decisions

   B The leadership style employed by the leader

   C The personality and characteristics of the leader

   D The relationship that the leader has with his or her followers

8 Transformational leaders are most likely to:

   A adopt an autocratic approach to leading others

   B share a vision and enable others to take on leadership responsibilities

   C set themselves up as heroic leaders

   D adopt a submissive approach to working with others.

9 Which of the following conflict management strategies is most likely to lead to a positive outcome for all parties?

   A Confronting

   B Avoiding

   C Smoothing

   D Collaborating

10 Which of the following is a key function of human resource management in maintaining an effective workforce?

   A Recruitment

   B Human Resource Planning

   C Compensation

   D Selecting the best employees to work for a company

Section 2: Structured questions

11 a State TWO assumptions made by Mayo's human relations model. [2]

  b i Explain the distinction that Herzberg made between 'hygiene' factors and 'motivators' in the context of work. [6]

    ii How could job enrichment be used in a specific work context to increase employee motivation and commitment? [8]

    iii Why might motivation be restricted in a 'bureaucratic organisation'? [4]

  c What advantages might flow from a bureaucratic organisational structure? [5]

12 a i Draw diagrams to illustrate the difference between a geographical and a functional organisational structure. [6]

    ii Identify TWO key advantages and ONE disadvantage of using a geographical organisational structure rather than a functional organisational structure. [6]

  b Evaluate the reasons why an organisation might choose to employ a matrix form of structure as it grows in size and explain the benefits of this structure. [10]

  c Identify ONE type of business organisation that might employ a decentralised structure and explain briefly the reasons why it might do so. [3]

13 a i What is a management style? [2]

    ii Compare and contrast TWO management styles. [6]

  b Would the use of a 'transformational' leadership approach achieve better results in large international companies than other forms of leadership? Discuss with reference to examples. [12]

  c Identify situations where other forms of leadership style may be more effective. [5]

14 a State THREE possible reasons for organisational change that stem from the external environment. [3]

  b How can a champion of change help to make the change process more effective? [2]

  c i Outline FOUR common barriers to change. [8]

    ii For each of the barriers that you have mentioned, discuss strategies that could be used to address resistance to change. [12]

15 a List the **main** areas of responsibility of a human resource department. [3]

  b Distinguish between recruitment and selection, and outline the main steps in the recruitment and selection process. [6]

  c An international hotel chain is keen to ensure continued development of its employees. Discuss THREE ways in which it can ensure the effective development of its employees. [12]

  d What are the **main** differences between training and development? [4]

> ☑ *Exam tip*
>
> When asked to discuss reasons for particular activities you should first identify or state the reasons and then follow with the relevant discussions. One mark is usually allocated to each reason identified. It is important to include relevant examples where they are warranted.

Further exam questions and examples can be found on the accompanying CD.

3 Business finance and accounting

General objectives

On completion of this module, you should be able to:

- understand the roles and functions of finance and accounting in the management of business with special reference to the Caribbean

- understand the impact of changes in finance and accounting practices on the overall operations of business

- develop analytical and interpretational skills relating to problem solving in finance and accounting.

Commercial banks are a major source of finance for businesses

Did you know?

In addition there is a simpler International Financial Reporting Standard for Small and Medium Enterprises (SMEs). The requirements are similar, but smaller companies do not have to provide as much detail as larger companies in relation to certain items that appear in the accounts.

Introduction

It is essential to have a good understanding of finance and accounts, as these are the foundations of any business. Accounting is the process of preparing, classifying, analysing and summarising the financial records of a business, using standard methods and procedures.

Need for finance and sources of finance

All businesses need finance – for example, when starting up, to pay for stocks or to invest for expansion purposes. A business can acquire finance from a range of sources depending on whether the finance is required for short-term purposes (for example, to pay an invoice) or for long-term purposes (for example, to purchase a new factory unit).

Money and capital markets and international financial institutions

The money market, which consists of institutions such as credit unions and commercial banks, provides short-term finance for business. In contrast, the capital market (including institutions such as the stock exchange) provides longer-term capital for business. In the Caribbean region, international financial institutions (such as the World Bank) are also important in providing governments with capital for development.

Why does a business need accounting information?

- There is a legal obligation for a company to keep accounting records.
- Accounting records are the basis of financial reports, which provide information for:
  - managers to run the business (internal reporting)
  - investors to monitor their investments (published accounts).
- Accounting records help to control the financial resources of the business.
- Accounting records provide the tax authorities with reliable information to enable them to assess the amount of tax that is due.

Financial statements

Accountants need to be able to analyse financial statements in order to have an overview of the business, solve financial problems and control costs. They also need to provide financial information to managers and board directors, following internationally accepted practices and standards, to enable them to make financial decisions.

The way in which financial statements are set out should comply with International Accounting Standards, particularly International Accounting Standard 1 (IAS 1), as defined by the International Accounting Standards Board. IAS 1 is followed in this module.

Standard accounting practice requires a company to produce the following financial statements:

- an income statement – to record the sales and expenses of a business in order to be able to calculate profit or loss in a given trading period

- a statement of financial position (balance sheet) showing:
  - □ assets (what the business owns)
  - □ liabilities (what the business owes)
  - □ net assets of the business: that is, total assets − total liabilities (the value of the business)
- a statement of cash flow showing:
  - □ the inflows and outflows of cash in the business during the previous year
  - □ the cash balance at the start and end of the year.

In this module you will look at the different components of financial statements listed above and learn how businesses analyse them and use them to make essential calculations. For example, at a simple level we can calculate the gross and net profit of a business and the cost of sales from the income statement (see the 'Did you know?').

Using ratios and percentages

Although raw figures such as gross profit and net profit are helpful, accountants often prefer to translate these figures into ratios and percentages (ratio analysis) to make comparisons easier. However, alongside the advantages that it brings there are some limitations to the use of ratio analysis, which you will look at in more detail.

Budgets

Budgets are used to show how a business is performing against plans. Accountants and managers set out budgets at the start of a financial year. The budget can be used as an ongoing means of controlling the business, and actions can be taken if actual figures are behind budget.

Investment appraisal

Investment appraisal is the process of identifying likely returns on investment. In 3.24–3.27 you will look at and compare the different methods of investment appraisal used by businesses.

Keeping up to date with accounting practices

Accountants need to be familiar with current practices. Accounting standards ensure consistency in the way that accounts are set out and presented on a global scale. They are updated regularly. Many Caribbean businesses are part of large global concerns, so it is essential that accountants keep up to date with international standards for financial reporting.

Did you know?

The income statement of a business shows how a company generates profit. For example in the illustration below a supermarket chain makes sales of $1,000,000 in 2014. The costs of items it buys in to resell came to $600,000 leaving a gross profit of $400,000. The expenses of running the business e.g. management and marketing costs came to another $250,000 leaving a final net profit of $150,000.

Income Statement of JoJo Stores, 2014

	$000
Sales revenue	1,000
Cost of sales	(600)
Gross profit	400
Administrative expenses	(250)
Net profit	150

On completion of this section, you should be able to:

■ explain the need for capital.

> **KEY TERMS**
>
> **Financial capital:** the funds used for investment in a business. The term 'capital' is also used in accounting to refer to the value of the owner's investment in a business.

Did you know?

It is the availability of finance that determines whether a business gets off the ground. Small businesses usually access funds from the owner's capital and from friends and family, but in addition often require other sources of finance (e.g. borrowing from a bank).

> **KEY TERMS**
>
> **Assets:** items of value that a business owns, which generate future economic benefits.
>
> **Fixed assets:** the tools of the trade that remain in the business.
>
> **Current assets:** assets that will be used up in the everyday trading of the business.

Figure 3.1.1 The typical cycle of funds within a business

Introduction

All businesses need capital (funds). The term **financial capital** refers to sums of money (or other financial assets) that a business requires for investment in physical items (for example, machinery and equipment) and other costs associated with starting up and developing a business.

There are four main reasons why a business needs capital:

■ for start-up – to set up a business for the first time

■ for working capital – that is, finance to purchase raw materials and stock, which the business will convert into finished goods

■ for growth – for example, when a business seeks to expand the scale of its operations

■ for growth – to take over another business or to form a joint venture.

Start-up capital

The start-up capital for a small business is likely to come from the owner's own funds and any borrowing he or she can secure. The owners of a business carry the risk. Whilst the owner may make significant financial gains, he or she also risks losing any capital invested.

For a private or public company, the financial capital is provided by shareholders. Ordinary share capital is often called 'equity capital'. Ordinary shareholders have voting rights in the companies in which they invest. In contrast, preference shareholders (see 3.2) do not have voting rights and so have less influence on company policy. In addition to capital invested by owners and shareholders, businesses raise finance by borrowing, often in the form of loans from a bank or from other finance providers, such as government agencies and venture capitalists.

A start-up business needs to invest in **assets**. There are two types of asset: fixed assets and current assets. **Fixed assets** are the tools of the trade (that is, the premises, machinery and equipment). For example, a new, small, private, start-up hotel business would need to invest in premises and furniture (beds, sideboards, dining chairs and tables etc.). Fixed assets are retained in the business.

A business, such as a hotel, also needs **current assets** (for example, food and drink to serve in the restaurant). A hotel is both a service provider and a trading company purchasing goods for resale. Like many other businesses, it is involved in the purchase of stock and goods for resale. The typical cycle of funds within a business is illustrated in Figure 3.1.1.

Working capital

Many businesses supply goods on credit (for example, because hotel customers pay only on departure), so they need funds for **working capital** (that is, to buy in stock to supply to customers). Most businesses are likely to obtain some of this working capital from overdrafts and creditors.

Investment/expansion capital

Once a business is established, the owner may want to grow it in size. The owner of one hotel may want to have a second hotel and eventually a chain of hotels. Capital for expansion can be paid for out of the business's profits. This is referred to as organic growth. However, the problem with organic growth is that it can take a long time. For example, it may take a long time to build a new hotel.

Takeovers, where one company buys a majority holding (51 per cent of the shares) in another company, provide a quicker way of expanding a business. To raise money for expansion in the short term, a business may also sell more shares or it may borrow external finance (for example, from a bank, a venture capitalist or a government agency).

Venture capital

Venture capital is a good source of investment for a growing business. A **venture capitalist** is usually a wealthy individual (or group of individuals) who tries to spot new investment opportunities (both businesses and entrepreneurs). Venture capitalists have been particularly active in the Caribbean, providing capital to new biotech and energy companies. The venture capitalist provides some of the funds for the enterprise in return for a share of the returns. Venture capitalists make capital available at a number of stages during the development of the business, as shown in Table 3.1.1.

> **KEY TERMS**
>
> **Working capital**: the capital required to purchase stock (inventories). A more technical definition is:
>
> Working capital = Current assets − Current liabilities

> **KEY TERMS**
>
> **Venture capitalists**: businesses and individual entrepreneurs who provide capital to other businesses (often start-up businesses and small businesses seeking to expand) in return for a share in the equity of the business.

Table 3.1.1 Types of venture capital

Type of funding	Purpose
Seed funding	Enables an entrepreneur to investigate a potential new opportunity or innovation. The investor may be referred to as an 'angel investor'
Start-up funding	Supports product and market development
Growth funding	Supports the early sales and manufacturing operations (i.e. the stages when the business is not yet profitable)
Second-round funding	Provides working capital because the business is not yet profitable
Expansion funding	Supports the growth of the business – to accelerate the growth of a business that is becoming profitable
Exit funding	Provides the funds for the business to go through the procedures of becoming a public listed company

Summary table

Type of capital	Typical sources of funds
Start-up capital	Owner's funds (e.g. shareholders' equity and borrowings to get started)
Working capital	Capital used to purchase stock Also defined as current assets minus current liabilities
Expansion capital	Capital to grow the business either from profits or from raising new funds (e.g. through a share issue)
Venture capital	Finance provided by venture capitalists usually to enable small businesses to grow

Summary questions

1   Identify as many ways of using the term 'capital' as you can (in a business sense).

2   Who are venture capitalists? What type of help might they give to a start-up business?

3   How is working capital different from the type of capital that is tied up in fixed assets?

4   What is the difference between a shareholder and a lender?

Specific objective

On completion of this section, you should be able to:

■ differentiate between various sources of finance, including equity and debt.

KEY TERMS

Equity: owner's capital – in the form of ordinary shares.

Gearing: the proportion of capital on which fixed interest payments are charged.

Liabilities: sums of money that a business owes to an individual or other organisation. In accounts, liabilities (i.e. negative numbers) are put in brackets to show that they need to be subtracted from the business's assets.

Did you know?

Preference shares are not really considered to be equity. Instead they are equivalent to debt – because preference shareholders are entitled to a fixed return that the company must pay out before paying ordinary shareholders. Only some companies will offer preference shares.

KEY TERMS

Preference shares: shares that earn fixed dividends that are paid before those on ordinary shares.

Equity versus debt

A major decision for any business is how it should be financed. The business needs to decide what proportion of the finance should come from the owner's **equity** and what proportion should come from debt (that is, lenders outside the business). We use the term **gearing** to describe the extent to which a business is financed externally. A business with a high proportion of capital from external sources is said to be highly geared or have a high gearing ratio. A business with a low proportion of capital from external sources is said to have a low gearing ratio (see 3.16). This is illustrated in Figure 3.2.1.

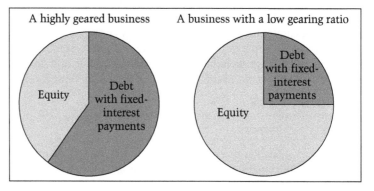

Figure 3.2.1 *High and low gearing ratios*

Forms of equity

Capital

Ordinary share capital is often called equity capital and can be likened to an owner's equity in a private house. Equity for the householder is the difference between the value of the house and the mortgage secured against it. In the case of a company, equity (the value of the ordinary shares) represents the difference between the value of assets owned by the business and the value of any outstanding loans and **liabilities** to other parties (Figure 3.2.2). For example:

	$000
Assets: fixed and current	200,000
Liabilities	(50,000)
Equity	150,000

Figure 3.2.2 *Calculating equity*

Shares

Holders of ordinary shares are able to vote at the company's annual general meetings. The influence that an ordinary shareholder has is directly proportional to the number of shares he or she holds. Ordinary shareholders are also entitled to a share of the business's profit after all other investors have been paid. They receive this in the form of a dividend payment. They can expect a high return when the company makes good profits. But in years when the company makes low profits, they may only receive a low dividend and in some years they may receive nothing at all. Ordinary shareholders are therefore the real risk-takers within a company.

Profit retained in the business

The equity section of the balance sheet shows accumulated profit that is retained in the business. In addition to ordinary shares, accumulated profit is counted as equity because it represents part of the owner's interest.

Forms of debt

Debentures/bonds

A debenture (also referred to as a company bond) is a loan made to a company under terms set out in a certifying document. Typically, the loan involves a fixed rate of interest and is repaid (redeemed) by the company on a predetermined date. Sometimes the loan is 'secured' against specified assets of the business in case the company runs into financial difficulties.

Other financial liabilities

- Long-term liabilities take the form of longer-term debt (debt that must be repaid in over one year).
- Short-term liabilities are debts that must be paid back in less than one year.

Sources and uses of finance

It is helpful to distinguish between a source of finance (the supplier of finance) and the use of that finance (that is, the type of finance provided and the purpose for which it is used), as shown in Table 3.2.1.

Table 3.2.1 Examples of sources and uses of finance

Source of finance	Use of finance
Bank or building society loan	Mortgage to build a new factory (long term)
Supplier offering trade credit	Trade credit for supplies of goods (short term)
Finance house providing hire purchase	Hire purchase agreement for purchase of a vehicle (medium term)

Summary table

Equity versus debt		
Type	**Source**	**Name of provider**
Equity	Finance put into the business by owner's contributions (e.g. by shareholders)	Shareholders or owners
Debt	Finance brought into the business from outside borrowing	Lenders

Summary questions

1. What are the main challenges facing a business with a high gearing ratio?

2. What are the main issues facing a business with a low gearing ratio?

3. Hovill has set up a new biotech business that she wants to expand quickly. In contrast, Michael has set up a new recording studio and does not want to take any risks with the financial structure of the company. Explain whether Hovill or Michael will be more tempted to choose a high gearing structure. Explain your reasoning.

Did you know?

Convertible debentures are an attractive option for investors because they can be converted into shares at some future date and at a predetermined price. Debenture holders therefore have fixed income in the short term with the possibility of capital gains at low risk in the long term.

KEY TERMS

Convertible debenture: a document stating that the company has received a loan from an individual that will be paid in the future by converting the loan into shares in the company.

3.3 Criteria for seeking finance and short-term finance

Specific objective

On completion of this section, you should be able to:

- explain the main criteria that businesses use when seeking short-term finance.

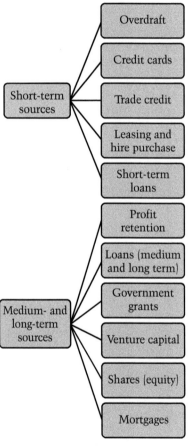

Figure 3.3.1 *Sources of finance*

KEY TERMS

Commercial banks: high street banks that provide bank accounts, loans and other forms of finance to personal and business customers.

There are a number of factors that a business needs to consider when seeking finance, including:

- The purpose of raising finance: for how long does the business need the finance? Does it need short- or long-term finance? Is the finance needed for starting up a business or expansion?
- Does the business want to raise the funds from its own resources (equity) or externally (debt)?
- Under what terms is the business prepared to repay the loan?
- How much interest needs to be paid on different forms of borrowing both now and in the future (i.e. current and future interest rates)? The higher the rate of interest, the less attractive the source of finance.
- Attitude to risk: is the business prepared to borrow a higher amount at higher rates of interest from a more risky source, or is it happy to borrow less at a lower rate of interest from a more secure source?

The most important decision relates to the time period over which a company wishes to borrow money. Figure 3.3.1 shows the different sources of short-term and long-term finance. Here we will focus on short-term finance. Medium- and long-term finance will be discussed in detail in 3.4.

Sources of short-term finance

The main sources of short-term finance are trade creditors and commercial banks, which provide a variety of types of finance as shown in Figure 3.3.1.

Overdrafts

An overdraft is the most frequently used form of short-term bank finance and it is used to ease cash-flow problems. It is an arrangement under which a **commercial bank** extends credit up to an agreed limit. The customer cannot withdraw funds beyond this limit. Interest is calculated on the overdraft on a daily basis and the amount of interest depends on the level of the overdraft. Often a bank makes a special charge for arranging an overdraft. An overdraft may be particularly helpful to a start-up business and for businesses needing finance for working capital.

Credit cards

A credit card provides a user with the facility to draw credit on a bank up to an agreed limit. The customer has the option to settle the balance at the end of the month without charge. However, if customers do not repay at the end of the month, they have to pay a substantial interest rate. Total repayment involves paying off any outstanding credit.

Trade credit

This is where supplies have been bought with an agreement to pay the supplier at a later date (for example, after 30, 90 or 180 days). Credit periods are usually governed by the type of business and the relationship between the purchaser and the supplier. A start-up business typically receives credit on less favourable terms than an established business. If the credit is not paid for within the stipulated period (such as one month) the interest rate may increase significantly (for example, from 5 per cent to 10 per cent).

Leasing and hire purchase

Hire purchase allows the business to use an asset without having to find the money for it up front. A finance house buys the asset (for example, a car or truck) from the supplier and retains ownership of it until the business has made the payments required under the hire purchase agreement. At the end of the agreement, ownership of the asset passes to the business (providing all payments have been made). However, by this point the value of the item is likely to have depreciated substantially.

Alternatively, a business can lease an item, enabling it to use the item for a set period but never to own the item. For example, a business may lease computers. Typically, leasing and hire purchase agreements are over a two- or three-year period. However, to be considered as short-term finance an asset on hire should really be paid for within the next 12-month period.

Short-term loans

Short-term loans are loans that a business needs to repay within a year. Businesses use short-term loans to finance working capital or for small investments. A disadvantage of short-term loans is that they need to be repaid within a short period.

Did you know?

An operating lease is for smaller items usually leased over a shorter period of time, whereas a capital or finance lease is for larger items leased over a longer period of time.

Summary table

Type	Source	Benefits	Disadvantages
Overdraft	Commercial bank	■ Facility to withdraw more money from a bank than has been deposited ■ Interest is only charged on the days that you are overdrawn, allowing flexible credit management	■ Bank can demand repayment at any time ■ High penalties for exceeding overdraft limits
Credit card	Commercial bank	■ A means of card payment allowing borrowing up to a prearranged sum ■ A useful source of additional working capital	■ Makes it easy to borrow money and can therefore encourage unnecessary borrowing ■ Interest is high on balances that are not paid off at the end of the month
Trade credit	Trade creditors	■ A means of buying supplies on credit	■ If the amount owing is not paid within the stipulated period, the interest rate increases
Hire purchase and leasing	Finance company/lessor	■ Enables the hirer or lessee to make use of capital items for which it has not yet paid	■ Hire purchase: depreciation by the time the company owns the item ■ Leasing: company never owns the item
Short-term loan	Commercial banks	■ Provides start-up capital, working capital and small-scale expansion capital	■ Short repayment period

Summary questions

1 Suggest two ways a retailer can finance the purchase of new stock.

2 Suggest three ways a small, start-up business can finance the acquisition of computing equipment.

3 What is short-term finance and why is it so important for growing businesses?

Did you know?

Depreciation is the reduction in the value of an asset that results from wear and tear. Each year a calculation is made to assess the sum of depreciation of fixed assets in a business.

KEY TERMS

Medium-term finance: finance typically taken over one to five years.

Long-term finance: finance typically taken over five years or longer.

Did you know?

Development Funds are organised funding arrangements for development purposes. For example, the Caribbean Regional Development Fund (based on funds provided by CARICOM member countries) provides support for government and businesses in the Eastern Caribbean to support job creation schemes and infrastructure development. Similarly, the Tourism Investment Fund provides funding for businesses in the Caribbean to improve aspects of tourism.

KEY TERMS

Government grant: a sum of money provided to businesses and other organisations by the government to fund specific targeted activities (e.g. to set up a new business). The grant is not expected to be repaid.

'Soft loans': loans that have easy repayment terms (e.g. low or no interest spread over a longer period of repayment than other forms of borrowing).

Sources of medium- and long-term finance

In addition to family and friends there are a number of other important sources of **medium-term finance** and **long-term finance** (see Figure 3.3.1 in 3.3).

Small business associations

Throughout the Caribbean, there are a number of small business associations, such as the Small Business Association of Jamaica. These not-for-profit organisations provide some capital to help small businesses that have great new ideas.

Profit retention

Profit that has been ploughed back into a business is one of the most important sources of finance. This source of finance only becomes available once the business has been trading for a certain period of time. Advantages are that the business does not have to pay interest on this form of finance and that it is useful for financing expansion and growth. However, retaining profits in the business means that less profit can be distributed to the owners of the business.

Loans (medium- and long-term)

Interest is the charge for borrowing money. The rate of interest depends on the level of risk involved with the loan. For example, longer-term loans made to small businesses with unproven track records are considered a higher risk. Borrowing is essential during the start-up stage of a business and for ongoing growth. Long-term loans can increase the gearing of a company because interest payments need to be made over a long period.

Commercial banks

A major source of loans, commercial banks look after money paid in by depositors and lend some of these funds to individuals and businesses seeking funds. They help businesses (particularly start-up businesses) by providing advice and helping with business planning, as well as funds and a range of banking facilities (for example loans, credit cards and safe deposits). However, they are cautious lenders, so it may be difficult for a business to borrow for what might appear to be a risky venture.

Government grants

Government grants, 'soft loans' and subsidies are another important source of medium- and long-term finance. Grants can be obtained from national governments and through development banks such as the Caribbean Development Bank (see 3.5). However, government grants are only available for specific projects and conditions may be attached which specify what the money can be spent on.

Venture capital

Venture capital companies provide finance in return for a shareholding in an organisation and an element of control. They can provide billions of dollars of investment capital. A disadvantage is that the investor often demands a high percentage of the business, depriving the owner of some profit in later years.

Shares (equity)

Once a business becomes incorporated as a company, it will have access to share capital. A share in a limited company is a tradable security that (subject to certain restrictions) can be bought and sold without affecting the business itself. Shareholders enjoy limited liability (see 1.2). Limited liability encourages shareholders to invest in companies. Share capital can be used at all stages of business growth after the company becomes incorporated. However, relying on shares to fund a business limits access to funds.

Mortgages

A mortgage is a loan secured against a property or land. The size of the mortgage depends on factors such as the value of the property, the length of repayment period (often 25 years or longer) and the income and credit record of the borrower. Mortgages provide a long-term drain on the profits earned by a business.

Did you know?

Banks and credit unions are risk averse. In addition to requiring a detailed business plan, they do not generally lend more than the owners are putting into a business themselves. Security is also usually required.

Summary table

Type	Source	Benefits	Disadvantages
Profit retention	Business itself	■ Capital is provided internally so there are no repayments or interest charges	■ Less profit may be distributed to the owners of the business
Long-term loan	Bank or credit union	■ Funds for expansion are provided by a reliable source ■ Repayment terms are agreed for a specified length of time	■ May raise the gearing ratio of the company as interest needs to be paid over a long period of time
Government grants	Government and development banks	■ There is no expectation that the grant will be repaid	■ Only available for specific projects or activities ■ May come with conditions determining on what the money can be spent
Venture capital	Venture capitalist	■ In addition to providing funds, venture capitalists often contribute business knowledge	■ Venture capitalists typically demand a high percentage of the equity of the business
Shares	Shareholder	■ Access to long-term funds ■ With equity capital, there is no requirement to make payments from profits each year	■ Business might grow slowly because of limited access to funds
Mortgage	Bank/building society	■ Access to substantial sums of capital for long periods	■ Provides a long-term drain on profits as a result of the lengthy repayment period (20 years or more)

Summary questions

1   Categorise the different types of finance outlined in 3.3 and 3.4 into short, medium and long term.

2   Which types of long-term finance are secured against specific assets?

3   Which types of long-term finance might you draw on to finance a new hotel? Identify the sources and the types of finance that you would require.

On completion of this section, you should be able to:

- discuss the roles, functioning and working of money and capital markets and international financial institutions with special reference to the Caribbean.

KEY TERMS

Capital market: a financial market for the buying and selling of long-term debt. Institutions in the capital market include those trading shares on the stock exchange, investment banks and private equity firms.

Money market: a market made up of organisations that channel short-term finance (provided by savers) into businesses and other borrowers.

Foreign direct investment (FDI): the investment of capital by a business in one country into another country (e.g. through investment in plant and equipment in another country, or by buying shares in overseas companies).

Did you know?

Jamaica is one of the prime destinations for FDI in the Caribbean. Typical areas of foreign investment include shipping, call centres and hotels. The Jamaica Promotions Corporation (JAMPRO) was set up by the Jamaican government to encourage FDI.

You have seen that businesses require finance for short-, medium- and long-term purposes. This distinction mirrors the broad markets in which finance is provided in an economy.

The capital market

The **capital market** is made up of financial institutions that provide long-term finance for business and for the government: for example, the stock exchange (where equities can be traded) and private equity companies investing in businesses.

The money market

The **money market** comprises financial institutions that provide short-term finance for business and the government: for example, the commercial banks and credit unions. The money market deals in transactions and short-term debt that become due for payment in less than one year.

Many financial institutions, particularly banks, operate in both the capital market and the money market. When they are dealing in long-term transactions they are operating in the capital market and when they are dealing in short-term transactions they are operating in the money market.

The bond market

The bond market is where companies and governments can borrow money from investors with surplus funds. The investor buys a bond which is repaid at a later date. The investor receives a return (interest) on the bond. Some short-term bonds are sold on the money markets (for example, when the government issues treasury bills) whereas longer-term bonds (for example, government securities and corporate bonds) are sold on the capital market.

Sources of capital

Foreign direct investment in the Caribbean

The Caribbean is subject to considerable international investment. **Foreign direct investment (FDI)** is long-term investment in a company that operates in a different country from that in which the investor is based. The investor acquires a controlling interest (defined as 10 per cent or more of the shares) in the company.

Regional and international financial institutions

Caribbean Development Bank

The Caribbean Development Bank (CDB) has its head office in Wildey, St Michael (near Bridgetown), Barbados. It provides capital for a range of development projects in the Caribbean, mainly to government but also to community groups for projects involving the development of industry and agriculture, and setting up small enterprises, typically in poorer communities.

The aims of the CDB include:

- promoting investment in the Caribbean
- bringing financial resources into the Caribbean from outside (for example, from the World Bank)
- supporting the development of financial institutions in the Caribbean
- helping borrowers to develop their economies and to increase trade.

World Bank

The World Bank is an international organisation that provides funds to national governments and development agencies, often for major development projects such as building schools and hospitals. It works with national governments, aid agencies and environmental groups to establish development priorities, which are then funded or part-funded by the World Bank. Before the World Bank lends money to borrowers it will first need to carry out feasibility studies and economic appraisal in order to check that the investment will yield an appropriate return.

Investment banks and private equity firms

Investment banks and **private equity** firms are international institutions that seek out investment opportunities usually involving considerable sums of capital. These institutions may invest in companies in Caribbean territories, such as hotel chains, where the prospects of making a financial return are good.

International Monetary Fund

Whereas the World Bank and the CDB are mainly concerned with providing long-term capital investment, the International Monetary Fund (IMF) may provide shorter-term support. The IMF provides loans to countries with balance of payments and other problems to help them to restructure their economies. Most, if not all, Caribbean countries have borrowed from the IMF in recent times – for example, to help to resolve financial difficulties after a severe hurricane. The IMF works with Caribbean countries to create economic stability and reduce poverty.

The World Bank and the IMF also provide technical and managerial advice to governments to support development programmes. These institutions appraise economies to identify their readiness for particular types of support, and conduct feasibility studies to identify the benefits of, for example, an irrigation system or building new roads.

Summary table

Type of market	Type of investment	Institutions that make up the market
Capital markets	Long-term investment funds	■ Stock exchange ■ Private equity firms ■ World Bank ■ Development banks (e.g. CDB)
Money markets	Shorter-term finance	■ Commercial banks and credit unions ■ IMF
Bond markets	Short- and long-term investment	■ Investors with surplus funds

Did you know?

International development bank (IDB) is a generic term for a financial institution that seeks to support economic growth and social development in a particular region or country. The IDB in the Caribbean is the Caribbean Development Bank (CDB).

KEY TERMS

Private equity: money invested by wealthy individuals and institutional investors to purchase businesses. Typically, they improve the performance of a business that they have acquired before selling it on.

Summary questions

1 Which type of market (capital market or money market) is likely to be involved in the following?

  a A short-term business loan

  b The issuing of shares in a company

  c A development loan to a Caribbean country for reconstruction after a hurricane

  d A takeover of a Caribbean company by private equity

  e A seed loan to launch a new business

2 How may a commercial bank operate in both the capital and money markets?

3 Describe the roles of the Caribbean Development Bank and International Monetary Fund.

Functioning and workings of money and capital markets: the stock exchange

Specific objective

On completion of this section, you should be able to:

■ discuss the roles, functioning and working of the stock exchange in the Caribbean.

The stock exchange

The stock exchange is a place in which shares in public companies are traded. Many countries now have a stock exchange – a very important institution for raising funds for business. Well-known examples are the New York, Hong Kong and London stock exchanges.

In the Caribbean, the principal stock exchanges are the Jamaica, Barbados, and Trinidad and Tobago stock exchanges and the Eastern Caribbean securities market.

CASE STUDY

The Jamaica Stock Exchange

The Jamaica Stock Exchange, known as the JSE, was set up in 1968 and is located at 40 Harbour Street in Kingston. Its objective is to promote the orderly development of the highest standards for its members. Its rules are designed to ensure public confidence in the exchange and in public companies.

The people who trade in shares are broker members of the exchange. They perform two functions (see Figure 3.6.1):

■ to act as agents who hold a stock of shares that they can sell to clients

■ to buy and sell shares on behalf of people or institutions.

Shares are bought and sold by broker members on behalf of their clients. Since 2000, the exchange has had an automated trading platform – an electronic system that records and processes all of the transactions that are made by the brokers. This enables swift processing and accurate transactions.

Figure 3.6.1 *The stock exchange as a marketplace*

For a company to have its shares traded on the JSE, it must have a minimum of $200,000 worth of capital and at least half of this must be issued in the form of ordinary shares. A minimum of 100 shareholders in the company must hold no less than 20 per cent of the ordinary shares that have been issued in the company. Public companies must produce an annual financial statement and circulate it to shareholders.

1 Why might a business want to become a public company and have its shares traded on the stock exchange?

2 In what ways is the JSE regulated? What is the purpose of this regulation?

Did you know?

The Stock Exchange Council is the body that oversees the orderly running of the stock exchange. It establishes standards that companies should meet if their shares are to be traded.

Trading shares

The stock exchange is a market for second-hand shares – that is, shares that a company has already issued. The shares are first issued by a company: for example, by offering them for sale to the general public or by agreeing to have them placed with large financial institutions such as pension funds. The holders of these shares can then trade them on the stock exchange. Shareholders are rewarded by means of dividends and by growing demand increasing the price of the shares that they already hold.

The functions of the stock exchange

The main purpose of the stock exchange is to help public companies raise capital. Financial capital is the money that a business raises from selling shares. The capital can then be used to purchase physical plant, such as buildings and machinery.

The existence of a stock exchange gives the public and the financial institutions confidence that they can:

- buy new shares
- sell their shares when they want to.

A shareholder in a company is a part-owner of that company. The rewards from holding shares are that:

- every six or 12 months, shareholders receive a payment known as a dividend, which is their share of the profits
- shareholders may benefit from the rising value of their shares
- some companies offer special concessions to their shareholders, such as cheap flights for holders of airline shares or discount vouchers to use in the company's stores.

Shareholders are protected by limited liability. As defined in 1.2, this legal protection limits the amount that a shareholder might lose to the value of their shareholding, if the company gets into financial difficulty. The shareholder does not have to pay any more to cover the company's debts. Stock exchanges also protect shareholders with strict rules that set out what a company must do in order for its shares to be listed on the stock exchange. Limited companies are required to produce an annual report for shareholders and to have their accounts checked each year by an independent auditor.

Summary table

Function of the stock exchange	How it enables this
Provides a marketplace	Enables shares to be bought and sold
Enables investment	Allows companies to sell shares, by trading them on the stock exchange, to finance their business
Provides regulation	Stocks and shares are traded in an orderly fashion, conforming to specified practice and standards
Gives investors confidence	A body (e.g. the Stock Exchange Council) oversees the orderly running of the stock exchange

Summary questions

1 What work do broker members carry out on a stock exchange?

2 A stock exchange can be described as 'a market for second-hand shares'. What do you understand by this statement?

Did you know?

An institutional investor is an organisation such as a pension fund, unit trust or investment company. It is set up for a particular purpose and has access to large sums of money that it can reinvest. For example, people saving for future pensions pay regular sums into the pension fund and these sums are then reinvested on the stock exchange.

Figure 3.6.2 Traders at a stock exchange are called broker members

Did you know?

The stock exchange also plays an important role in helping the government to raise finance through selling bills and bonds. Institutional and other investors lend money to the government, knowing that they are almost certain to be paid back. In most countries, government bonds are more secure than shares in companies, although the return on a government bond may be lower than a dividend on a share in a company.

What is accounting?

Accounting is the process of using accepted methods and procedures to prepare, classify, analyse and summarise the financial records of a business.

Who uses accounting information and why?

There are a number of different individuals and groups (users) who have a stake in how a company is run:

■ Internal users are individuals and groups within an organisation, such as managers and shareholders (investors).

■ External users are individuals and groups outside the organisation, such as suppliers, customers and the local community.

These users utilise accounting information in different ways.

Take a gold mining company as an example. At the end of each financial year the company produces a set of accounts that are used by a number of stakeholders, as shown in Figure 3.7.1.

Figure 3.7.1 *The stakeholders who would use a gold mining company's accounts*

Shareholders

The main concern of shareholders is that the company is managed well by the board of directors. Accounts should allow them to see for themselves how well the business is being managed. They should be presented in a way that is clear and enables comparisons to be made between one period and the next. The company's annual report and accounts focus on:

■ the financial performance of the company, measured in terms of the sales and profits of the company – in the case of the gold mining company, shareholders want to see an increase in sales of gold and other minerals, and the costs of mining kept under control

- the net wealth of the business – comparing the value of all of the assets of the company with the value of all of its liabilities
- the **solvency** of the business – whether the company has a sufficient cash balance to keep on trading
- the directors' benefits – shareholders want to check that the renumeration and benefits of the directors are in line with the achievements of the company and that directors are not rewarding themselves disproportionately to the success of the business.

Creditors

Creditors are financial institutions and other businesses that supply a business with credit. For example, banks and finance companies lend money which needs to be repaid at a future date. Before making a line of credit available, the creditor might want to check the financial statements of the purchaser to check whether they are likely to be able to pay when the credit becomes due for payment.

Suppliers are also creditors as they supply a business with goods and services on credit terms so that payment is only made at a future date (for example, a supplier supplying agricultural produce to a food processing company). They are therefore interested in their customer's solvency to ensure they receive payment.

Other users of accounting information

Other stakeholders within a business also have an interest in the accounts.

- Customers want to have confidence in the financial stability of the company to ensure continuing supplies.
- Employees want to know that their employer is financially stable and is able to offer a secure future. If profits are good, they may be encouraged to press for wage increases, bonuses or share options.
- The government needs to be able to assess tax liabilities on the basis of published financial information. It may also want to assess whether the company is entitled to a grant or subsidy.
- Members of the local community in which a company is established may want to read the accounts to check the viability of the company, particularly if it is an important provider of local jobs. They might also want to check how much profit the company is making from operating in their area.

> **KEY TERMS**
>
> **Solvency:** the ability of a company to cover all of its pressing liabilities (short-term liabilities) with short-term assets, so that it can carry on trading.

> ☑ *Exam tip*
>
> Remember to always read through the entire question before attempting a response.

Summary table

The users of accounts	The stakeholders who make use of company accounts include:
	■ shareholders ■ creditors ■ suppliers ■ members of the local community ■ customers ■ employees ■ government
The purposes of accounts	The reasons why accounts are kept vary according to the users of the accounts, e.g. shareholders use them to check on how their stake in the business is being protected; suppliers use them to check whether a business will be able to pay for orders.

Summary questions

1 For what purposes do shareholders use accounts?

2 To what extent are the uses of accounts similar for all stakeholders?

3 What specific information do suppliers look for in a set of accounts?

4 What specific information do government tax officers look for in a set of accounts?

	31 March 2013 $000
Sales revenue	4,901.4
Cost of sales	(2,689.5)
Gross profit	**2,211.9**
Operating expenses	(1,614.7)
Operating profit	**597.2**
Net interest	15.3
Profit before tax	**612.5**
Taxes paid	(104.3)
Net profit	**508.2**

Figure 3.8.1 *Income statement for Sea Sea Cosmetics*

Financial statements provide users with a great deal of information about the financial health of a company and how well it is performing.

The **income statement** is one of the most frequently used financial statements. It shows the profit or loss earned by a business in a particular accounting period (often a year, although they can be published for shorter periods, such as six months).

A company makes a profit or loss as a result of making and selling items, producing a service or trading (that is, buying in items and then selling them at a higher price). In order to work out profit, we take away from the value of the sales the cost of making those sales and the expenses of running the business.

Figure 3.8.1 shows the income statement of a cosmetics manufacturer and retailer in 2013. The company specialises in skincare, fragrances, make-up and haircare. The figures are for the year leading up to 31 March 2013.

You should be able to see that the term 'profit' is used in four ways in Figure 3.8.1.

Gross profit

Gross profit is calculated by deducting Sea Sea's cost of purchasing items to make and resell from the sales that it makes in the 12 months leading up to 31 March 2013.

> Sales revenue − Cost of sales = Gross profit
>
> 4,901.4 − 2,689.5 = 2,211.9

Sea Sea's cost of sales would include, for example, the ingredients it puts into its perfumes.

Operating profit

Operating profit is calculated by deducting the operating expenses (that is, the costs of running the business, such as heating and lighting of the retail stores, marketing costs, etc.) from the gross profit.

> Gross profit − Operating expenses = Operating profit
>
> 2,211.9 − 1,614.7 = 597.2

The figure for operating profit is very important because it shows how well the managers are running the main activities of the business.

Profit before tax

This shows profit including any interest from money deposited in the bank or any interest it may be paying. In this instance the company is earning interest of $15,300.

> Operating profit +/− Net interest = Profit before tax
>
> 597.2 + 15.3 = 612.5

Net profit

The business also pays some taxes on its profits to the government. The term 'net' in **net profit** shows that deductions have been made from the gross profit the business made.

Profit before tax − Tax = Net profit

612.5 − 104.3 = 508.2

Making comparisons

It is essential that the presentation of income statements is consistent, as users want to be able to make comparisons of profits between companies and over periods of time. For example, using Figure 3.8.2 we can compare Sea Sea's profit figures in 2013 with those in 2014.

	31 March 2013 $000	31 March 2014 $000
Sales revenue	4,901.4	6,405.1
Gross profit	2,211.9	2,896.7
Operating profit	597.2	828.2
Profit before tax	612.5	834.8
Net profit	508.2	689.7

Figure 3.8.2 *Sea Sea's profit figures in 2013 and 2014*

In terms of the raw figures, you can see that all of the profit totals have increased in 2014 compared with 2013. This is not surprising because Sea Sea's sales have increased. More sales typically lead to more profits.

Did you know?

To arrive at profit before tax, positive net interest should be added to operating profit. If net interest is negative because the company pays out more interest than it receives, this should be deducted from operating profit to arrive at profit before tax.

KEY TERMS

Net profit: the profit of a business after the cost of sales and other expenses have been deducted.

Did you know?

In an income statement, the sales are often referred to as the 'top line'.

The 'bottom line' is the net profit (i.e. the profit after all deductions have been made).

Summary table

The income statement sets out:		
1 The sales made by a company during a particular time period	**4** The expenses from running the business	**7** **Profit before tax** (i.e. 5 +/− 6)
2 The cost of making those sales	**5** The **operating profit** (i.e. 3 − 4)	**8** Taxes paid
3 The **gross profit** from making those sales (i.e. 1 − 2)	**6** The net interest	**9** **Net profit** (i.e. 7 − 8)

Summary questions

1 What is the difference between gross profit and net profit?

2 Explain why the figure in the bottom line of an income statement should be lower than the figure in the top line.

3 How is the cost of sales different from operating expenses?

4 What period of time is covered by an income statement?

Did you know?

The trading account part of an income statement (for a retailer or other trading company) consists of:

Sales

less Cost of sales

= Gross profit

3.9 Components of financial statements: balance sheet

Components of financial statements: balance sheet

Specific objective

On completion of this section, you should be able to:

- appraise the components of the balance sheet.

KEY TERMS

Balance sheet (statement of financial position): one of the main financial statements, showing the financial situation of a business at a particular date. It summarises the assets and liabilities of a business as well as the owner's capital.

The purpose of a balance sheet

The **balance sheet** (also known as the **statement of financial position**) shows the state of a business's finances at a given point in time (that is, at the end of a month or year). Analysis of a balance sheet allows stakeholders to assess the financial health of a business. The balance sheet gives a summary of the business's:

- assets
- liabilities
- capital.

Figure 3.9.1 shows the basic structure of a balance sheet.

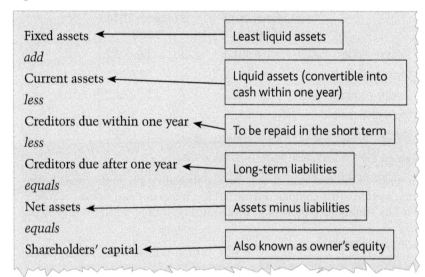

Figure 3.9.1 *The basic structure of a balance sheet*

A more detailed picture of a balance sheet is shown in Figure 3.9.2.

	$000	$000
Fixed assets		1,150
Current assets		
Inventories	500	
Trade receivables (debtors)	1,000	
Cash at bank and in hand	50	
	1,550	
Current liabilities		
Trade payables (creditors to be paid in under a year)	(800)	
Net current assets		750
Total assets *less* current liabilities		1,900
Trade payables (creditors to be paid in over a year)		(300)
Total net assets		1,600
Owner's equity		1,600

Figure 3.9.2 *A more detailed balance sheet for Sea Sea*

Did you know?

You can work out subtotals by using two columns. In the balance sheet you can see that the left-hand column has been used to calculate current assets − current liabilities (i.e. net current assets). The total from this calculation (750,000) is then transferred to the right-hand column.

In published accounts, the balance sheet includes comparative figures for the previous year and 'notes to the accounts' to explain the composition of individual balances.

Assets and liabilities

As mentioned previously, the balance helps us to see how much a business is worth at a particular moment in time – in this case, $1,600,000. To arrive at this total we need to subtract all of the liabilities (what the business owes) from the assets (what the business owns or is owed by others).

Assets

- The value of fixed assets = $1,150,000. This includes equipment and fixtures used by Sea Sea.
- Add the current assets = $1,550,000. Current assets include inventories (stock waiting to be sold), trade receivables (money owed to Sea Sea by debtors) and cash.

Liabilities

- Deduct any current liabilities that Sea Sea has (which need to be paid back in less than 12 months). These amount to $800,000.
- Deduct the long-term liabilities (**fixed liabilities** to be repaid in over 12 months), which are $300,000.

We can now subtract all of the liabilities from all of the assets:

$1,150,000 + $1,550,000 − ($800,000 + $300,000)

$2,700,000 − $110,000 = $1,600,000

The figure of $1,600,000 represents the net assets of the business.

> **KEY TERMS**
>
> **Fixed liabilities**: include outstanding liabilities of a company that need to be repaid. There is a minimum of 12 months before payment becomes due.

Subtotals in the balance sheet

We can also use the balance sheet to show some subtotals. For example, net current assets shows the current assets minus the current liabilities:

$1,550,000 − $800,000 = $750,000.

We can also show total assets minus current liabilities:

$1,150,000 + $1,550,000 − $800,000 = $1,900,000.

Owner's equity

The final section of a balance sheet shows the owner's equity. Sea Sea is worth $1,600,000 on the balance sheet (all assets − all liabilities). This is the capital available to the owners (which could be the shareholders).

Summary table

Assets of a business	Liabilities of a business
Fixed assets	Fixed liabilities
Current assets	Current liabilities
Total assets	Total liabilities
Net assets = Total assets − Total liabilities	

Summary questions

1 What is likely to cause the net assets of a business to rise from one year to the next?

2 Why is it important to make a distinction between assets and liabilities that are due in over 12 months and those that are due in less than 12 months?

3 Why might increasing liabilities be a cause for concern?

Components of financial statements: cash flow statement

Specific objective

On completion of this section, you should be able to:

- appraise the components of a cash flow statement.

All businesses need to have cash in order to carry on trading. Without cash a business is not able to buy supplies or pay wages. The income statement that we examined in 3.8 records sales and purchases when they take place. However, many business transactions are not paid for in cash (for example, goods may be supplied on credit but never paid for) and so the income statement does not accurately represent the cash movements in and out of a business. The **cash flow statement (statement of cash flows)** gives a much clearer overview of the movement of cash (see Figure 3.10.1).

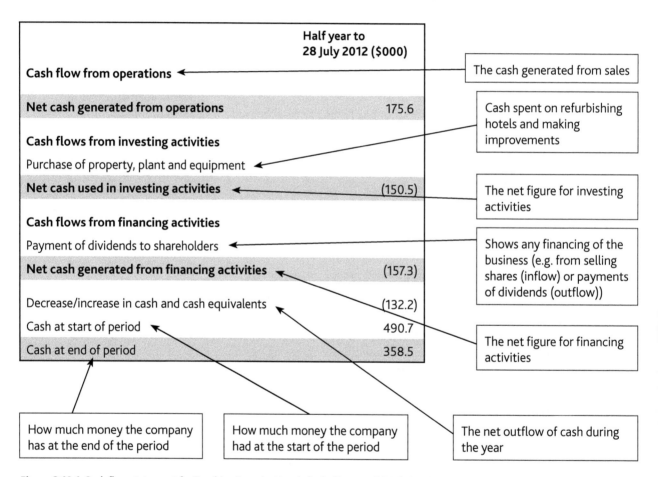

Figure 3.10.1 *Cash flow statement for Sunshine Serenity Hotels for half year to 28 July 2012*

Structure of the cash flow statement

The cash flow statement shows three main types of cash movement:

- **Cash flows from operations:** the flow of cash into a business from sales of goods and services. This is almost certain to be a positive amount. You can see in the cash flow summary (Figure 3.10.2) that in the six months to 28 July 2012, Sunshine Serenity Hotels had a net inflow of cash from operations of $175.6 million.

- **Cash flows from investing activities:** during the same period Sunshine Serenity Hotels was refurbishing its hotels. This is an investment in improvements and cash flows from investing activities appear as a negative outflow of cash in the cash flow statement. The outflow was $150.5 million.
- **Cash flow from financing activities:** the final movement of cash is purely of a financial nature. Some cash flows from financial activities are inflows to a business (for example, cash borrowed), whereas other financial flows are outflows (for example, the payment of interest on borrowing). In some years there will be outflows for financial purposes and in some years there will be inflows. In the six-month period shown in Figure 3.10.2, there was a net outflow of cash of $157.3 million.

Finally, we can balance up our statement of cash flows. This is a simple process. All we have to do is to adjust the balance we had at the start of the year by the net cash movements during the year.

In the summary shown in Figure 3.10.2, Sunshine Serenity Hotels started the year with $490.7 million of cash. During the year there was a net outflow of cash of $132.2 million, leaving the company's cash balance at the end of the year standing at $358.5 million.

Although the business has had a net outflow of cash during the year, it has plenty left at the end (see Figure 3.10.2) – although it would not want the balance to keep reducing.

	$000
Starting balance	490.7
+	
Inflow from operations	175.6
−	
Outflow from investment	(150.5)
−	
Outflow from finance	(157.3)
=	
End balance	358.5

Figure 3.10.2 Summary of the cash flow of Sunshine Serenity Hotels

Figure 3.10.3 When Sunshine Serenity Hotels refurbishes its property this will result in an outflow of cash under the heading investment activities

Summary table

Typical outflows of cash	Typical inflows of cash
Outflows of cash for investment activities	Inflows of cash from operations
Outflows of cash for financial activities (e.g. interest payments)	Inflows of cash from financial activities (e.g. borrowing)

Summary question

1 Which of the following would lead to inflows of cash and which would lead to outflows of cash?

  a Repayment of a loan

  b Interest payments

  c Payment of dividends to shareholders

  d Cash flows from operations

  e Cash flows for purchase of equipment

  f New borrowing from a bank

  g Sale of new shares in a business

Did you know?

IAS 1 does not prescribe the format of the balance sheet, so when you look at companies' balance sheets you will find that they do not always present the items in the same order. For example current assets can be presented before non-current assets or vice versa. The same is true of liabilities and equity.

Did you know?

The term 'comprehensive income' shows that the income specified in the statement comprises all sources of income including operating income (e.g. from sales) and financial income (e.g. from interest received).

Single-step income statement
Statement of comprehensive income setting out all gains and losses.
Sales
− cost of sales
+ any additional income
− any additional costs
= profit or loss for the year

Figure 3.11.1 *A single-step income statement*

International Accounting Standards and IAS 1

Major businesses across the globe are expected to present their financial statements in accordance with accounting standards set out by the International Accounting Standards Board. The International Accounting Standard (IAS) 1 *Presentation of Financial Statements* requires a complete set of financial statements to include:

- a statement of financial position (balance sheet, see 3.9)
- a statement of profit or loss and other comprehensive income
- a statement of cash flow.

By having a standard way of setting out these financial statements, it is possible to make comparisons:

- between the financial statements of a business from year to year
- between the financial statements of a business and the financial statements of other businesses.

Collectively, the statements listed above enable a company to provide financial details about:

- assets (statement of financial position)
- liabilities (statement of financial position)
- equity (statement of financial position)
- income and expenses, including gains and losses (income statement)
- cash flows (statement of cash flows, see 3.10).

The statement of financial position

A business must normally present a classified statement of financial position, separating out current and non-current assets and liabilities.

Statement of comprehensive income

A company is required to present a statement of comprehensive income, which should include the profit or loss for that period plus other comprehensive income recognised in that period. Typically, the bottom line of an income statement should read 'profit or loss'.

A company has a choice of presenting:

- **a single-step statement of comprehensive income:** an income statement showing how the profit or loss is made during the period (see Figure 3.11.1) or
- **two statements (or a two-step income statement):** a statement of comprehensive income that starts with the profit or loss (bottom line of the income statement) and displays components of other comprehensive income, such as currency exchange differences that arise when the results of overseas subsidiary companies are translated – for example, into Barbados dollars for the group accounts of a Barbados-based company with subsidiaries in other countries (see Figure 3.11.2).

Two-step income statement
Income statement ending with profit or loss.
Statement of comprehensive income. First line is profit or loss from the income statement and then it sets out other components of comprehensive income.
Step 1
Sales
− cost of sales
+ any additional income
− any additional costs
= profit or loss for the year
Step 2
Profit or loss for the year (from bottom of step 1)
+/− other forms of income (e.g. currency exchange differences from subsidiaries)
= total comprehensive income

Figure 3.11.2 *A two-step income statement*

Relationship between the statement of financial position and the statement of comprehensive income

The statement of comprehensive income shows all of the gains and losses that a company has made in a particular period. These include those that appear in both the income statement (to record profits and losses) and other gains and losses that are only recorded in the statement of financial position: for example, gains or losses from the company's pension scheme and exchange differences that arise from translating the financial statements of a foreign operation. In addition, the statement of comprehensive income feeds information into the statement of financial position, as the net profit (or loss) each year is transferred from the statement of comprehensive income to the foot of the statement of financial position. As profit enables a company to grow, it increases the net worth of the company as reflected in the statement of financial position.

Summary table

International Accounting Standard 1 (IAS 1)	Sets out the overall requirements for the presentation of financial statements Ensures consistency in presentation so that financial statements can be compared between periods and entities
Income statement	Sets out how the profit or loss is achieved
Statement of comprehensive income	Shows gains and losses recorded in the income statement and in the statement of financial position

Summary questions

1 What additional information is provided in a two-step income statement that is not available in a one-step statement? From where would this additional information be accessed?

2 Why might currency exchange differences be significant when examining the income of Caribbean-based companies?

3 How do international standards help to regularise the presentation of financial statements in the Caribbean?

Financial statements analysis: use of accounting ratios

On completion of this section, you should be able to:

■ interpret and analyse key financial statements through the use of ratio analysis by understanding how accounting ratios are used, their advantages and limitations.

KEY TERMS

Benchmark: a standard that other organisations or parts of an organisation seek to emulate.

What is an accounting ratio?

An accounting ratio is a comparison of two items from the financial statements of a business.

A ratio can be set out as:

$$\frac{\text{Value 1}}{\text{Value 2}} \quad \text{or} \quad \text{Value 1 : Value 2}$$

For example, we could set out a ratio showing the gross profit that we make from sales in the following way:

$$\frac{\text{Gross profit}}{\text{Sales}} \quad \text{or} \quad \text{Gross profit : Sales}$$

So, for example, if sales = \$100,000 and gross profit is \$20,000, the gross profit ratio could be set out as:

$$\frac{20,000}{100,000} \quad \text{or as} \quad 20:100$$

What is clear from both of these presentations is that gross profit is 20 per cent of the sales value.

Comparing with a benchmark

On its own, an accounting ratio has little meaning. For example, if gross profit represents 20 per cent of sales, is this good or bad? True analysis is possible only if a ratio is compared to a **benchmark** – for example, the same ratio calculated for:

■ a different period, such as the previous year (this will provide information about trends)

■ a comparable business (this will provide a means of comparing the financial performance of different companies).

Ratios may be calculated for business units within the same company, such as individual shops within a retail chain, or for similar firms trading during the same period.

A benchmark makes it possible to identify what is achievable by the most successful business or by similar businesses in the same industry. So, for example, the gross profit ratios for two comparable businesses for 2011 and 2012 are shown in Table 3.12.1.

You can see from these figures that not only has the gross profit ratio of Top Stores improved from 2011 to 2012, but it is also doing better than Superior Stores if this ratio is used as an indicator.

Table 3.12.1 Gross profit ratios for 2011 and 2012 for two comparable businesses

	2011	2012
Top Stores	20 : 100	21 : 100
Superior Stores	18 : 100	18 : 100

What do ratios measure?

In 3.13–3.17, you will look at four main types of ratio. You will look at those used to:

■ measure profitability

■ measure the efficiency of business activity

■ measure liquidity (that is, the ability of a business to meet pressing liabilities in the short term)

■ help shareholders assess returns on the investments they make or are thinking of making.

The figures used within the ratios are extracted from:

- the income statement
- the balance sheet (statement of financial position)
- a combination of the income statement and the balance sheet.

Table 3.12.2 gives some examples of different ratios and the source of the figures needed to calculate them.

Table 3.12.2 *Examples of different accounting ratios*

Ratio	What it shows	Source of figures
Profit : Sales	The profit made on every $1 of sales	Income statement
Current assets : Current liabilities	Whether the business has enough current assets to cover current liabilities	Balance sheet
Profit : Owner's equity in the business	How much profit is made for every $1 invested in the company by the owners	Income statement and balance sheet

Advantages and limitations

Ratio analysis makes it possible to:

- compare the performance of a company from one year to the next
- compare one company's performance with another's more effectively than by using just figures.

A limitation of ratio analysis is that ratios can be calculated in different ways depending on the figures used. For example, when calculating gearing, there are different ways of calculating a company's debt.

Another limitation is that ratios tend to emphasise short-term results rather than long-term performance. The information that becomes available in published accounts is often several months old. Published accounts therefore need to be sufficiently detailed for businesses to calculate ratios accurately. In addition, comparison of ratios between companies is difficult because the business activities of firms are rarely identical.

Did you know?

Ratios that compare profit (from the income statement) and capital invested (from the balance sheet) allow investors to compare different companies' performance and to choose the most profitable investment opportunity.

Summary table

Type of ratio	Example	Type of ratio	Example
Profitability	**Net profit ratio:** net profit as a percentage of sales	Efficiency	**Stock turnover:** $\dfrac{\text{Cost of sales}}{\text{Stock}}$
Liquidity	**Current ratio:** Current assets : Current liabilities	Returns to shareholders	**Earnings per share:** $\dfrac{\text{Net profit}}{\text{Average number of ordinary shares in issue (shareholders)}}$

Summary questions

1 What ratios can be calculated from the income statement?

2 Identify two ratios that could be extracted from a balance sheet.

3 Identify two ratios that could be calculated using information from both an income statement and a balance sheet.

Liquidity ratios are calculated using figures from the balance sheet.

However profitable a business is, it must always have enough cash (liquidity) to be able to pay its suppliers and employees on a day-to-day basis.

In order to analyse liquidity ratios, we will use the section of the balance sheet for Sea Sea Cosmetics, shown in Figure 3.13.1, which deals with current assets and current liabilities.

	$000
Current assets	
Inventories	500
Trade receivables (debtors)	1,000
Cash at bank and in hand	50
	1,550
Current liabilities	
Trade payables (creditors to be paid in under a year)	(800)

Figure 3.13.1 *Sea Sea's balance sheet at 31 December 2013*

Figure 3.13.2 *Stock waiting to be sold is a current asset as it will soon be sold for cash*

Current ratio

The current ratio compares current assets ($1,550,000) with current liabilities ($800,000). This shows that for every $1 of current liabilities, Sea Sea has roughly $2 of current assets on 31 December 2013. This shows that the company can meet any pressing payments (for example, any invoices that need paying).

The actual ratio is:

> Current assets : Current liabilities

$1,550,000 : $800,000

i.e. $\dfrac{1,550}{800} = 1.9375$

For every $1 of current liabilities, Sea Sea has $1.9375 of current assets.

What constitutes an appropriate current ratio depends on the type of business. In businesses where creditors are likely to press for payments, it is important to have a favourable current ratio (i.e. more than 1 : 1). In assessing current ratios it is perhaps more important to identify what is happening to the ratio over time. When the current ratio falls, this can indicate that the company is less able to meet pressing liabilities.

Acid test ratio

The current ratio compares *all* current assets to short-term creditors whereas the acid test ratio compares only cash and other **monetary assets** to short-term creditors.

The **acid test ratio** calculation does not consider stock to be a current asset. This is because if stock needs to be sold in a short period of time, it can only be sold at a discount. If you have to meet pressing liabilities, you should not rely on selling stock to provide you with the cash you need.

The acid test ratio is:

$$\frac{\text{Current assets} - \text{Stock}}{\text{Creditors due in less than one year}}$$

Using the example of Sea Sea:

- Current assets − Stock = 1,050
- Current liabilities = 800

So the acid test ratio is:

$\frac{1,050}{800}$ or $1,050 : 800 = 1.3125$

This shows that the business has enough current assets to cover its short-term liabilities (for every \$1 of current liabilities, it has over \$1.3 worth of cash and trade receivables).

KEY TERMS

Monetary assets: assets with an obvious cash value (e.g. trade debtors who will pay in the next month or so).

Acid test ratio: a ratio measuring those assets that can be most easily turned into cash in the short term (cash + debtors) against the short-term liabilities of a business:

Acid test ratio = (Cash + debtors) : Current liabilities

Did you know?

The acid test ratio is also called the 'quick ratio' because it is concerned with monetary assets that can be turned into cash quickly.

Summary table

Ratio	What it measures
Current ratio	Current assets : Current liabilities
Acid test ratio	Monetary assets : Current liabilities

Summary questions

1 Why is it important for a business to have sufficient current assets to cover current liabilities?

2 A business has inventories of \$1,000, trade receivables of \$600 and cash of \$400. It has trade payables of \$1,000. Work out the current ratio and the acid test ratios. Do these pose any problems for the business? How would this depend on the type of business being considered?

On completion of this section, you should be able to:

■ interpret and analyse key financial statements through the use of ratio analysis by calculating and interpreting profitability.

Did you know?

Calculating profit as a percentage enables a business to see how much profit it has made for every $1 of sales.

Profit is an indication of a business's competitive position. The ideal position is for profits to be high in relation to sales and for competition to be weak.

Profitability ratios generally take values in the profit and loss account and express them as a percentage of sales revenues. Profitability ratios can be calculated at a number of points in the income statement: that is, gross profit margin, operating profit margin and net profit margin.

In order to assess profitability we will use the income statement for Sea Sea Cosmetics shown in Figure 3.14.1.

	31 March 2013 $000	31 March 2012 $000
Sales revenue	4,901.4	4,800.0
Cost of sales	(2,689.5)	2,650.0
Gross profit	**2,211.9**	**2,150.0**
Operating expenses	(1,614.7)	(1,500.0)
Operating profit	**597.2**	**650.0**
Net interest	15.3	15.3
Profit before tax	**612.5**	**660.3**
Taxes paid	(104.3)	(110.0)
Net profit	**508.2**	**550.3**

Figure 3.14.1 Sea Sea's income statement

Gross profit margin

The gross profit margin is a particularly important figure for a trading company, such as a retailer. It shows how much profit a business makes when the cost of sales has been deducted from the sales. As a percentage, it is calculated as follows:

$$\text{Gross profit margin} = \frac{\text{Gross profit}}{\text{Sales}} \times 100$$

Using the figures above, Sea Sea's gross profit margin for 2013 is:

$$\frac{2,211.9}{4,901.4} \times 100 = 45.13\%$$

In 2012 Sea Sea's gross profit percentage was 44.79 per cent. So you can see that Sea Sea's gross profit margin has improved from 2012 to 2013, which is a good sign. For a retailing company this may mean that it has been able to buy in goods more cheaply (reducing costs), or perhaps its prices have been more attractive to customers.

Operating profit margin

The operating profit margin shows profit after the costs of running the business (heating and lighting costs, marketing costs, etc.) have been deducted. As a percentage, it is calculated as follows:

$$\text{Operating profit margin} = \frac{\text{Operating profit}}{\text{Sales}} \times 100$$

Sea Sea's operating profit for 2013 is:

$$\frac{597.2}{4,901.4} \times 100 = 12.2\%$$

If we compare this with the corresponding figure in 2012 (650 as a percentage of 4,800, or 13.54 per cent), we can see that operating profit has reduced. This might be because operating costs have increased substantially between 2012 and 2013. For managers this is a warning sign that the business may need to identify ways of cutting costs.

Net profit margin

Finally, we can calculate bottom line profitability: that is, the amount of profit after all expenses (such as taxes) have been deducted from sales. As a percentage, the net profit margin is calculated as follows:

Net profit margin $= \dfrac{\text{Net profit}}{\text{Sales}} \times 100$

For 2013 this is:

$$\frac{508.\,2}{4,901.4} \times 100 = 10.4\%$$

Again we would need to compare this with the net profit margin from the previous year. This measure is used by companies to see how their profit is improving over time.

Return on capital employed (ROCE)

This is a profitability ratio that tells us how effectively a business is running its operations. ROCE indicates how well the business is using the funds that have been made available to it, by measuring profitability (operating profit) as a percentage of funds from owners and other lenders.

Return on capital employed (ROCE) $= \dfrac{\text{Operating profit}}{\text{Total capital employed}} \times 100$

Total capital employed comprises owner's equity plus the debt owed by the business, such as loans, which is set out in the balance sheet.

If a company has an operating profit of $500,000 and employs capital of $5 million, then the return on capital employed is:

$$\frac{500,000}{5,000,000} \times 100 = 10\%$$

Summary table

Profitability ratio	What it measures
Gross profit margin	Gross profit as a percentage of sales
Operating profit margin	Operating profit as a percentage of sales
Net profit margin	Bottom line as a percentage of sales
Return on capital employed (ROCE)	Operating profit as a percentage of capital employed

When writing responses to questions that require calculations it is important that you include formulae where warranted. One or two marks are usually allocated to this.

Summary questions

1 Figure 3.14.2 shows Sea Sea's profit margins in 2012 and 2013. Show how these are calculated.

2 Why might the gross profit margin improve while other margins fall?

3 What does ROCE measure? Why is it an important profitability ratio?

	2013	2012
Gross profit margin (%)	45.13	44.80
Operating profit margin (%)	12.18	13.54
Net profit margin (%)	10.36	11.46

Figure 3.14.2 *Profit margins for Sea Sea in 2012 and 2013*

Specific objective

On completion of this section, you should be able to:

- interpret and analyse key financial statements through the use of ratio analysis by calculating and interpreting efficiency.

Did you know?

Sometimes stock turnover calculations are based on average stock for the year. To find out the average stock, look for the figure for inventory at the start of the year, add it to the inventory at the end of the year and divide by 2.

Did you know?

In making calculations for stock turnover period, we divide the bottom part of our calculation by 365 to represent the number of days in the year. This gives us a final figure in days.

Efficiency ratios measure how well a business is using its assets. Businesses use a number of efficiency ratios, but the most important ones that you will need to be able to calculate are:

- stock turnover ratios – how quickly a business is replacing inventories
- debtor day ratios – how long it takes debtors to settle their debts with the business.

These types of ratio are referred to as 'activity ratios' because they measure business activity.

Stock turnover ratios

Figure 3.15.1 *The stock turnover ratio measures how quickly a business replaces stock in a given period of time*

Stock turnover, as the name suggests, is a measure of how quickly a business is turning over its stock (inventories). In order to make this calculation, you need to extract the figures for:

- cost of sales from the income statement – this shows the value of sales made during the year in terms of the cost of buying the stock for those sales
- stock shown in the balance sheet (as inventories).

The stock turnover ratio is calculated as follows:

$$\text{Stock turnover} = \frac{\text{Cost of sales}}{\text{Stock}}$$

So, for example, if a shoe shop bought in $100,000 of shoes during 2013 (cost of sales) and on 31 December had stock (inventories) of shoes of $10,000, its stock turnover would be:

$$\frac{100,000}{10,000} = 10$$

The stock turnover period can also be calculated to see whether a business is holding stock for too long. It is calculated as follows:

$$\text{Stock turnover period} = \frac{\text{Stock}}{\text{Cost of sales per day}}$$

So in our example of the shoe shop this would be:

$$\frac{10,000}{100,000} \times 365 = 36.5 \text{ days}$$

When assessing stock turnover, it is important to check whether the number of days is increasing or decreasing over time. If it is increasing, the business may be holding too much stock, or stock of the wrong type. Generally, a low stock turnover period is preferable: in other words, inventory should be held for the shortest time possible.

Debtor day ratio

Most businesses make a large proportion (sometimes all) of their sales on credit. The debtor day ratio is a measure of the average time payment takes.

When the debtor day ratio increases, this may indicate that debtors are more likely to default on payment. A rising debtor day ratio means that a business's liquidity ratio might fall. A falling debtor day ratio shows that a business is being paid quicker, which helps to increase the liquidity ratio.

There are two ways in which debtor day ratios are used:

1 Debtor collection days (the number of days that debtors take to pay):

$$\frac{\text{Trade debtors}}{\text{Sales}} \times 365$$

2 The percentage of sales still unpaid:

$$\frac{\text{Trade debtors}}{\text{Sales}} \times 100$$

Creditor day ratio

The creditor day ratio is similar to the debtor day ratio. It indicates the extent to which a business is taking advantage of credit offered by suppliers. It measures the average time it takes a business to settle debts and is calculated as follows:

$$\text{Creditor day ratio} = \frac{\text{Trade payables}}{\text{Cost of sales}} \times 365$$

Increasing creditor days indicate that a business is taking longer to settle its debts.

Summary table

Efficiency ratio	Calculation
Stock turnover	$\dfrac{\text{Cost of sales}}{\text{Stock}}$
Debtor days	$\dfrac{\text{Debtors}}{\text{Sales}} \times 365$
Creditor days	$\dfrac{\text{Trade payables}}{\text{Cost of sales}} \times 365$

Summary questions

1 A business reports that during the year debtor days increased, while creditor days fell and stock turnover increased. Comment on whether these changes are favourable or unfavourable and what would have been involved in each instance.

2 A business has the following figures (extracted from the financial statement in $000): sales 1,600, cost of sales 850, stock 425, debtors 375 and trade creditors 150. Calculate the stock turnover, debtor days and creditor days.

Specific objective

On completion of this section, you should be able to:

- interpret and analyse key financial statements through the use of ratio analysis by calculating and interpreting gearing ratios.

What is gearing?

Gearing is used by businesses to show how much capital comes from:

- ordinary shareholders
- loans and preference shares.

Gearing ratio

The **gearing ratio** measures the level of external borrowing (debt) that a company has (that is, loans) against the capital employed in the company (Figure 3.16.1).

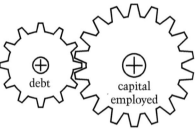

Figure 3.16.1 *The gearing ratio compares the debt to the capital employed within a business*

There are a number of ways of presenting gearing ratios but two of the most popular that you should be familiar with are:

1 $$\frac{\text{Long-term debt (e.g. loans on which interest must be paid)}}{\text{Capital employed}} \times 100$$

2 External finance : Owner's equity

In this section, you will concentrate on the first calculation. However, the second ratio is used by businesses to compare the proportion of capital that is raised externally with that which is raised internally. If this ratio increases over time, it shows that the company is exposed to interest repayments, which will grow proportionately as the external debt increases.

High gearing ratios indicate that the business has raised a high percentage of capital from external sources. If a business progressively increases the proportion of its capital raised from external sources, this puts it at financial risk.

CASE STUDY

The gearing effect

The way that the capital of a company is structured affects the variability of the return for investors and the degree of risk involved.

In general, investors receive financial returns in line with the risks they take. For example, loan stockholders and preference shareholders are first in the queue for returns because their investment is a lower risk. Ordinary shareholders are last in the queue (and as a result they take the highest risk with their investment) and only receive a share of the profit after all other claims have been met.

When a company has a high gearing ratio, it might mean that there is little left for the ordinary shareholders when loan stockholders and preference shareholders have been paid. The higher the gearing, the lower the likelihood that ordinary shareholders will receive a good return on their investment.

1 How may shareholders in a company with a low gearing ratio benefit?

2 How may shareholders lose out in a company with a high gearing ratio?

3 Explain why shareholders may prefer to see the gearing ratio fall.

In order to calculate the gearing ratio, you need figures for:

- debt
- capital employed.

Debt

Debt is the long-term debt of the business and this figure can be found in the balance sheet.

Capital employed

The amount of capital employed can be calculated using the following formula:

Capital employed = Fixed assets + (Current assets − Current liabilities)

This is referred to as the net assets approach to calculating capital employed. You are measuring the amount of capital that the business is employing in the form of fixed capital and working capital.

CASE STUDY

Caribbean News

Caribbean News is a magazine publisher operating in the Caribbean that publishes a range of trade journals and magazines. It supplies newsagents and booksellers with periodicals on a credit basis. It has a number of printing presses in various territories in the Caribbean as well as distribution outlets and warehouses.

On 31 December 2012 its balance sheet showed that it had fixed assets worth $500,000. The balance sheet also indicated that it had a healthy level of current assets ($100,000) when compared

with current liabilities ($50,000). In order to start up the enterprise and then to build it up over time, the company has engaged in some borrowing – principally from banks. Its present long-term liabilities (as at 31 December 2012) amount to $225,000. It should be noted that on 31 December 2010 the company had fixed assets of $400,000 and net current assets of $20,000, while its long-term liabilities were $400,000.

1 What happened to the gearing ratio of Caribbean News between December 2010 and 2012?

2 What are the implications of this change in the gearing ratio for shareholders of Caribbean News?

Summary table

Information needed to calculate the gearing ratio	Calculation
Gearing ratio = $\dfrac{\text{Debt}}{\text{Capital employed}}$	
Debt	Amount of long-term debt can be found in the balance sheet
Capital employed	Fixed assets + Working capital
Working capital	Current assets – Current liabilities

Summary questions

1 What problems do you associate with rising gearing ratios?

2 Why are shareholders interested in the level of gearing in a company?

3 How would you measure the gearing ratio?

4 What is the difference between the internal capital of a company and the external capital?

Did you know?

A distinction can be made between investors (those contemplating buying shares in a company or in other financial assets) and shareholders (those who already own shares in a company).

Shares

Shareholders benefit when shares that they hold in a particular company increase in value over time. For example, an investor may buy 100 shares in 2010 for $20 each. By 2013 the share price on the Jamaica Stock Exchange may have risen to $25 because everybody thinks that the company is a good investment. So the original holding of shares is now worth $2,500 (100 × $25) instead of the original purchase price of $2,000 (100 × $20). The shareholder could make a capital gain from selling his or her shares. In addition the shareholder benefits from receiving a share of the company profits each year in the form of a dividend. For example, for each share held the company might pay a dividend of $1 at the midpoint of the year and again at the end of the year. The dividend is the reward to shareholders for the risk they take in investing in a company.

Figure 3.17.1 *A shareholder's level of ownership in a company is detailed in his or her share certificate*

Types of investor/shareholder ratio

In order to make decisions, investors need information about the returns on different types of share. For example, they may want to compare the returns on ordinary shares, preferences shares and loan stock. A number of different investor/shareholder ratios can be used.

Shareholder return

Total ordinary **shareholder return** is one way of calculating how well shareholders are doing. It is calculated as follows:

$$\text{Shareholder return (\%)} = \frac{\text{(Dividend + Change in share price)}}{\text{Share price}} \times 100$$

Earnings per share (EPS)

The calculation of earnings per share allows potential investors to assess the amount of profit generated for every share in issue. It is calculated as follows:

$$\text{Earnings per share} = \frac{\text{Net profit}}{\text{Average number of shares on offer}}$$

Looking back to 3.8, we can see that on 31 March 2013 Sea Sea Cosmetics made a net profit of approximately $500,000. If the company had 100,000 shares in issue, then the earnings per share would be $5.

Dividend yield

In order to calculate the dividend yield, more information is needed than is provided in a set of financial statements. It is necessary to know the current market price of the share, which often changes from day to day.

When shareholders invest in shares, they pay for the shares in cash. For example, they may purchase shares at $20 each. Let us assume that a company pays out a dividend of $1 per share. Assuming that the share price remains the same, the dividend yield will be 5 per cent (i.e. $\frac{1}{20} \times 100$ = 5%). However, the market price of shares changes regularly and this will affect the dividend yield on those shares. So, for example, if the market price rises to $25, the dividend yield on the shares will fall to 4 per cent (i.e. $\frac{1}{25} \times 100 = 4\%$). So someone purchasing the shares for $25 would only receive a yield of 4 per cent. The dividend yield therefore varies because the price of shares changes over time, as does the amount the company pays out in dividends. At any one time the dividend yield can be calculated as:

$$\text{Dividend yield (\%)} = \frac{\text{Dividend per share}}{\text{Market price of share}} \times 100$$

A high dividend yield is sometimes seen as being attractive to investors because it often indicates that a share price is undervalued (and therefore likely to rise in the future). Similarly, a low yield may indicate that a share is overvalued (and therefore likely to fall in the future).

As well as knowing the dividend yield for particular companies, investors may also want to know the average yield of a range of shares (for example, particular groups of company shares listed on the Dow Jones or on the Jamaica Stock Exchange). To calculate the average yield of shares, you need to calculate the average dividend per share and the average market price of shares quoted on the exchange at a particular moment in time.

Summary table

Shareholder ratio	Calculation
Shareholder return (%)	$\frac{\text{Dividend + Change in price}}{\text{Share price}} \times 100$
Earnings per share	$\frac{\text{Net profit}}{\text{Average number of shares on offer}}$
Dividend yield (%)	$\frac{\text{Dividend per share}}{\text{Market price of share}} \times 100$

Summary questions

1 Shares in Grenada Stores were issued at $1 each in December 2011. In 2012 the price of these shares rose to $1.20. The total dividend paid in 2012 was 20 cents per share. What was the dividend yield for 2012?

2 Grenada Stores made a net profit of $10,000 in 2012. The number of individual shares in the company is 1,000. What are the earnings per share?

3 The dividend per share in Grenada Stores has increased, although the dividend yield has fallen. At the same time the earnings per share continues to rise. Why might a shareholder be interested in this information in 2014?

Did you know?

Shareholders are interested in the calculation of dividend yield because it shows them how much the company is paying in dividends as a percentage of the market price of shares.

Did you know?

Another useful shareholder ratio is dividend cover. It measures how many times a company's total ordinary dividend could have been paid out of the current year's net profit. The result gives an indication of the company's potential to maintain dividends in the future:

$$\frac{\text{Dividend}}{\text{cover}} = \frac{\text{Net profit}}{\text{Ordinary dividend paid}}$$

The ordinary dividend is the dividend paid to ordinary shareholders.

On completion of this section, you should be able to:

■ explain the purpose and nature of budgeting.

Budget: a plan for the future, usually set out in numbers.

Variance: the difference between what actually happens and what is budgeted to happen.

Budgets help businesses to keep track of their finances and allow them to predict financial outcomes, which can help with decision making and planning. Five main budgets are created and used by businesses: sales budget; production budget; materials/purchases budget; labour budget; and cash budget.

It is important to understand that all of the different budgets need to be integrated to create an organisation-wide budget.

The purpose of budgeting

The main purpose of budgeting is to enable a business to plan ahead. Budgeting forces busy managers to think about the company's aims and objectives, and to create plans to achieve them.

Budgets also provide numerical targets. Once budget plans are in place, it is possible to monitor progress towards achieving these targets. A budget should be reviewed regularly to measure performance against the plan and identify **variances**.

Variances typically occur when a business has underestimated its costs, for example because of inefficient use of resources or a project taking longer than expected. A business might also overestimate the sales it budgets to make. Business people tend to be optimistic and forecast greater demand for their product than actually materialises. In order to sell more, a business may have to reduce prices and as a result sales revenue falls compared to budgeted figures. Variances may also occur as a result of changes in the external environment. For example, a rise in oil prices may raise costs, or a recession in the economy may reduce expected sales.

As you can see in Table 3.18.1, the variance may be favourable or adverse.

Table 3.18.1 *Variance may be favourable or adverse*

	Actual greater than budget	**Actual lower than budget**
Sales/turnover/income	Favourable	Adverse
Cost/expenses	Adverse	Favourable

Budgets should be flexible so that they can be revised if it looks like actual results will be substantially different from those in the budget.

The budgeting process

Figure 3.18.1 shows the process of creating a budget.

A master budget

A master budget is a summary of the plans (budgets) for the various parts of a company. The master budget is used to create projected financial statements (for example, what the income statement will look like at the end of the year if things go to plan).

The sales budget

This is a detailed plan showing expected sales figures for a period (see 3.19). It is important to start with the sales budget because it feeds into all other budgets. For example, the sales budget determines the quantities of goods that need to be produced (the production budget)

Set aims and objectives for the business (e.g. to increase profits by 10 per cent this year)

↓

Identify budgeting assumptions

↓

Prepare draft budget showing outcomes (e.g. profit, cash flow)

↓

Does it meet aims and objectives?

No → Yes

↓

Finalise budget

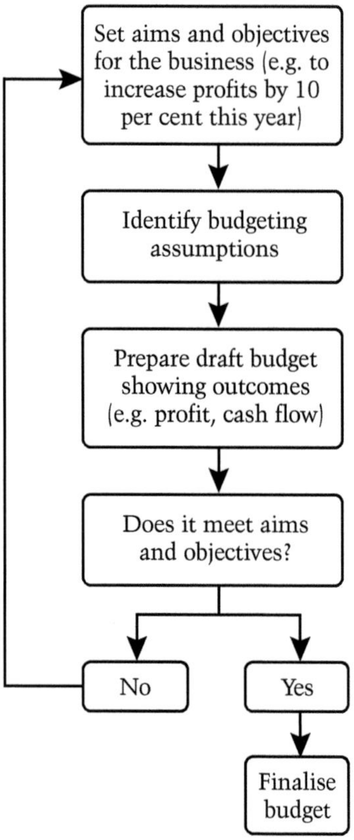

Figure 3.18.1 *The process of creating a budget*

and this determines how many raw materials need to be purchased (the raw-materials budget).

The production budget

This is an estimate of the number of units that need to be manufactured in order to meet the sales targets (set out in the sales budget).

The materials/purchase budget

The production budget is the starting point for determining the quantities of raw materials and components that need to be purchased. The direct materials budget will vary according to the amounts needed for production.

The labour budget

The labour budget outlines the estimated costs associated with employees and management within an organisation. In order to deliver the master budget and achieve the sales and production budgets, an organisation needs to ensure that it has the right people in the right places doing the right tasks.

The capital budget

The capital budget is a prediction of a company's long-term investments in equipment or plant, such as machinery, buildings and vehicles.

The cash budget

The cash budget predicts a company's inflows and outflows for a particular period of time. It usually covers a period in the short-term future. The cash budget helps the business to determine when income will be received and when expenditure will take place. This helps to make sure that there is enough cash for liquidity purposes (see 3.19).

Other budgets

Other budgets created within companies include:

- marketing budgets – used to plan advertising campaigns, market research and other marketing activities
- project budgets – used for specific projects, such as planning expenditure on new information technology upgrades.

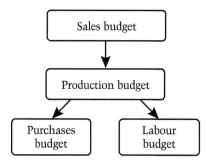

Figure 3.18.2 *The sales budget feeds into all other budgets*

Summary table

Budget	Purpose
Sales budget	Planning future sales
Production budget	Production plan to meet sales targets
Purchases budget	Plan for raw materials and stock required for production
Labour budget	Human resource planning
Capital budget	Plan for fixed assets
Cash budget	Plan for inflows and outflows
Master budget	Organisation-wide, overarching plan

Summary questions

1 A furniture manufacturer has budgeted to sell 1,000 chairs next month. Explain how the sales budget for the chairs feeds into other budgets. Illustrate your answer in the form of a diagram.

2 What is a variance? How might variances in sales cause problems for other budgets? How might managers plan to cope with variances?

3 What are the main benefits of budgeting?

3.19 Cash and sales budgets

Specific objective

On completion of this section, you should be able to:

- explain the purpose, nature and usefulness of cash and sales budgets.

KEY TERMS

Disbursement: money paid out or spent.

Did you know?

A cash budget not only shows the inflows and outflows of cash from normal business transactions, but also sets out borrowings and repayments (in a separate financing section).

The cash budget

The cash budget is a prediction of future inflows (cash receipts) and outflows (expenditures) for a particular time period. It usually covers a relatively short period of time (up to a year). The cash budget helps a business to make sure that it has enough cash inflows to meet its cash outflows. The business can use the cash budget to identify times when potential cash shortfalls might arise (so that it can take steps to access outside finance).

There are four main sections to the cash budget:

- receipts (inflows) – including sales but excluding finance
- **disbursements** (outflows) – payments for raw materials, capital equipment and labour, and withdrawals of cash by the owner
- cash surplus or (deficit) – shows the starting balance plus receipts minus disbursements over a particular period
- financing section – shows any borrowing or repayment required to make sure there is enough cash to meet requirements.

Figure 3.19.1 shows the first three sections of a cash budget.

	$
Cash balance at start (1)	85,000
Add receipts (2)	460,000
Total cash available (3)	545,000
Less disbursements (4)	(705,000)
Excess or (deficiency) of cash (5)	(160,000)

Figure 3.19.1 *The first three sections of a cash budget*

We can now add into the cash budget any financing (borrowing or payments made at the end of a period of time), as shown in Figure 3.19.2.

	Budget	Jan–Mar $	Apr–June $	July–Sept $	Oct–Dec $	Annual $
Opening balance (1)		85,000	80,000	80,000	81,000	95,000
Add receipts (2)						
Collections from customers	Sales	460,000	960,000	1,480,000	1,040,000	3,940,000
Total cash available (1 + 2 = 3)		545,000	1,040,000	1,560,000	1,121,000	4,035,000
Less disbursements						
Materials	Materials budget	99,000	144,600	200,100	158,700	602,400
Labour	Labour budget	168,000	384,000	432,000	228,000	1,212,000
Overhead costs	Overhead budget	136,000	193,600	206,400	152,000	688,000
Marketing costs	Marketing budget	186,000	261,800	369,500	258,300	1,075,600
Equipment purchases	Capital budget	100,000	80,000	40,000	40,000	260,000

	Budget	Jan–Mar $	Apr–June $	July–Sept $	Oct–Dec $	Annual $
Dividends		16,000	16,000	16,000	16,000	64,000
Total disbursements (4)		705,000	1,080,000	1,264,000	853,000	3,902,000
Surplus/deficiency of cash (3 − 4 = 5)		(160,000)	(40,000)	296,000	268,000	133,000
Financing						
Borrowings (at start)		240,000	120,000	–	–	360,000
Payments (at start)		–	–	(200,000)	(160,000)	(360,000)
Interest		–	–	(15,000)	(13,000)	(28,000)
Total financing (6)		240,000	120,000	(215,000)	(173,000)	(28,000)
Cash balance at end (5 − 6 = 7)		$80,000	$80,000	$81,000	$95,000	$105,000

Figure 3.19.2 Cash budget for the year ended 31 December 2013

This cash budget enables managers of the business to plan borrowing (and repayment of borrowing) to make sure there is enough cash at all times.

For example, by borrowing $240,000 at the start of the overall budget period, the business can be assured of having a cash balance of $80,000 (7) at the end of the first quarter, even though disbursements ($705,000) (4) are substantially higher than inflows of cash from sales ($460,000) during the period.

Calculating the cash budget

- **Receipts:** we add receipts (2) to our opening balance (1) to find out the cash available before disbursements.
- **Disbursements:** we can then calculate the impact of planned disbursements (4).
- **Cash surpluses or deficiencies:** the surplus or deficiency of cash (5) in any quarter will therefore be (3) – (4).
- **Financing:** the next part of the cash budget statement shows any borrowings or payments, as well as interest paid on money borrowed. When we add borrowing and take away payments and interest from the surplus or deficiency of cash, we arrive at a figure for the cash balance (7) at the end of a particular quarter (or year).

The sales budget

The sales budget is an estimate of future sales that can be broken down into units (for example, bottles of rum) and dollars. The sales budget is used to set sales targets.

The sales budget can be extracted from the cash budget.

	Jan–Mar	Apr–June	July–Sept	Oct–Dec	Total
Sales ($)	460,000	960,000	1,480,000	1,040,000	3,940,000

Figure 3.19.3 The sales budget extracted from Figure 3.19.2

Typical methods of sales forecasting include gathering the opinions of the sales force, market research and statistical methods such as recording trends.

Summary table

Cash budget
Opening balance
plus Receipts
= Total cash available
minus Disbursements
= Surplus/deficiency
plus Borrowing
minus Payments and interest
= Cash balance at end

Summary question

1 Prepare a cash budget for yourself for the next two quarters, assuming that you start off with $100 in your savings account:
   a What will be the value of your starting cash balance?
   b What is the value of your inflows?
   c What is the value of your disbursements? How much have you borrowed at the start of the period?
   d How much will you borrow during the period?
   e How much will you repay during the period?
   f Set out your cash balance at the start, at the end of the first quarter and at the end of the final quarter.

Specific objective

On completion of this section, you should be able to:

■ explain the purpose, nature and usefulness of production, materials and labour budgets.

Figure 3.20.1 *The production budget is a forward-looking plan that establishes how many goods need to be produced in future periods*

Did you know?

When requirements exceed capacity, a production manager may:

■ subcontract production

■ plan for overtime

■ introduce shift work

■ hire and/or purchase additional machinery.

Did you know?

■ A raw-materials budget should be extracted directly from the production budget, not from the sales budget. It will establish the cost of producing the quantities that have been budgeted.

■ A materials usage budget is set out in quantities.

■ A materials purchases budget is both quantitative and financial.

Deriving other budgets from the sales budget

It is helpful to create a sales budget before constructing a number of other interrelated budgets. Once you know how much you are likely to be able to sell, you can plan for production. Levels of production determine the requirements for inputs, such as materials, supplies and labour.

In calculating future sales, it is helpful to draw out projections based on likely trends. For example, if we know that a company currently sells 44,000 units at $1 each and that sales are projected to increase at 7 per cent per annum for the next few years, on this basis we can calculate that sales in units will be:

■ this year: 44,000

■ next year: 44,000 × 1.07 = 47,080

■ the following year: 47,080 × 1.07 = 50,376 etc.

This information can then be fed back into the production department.

The production budget

A production budget uses physical units of production rather than financial information. Production budgets need to be forward looking, identifying how many units of output need to be produced in future periods. A key physical constraint for a production manager is plant size. You cannot produce more items than you are physically capable of making in a given period of time. Production managers therefore often have to think ahead in periods when sales demand is likely to be lower and build up stock to satisfy periods of high demand. This forward-looking process is illustrated in the case study below.

> **CASE STUDY**
>
> ### Caribbean Finest Furniture's production budget
>
> Figure 3.20.2 shows the sales budget for tables sold by Caribbean Fine Furniture. The problem is that the company only has maximum production capacity of 1,000 tables per month. In January, when sales peak, demand will be 1,500 whereas production in that month can only be 1,000. The production manager will therefore have to build up extra stocks in October and November in order to have enough in stock in January.
>
> | Sales budget | | | | |
> |---|---|---|---|---|
> | September | October | November | December | January |
> | 500 | 500 | 750 | 1,000 | 1,500 |
>
> **Figure 3.20.2** *Sales of tables*
>
> 1 Why does the production budget need to be calculated from right to left rather using than the normal approach of moving from left to right?
>
> 2 How does the production budget facilitate production planning?
>
> 3 What problems may arise if sales are less than forecasted?

The production budget enables a company to plan the number of units of finished goods that it needs to produce. A simple way of calculating this for a specific time period is:

1 Budgeted sales of finished goods in units (taken from sales budget)
+
2 Desired inventory of finished goods at the end of the period
−
3 The starting inventory of finished goods
=
4 Finished goods units to be produced in that period

The materials budget

The materials budget is derived directly from the production budget. The amount of direct materials that go into units of production is calculated as follows:

1 Budgeted production of finished goods units × Raw materials required per unit
+
2 Required stock of raw materials at the end of the period
−
3 Starting inventory of raw materials
=
4 Units of raw materials that need to be purchased

If you want to work out step 4 in monetary terms then you simply multiply the number of units of raw materials that need to be purchased by the cost per unit. This gives the budgeted cost of raw materials in each period.

The labour budget

Similarly, human resource planners have to budget for the number of hours of labour they need for particular production processes. Again, the labour budget is derived directly from the production budget.

The purchases budget

This budget shows any goods or raw materials that need to be purchased for future sale by the business.

Summary table

Type of budget	From where is the information derived?
Sales budget	Sales forecasts and industry and market trends
Production budget	Sales budget
Materials budget	Production budget
Labour budget	Production budget

Did you know?

The purchases and inventory/materials budgets are often combined. The business needs to plan how much inventory to hold at particular times. The purchasing of materials and inventories is then planned to ensure that there is enough stock of the right kind at the right times.

Summary question

1 A&P Kites Ltd manufactures kites throughout the year. Sales are seasonal, with the main demand coming in the period just before Easter (i.e. February and March). The company always tries to have 50 kites in stock at the end of each month and has a maximum production capacity of 200 units. The sales forecast shown in Figure 3.20.4 has been prepared. Work back from March and calculate a production budget for the year.

	Units
April	50
May	50
June	50
July	50
August	50
September	50
October	50
November	50
December	50
January	50
February	500
March	500

Figure 3.20.4 Sales forecast for A&P Kites Ltd

The benefits of budgeting

Every organisation needs to create and monitor its budgets. Budgets enable clear planning to take place coupled with ongoing checks on performance. Budgeting:

- forces busy managers to think about the future and to formulate targets and plans
- helps to identify plans that will fail to deliver – for example, sales and cash budgets might reveal that a new product/service might be too risky, and it is better to fail on paper than in reality
- enforces consistency – in a large company with several departments, a focused master budget can make sure that each department is working towards the same goals based on the same assumptions about sales volumes, prices, costs, etc.
- makes it possible to measure performance (Figure 3.21.1) – actual performance (what happens in reality) can be compared with budgeted performance (set out in the budget plan)
- acts as a motivational tool:
  - □ by setting targets, people in an organisation have something to work towards
  - □ achieving budgeted targets is a reward in itself
  - □ bonuses can be awarded for achieving budgeted figures.

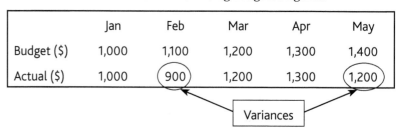

	Jan	Feb	Mar	Apr	May
Budget ($)	1,000	1,100	1,200	1,300	1,400
Actual ($)	1,000	900	1,200	1,300	1,200

Figure 3.21.1 *Budgets make it possible to spot variances between actual performance and budgeted performance*

Limitations of budgeting

- It is a time-consuming process. However, because it is such an effective management tool it can save a lot of time and money later on, as it gives managers a useful plan to work with. Additionally, it saves time by enabling a business to focus on what will work – rather than on carrying out activities that fail because of poor planning.
- There can be too much emphasis on short-term planning at the expense of longer-term planning. An annual budget usually becomes a strong focus for attention, whereas sometimes it may be more useful to take a longer-term view.
- Budgets are often inflexible. In the real world, circumstances change. However, businesses may stick to their original budget plans because managers are reluctant to give up the control that the budget appears to give them.

Assumptions

An important step in preparing a budget is to state the budget assumptions. This helps the user of a budget to understand how budget calculations have been made and whether they are valid. For example, in a sales budget, an assumption might be made that sales in January will be

1,000 units at $5 each, making a total of $50,000. Of course, it might be possible to question whether:

- 1,000 units can be sold in that period
- they can be sold for a price of $5 each.

Assumptions should be stated so that any limitations can be taken into consideration and questioned.

Other limiting factors

In the preparation of budgets, it is essential to ensure that departmental budgets are prepared in advance for each period. It is also important to recognise that unforeseen events (for example, a lack of skilled workers, a lack of machine capacity or a lack of funding to finance working capital) may impact on budgeted figures, and so contingency plans need to be put in place. For many businesses the level of sales may be a major limiting factor on budgets. For example, if production of non-perishable goods cannot keep up with sales during a particular month, it is necessary to plan to build up stocks during the preceding months.

CASE STUDY

Hair Extensions Ltd

Hair Extensions Ltd, as the name suggests, is a company supplying hair extensions to hairdressers. The company's budget for the four quarters of 2013 is shown in Figure 3.21.2.

($)				
Cost	Q1	Q2	Q3	Q4
Materials	600	600	300	600
Petrol	400	400	400	400
Direct labour	1,600	1,600	1,600	1,600
Promotion	400	400	400	400
Insurance	300	300	300	300
Rent of premises	800	800	800	800
Interest on loan	350	350	350	350
Total	**4,450**	**4,450**	**4,150**	**4,450**

Figure 3.21.2 2013 budget for Hair Extensions Ltd

Some of the actual costs, however, vary from those budgeted, as shown in Figure 3.21.3. Other costs (e.g. rent and interest) are as expected.

($)				
Cost	Q1	Q2	Q3	Q4
Materials	700	700	350	700
Petrol	450	460	470	480
Direct labour	1,500	1,500	1,500	1,600
Promotion	400	200	200	200
Insurance	350	350	350	350

Figure 3.21.3 Actual costs for 2013 for Hair Extensions Ltd

1 Using the information provided, identify quarters during which the company experienced favourable variances.

2 In each case, identify the areas where the favourable variances occurred.

3 Identify quarters where there were adverse variances. In each case, identify the possible causes of the adverse variances.

4 What would be the main benefits of budgeting for Hair Extensions Ltd?

5 What assumptions appear to have been made in terms of anticipating likely costs?

Summary table

Advantages of budgeting	Disadvantages of budgeting
■ Encourages planning and targets ■ Identifies what will work ■ Enables sharing of targets ■ Facilitates performance tracking ■ Tool for communication and motivation	■ Time consuming to create ■ Focuses on the short term ■ Lacks flexibility

Summary questions

1 Explain the following terms that are used in budgeting: budget assumptions, limiting factors, performance tracking.

2 'Detailed budgeting is too time consuming and costly to yield real benefits to an organisation.' What arguments would you put forward against this assertion?

Specific objective

On completion of this section, you should be able to:

- explain the purpose, nature and usefulness of budgetary control.

Did you know?

Responsibility centres are a useful method of budgetary control. A responsibility centre is a functional unit within a company. Examples of responsibility centres include:

- revenue centres, which measure output in monetary terms (e.g. the value of sales in line with the sales budget)

- profit centres, where performance is measured in terms of the difference between revenues and expenditures.

The manager is responsible for any variances within the responsibility centre. Responsibility centres make it possible to identify the reasons for variances (e.g. prices are not competitive, too much stock has been ordered) and to implement controls.

Budgetary control is the process of controlling budgets within an organisation. Managers have particular methods/processes that they use to control budgets. If negative cash flows and cash balances are predicted, managers can then take action, for example by:

- reducing or delaying expenditure
- obtaining cheaper supplies of materials and components
- renting or leasing equipment rather than buying it.

Methods of budgetary control

Variance analysis

Using variance analysis to control budgets involves comparing actual results with budgets to identify any variances (see 3.18). If adverse variances are observed, key individuals such as managers, who are responsible for controlling costs within the different budgets, are tasked with taking action to control the costs or revise the original budget.

For example, if actual sales in a particular period of time are less than budgeted sales, a sales manager might be tasked with encouraging the sales staff to improve performance (for example, by offering performance incentives). Alternatively, sales targets and sales revenues may be reduced or other actions taken, such as reducing prices or increasing promotional activity.

CASE STUDY

Exercising budgetary control

Table 3.22.1 shows some summary production figures (for a particular production line) that have been presented to the board of a manufacturing company.

Table 3.22.1 *Summary production figures for a particular production line*

Budgetary area	Budgeted figure	Assumptions	Actual
Sales	$10,000	5,000 units will be sold at $2 each	$8,000
Production	5,000 units	5,000 units to be produced at a cost of $1 each	4,000 units produced at $1.20 each
Raw materials	10,000 units	10,000 units of raw materials are required at 20 cents per unit	10,000 units purchased at 25 cents each
Labour	100 hours	100 hours are required at $2 per hour	Labour cost = $200

- The first column shows the budgetary area.
- The second column shows estimated sales figures within the budget, the estimated level of production required to meet the sales figures and the estimated requirements in terms of human resources and raw materials to produce the materials.

- The assumptions column shows the assumptions on which these figures were created.
- In most cases, the actual figures achieved (column 4) are different from those within the budget.

1 For each of the actual figures shown, state whether there is a favourable or adverse variance.

2 Why might the actual figures be different from those that were in the original budget?

3 What steps could managers take to act upon the variances you have identified?

Adjustment of funds

In this technique top management may decide to reallocate funds from one project to another. Management creates the budget based on the needs of the organisation for a particular period of time. Changes may have to be made if, for example, it is found that more money was allocated to one department or project and not enough to another. Here reallocation of funds is warranted. **Funds flow analysis** is deemed useful in adjustment of funds.

Zero-based budgeting

Zero-based budgeting starts each budget period afresh, not based on historical data. Every function within an organisation is analysed for its needs and costs. All expenses must be justified for each new period. Budgets are built around what is needed for the upcoming period, regardless of whether the budget is higher or lower than the previous one. In traditional budgeting, managers take into consideration variances and historical data based on the assumption that the baseline has already been approved. For zero-based budgeting no such assumptions are made. Every line item of the budget must be approved rather than only changes.

The role of the budget officer

A **budget officer** is responsible for the administration of a budget. He or she makes sure that deadlines are met and that necessary budgetary controls are in place. This involves working with managers responsible for budget preparation to make sure that the budget is produced appropriately and on time.

Summary table

KEY TERMS

Funds flow analysis: involves the study of how funds are allocated between different forms of assets and projects in order to identify the best uses for which the funds can be used.

Zero-based budget: a budget where every activity is questioned as if it is new. Each plan of action is justified in terms of total costs involved and total benefits to accrue, with no reference to past activities.

Budget officer: individual responsible for administration of a budget.

Summary questions

1 What steps would you take to control a budget variance?

2 Give three examples of situations where variances between actual and budgeted figures might occur. Which of these would be the most serious?

Purpose of budgetary control	Method of budgetary control	Usefulness of budgetary control
To enable managers to ensure that targets are being made and to take remedial action if actual performance strays from the plan	■ Identifying variance ■ Adjustment of funds ■ Zero-based budgeting	■ Helps to identify whether plans are being met ■ Enables managers to take control when variances occur ■ Provides accountability/responsibilities for budgets within an organisation ■ Helps managers and the organisation to meet targets

On completion of this section, you should be able to:

- identify the purpose of investment appraisal.

KEY TERMS

Investment: the purchase of fixed assets, such as buildings and equipment, in the present for benefits in the future.

Did you know?

Investments that businesses make today are repaid in the future. However, the further into the future we look, the less certain we can be of the likely returns.

KEY TERMS

Investment appraisal: methods of calculating the likely returns on an investment, which can be used to compare different investment options.

What is investment?

Investment is spending on capital goods (for example, machinery and vehicles) to allow increased production of goods and services in the future. Investment allows a business to grow and develop by adding to or replacing some of its operating assets.

Investment objectives

An investment objective is the end that a business seeks to achieve as a result of carrying out an investment – for example, to replace an existing asset that is based on old-fashioned technology.

The aim of an investment may be to:

- increase efficiency (for example, using a more modern and productive machine)
- expand capacity (to produce on a larger scale)
- replace existing assets that are no longer economical to use or that are obsolete technologically
- comply with health and safety regulations.

Investment appraisal

Investment appraisal is a means of assessing financially whether an investment is worthwhile.

Purposes of investment appraisal

There are two main purposes of appraising an investment:

- to identify whether the benefits of the investment outweigh the costs – the greater the benefits relative to the costs, the more rewarding the investment opportunity
- to compare alternative investment opportunities – a business can use capital for many different purposes, so it needs to assess which investments are likely to yield the 'best' returns.

What constitutes the 'best' return is open to discussion and will be explored in the next sections.

The limitations of appraising an investment

Investments that a business makes involve the outlay of cash in the present for benefits in the future. This raises a number of issues:

- The future is never predictable – estimates of future revenues and costs are likely to be less accurate the further into the future they go.
- Factors that are beyond a business's control can affect the project's success, such as:
  - changes in government and the law
  - fluctuating economic conditions, such as interest rates and exchange rates
  - changing market conditions, such as competition and consumer trends.

■ In cash terms, benefits in the future are not as valuable as benefits received today. For example, a business will incur interest charges on debt used to finance the project.

The planning horizon

A number of possible techniques are used to appraise an investment opportunity (these will be covered in 3.24–3.26). However, a common approach across the different techniques is to set a realistic **planning horizon** beyond which benefits are not taken into account.

This planning horizon depends on the nature of the project. For example, the appraisal of a new oil rig in the Caribbean Sea is likely to require a planning horizon of at least 10 years, whereas the planning horizon for an advertising campaign may look just one or two years ahead.

KEY TERMS

Planning horizon: the period over which the benefits and costs of an investment are calculated.

Figure 3.23.1 *Building an oil rig in the Caribbean Sea is an investment decision that would require a long-term planning horizon*

Summary table

What is investment appraisal?	A means to calculate the time taken for an investment to pay back initial outlay or to measure the return on investment.
What are the purposes of investment appraisal?	■ To compare the benefits of investments with the costs of investment ■ To compare alternative investment opportunities to identify the best use of investment funds
What are the difficulties associated with appraising investment?	■ Uncertainty of the impact of future events on returns ■ Changing conditions that impact on investment returns (e.g. economic climate, market conditions)

Summary questions

1 What is an investment? Provide examples of investments made by a firm in the Caribbean. Why would the firm want to make these investments? What would be the purpose of carrying out an investment appraisal on these investment projects?

2 Why does the planning horizon vary between different investment projects? Why would the planning horizon vary between an investment in a new factory and an investment in a new computer system?

On completion of this section, you should be able to:

- assess the average rate of return method for appraising an investment.

Year	$000
0	350
1	60
2	90
3	120
4	200
5	100

Figure 3.24.1 *Expected returns into the cricket business*

Figure 3.24.2 *The appraisal of an investment project to build a new cricket stand involves calculating returns in terms of future cash flows*

Did you know?

In investment appraisal we use the term Year 0 to refer to the time at which the investment took place. Since the end of one year is separated from the beginning of the next by only a day, the end of Year 0 is the same as the start of Year 1.

Did you know?

Average rate of return is also known as accounting rate of return.

Initial steps in appraising an investment

As discussed in 3.23, when appraising an investment, organisations need to consider whether:

- a project is worthwhile (that is, whether the return on investment is likely to be sufficient)
- one project is likely to yield a better return than another (for example, whether to invest in expanding the capacity of a cricket stadium or a new set of floodlights for the existing stadium).

Before deciding on which particular method of appraisal to use, an organisation must first identify the capital cost of the project. It must then identify the anticipated returns on the investment.

To explore an investment decision, let us use the example of a capital investment project to build a new stand for a cricket stadium.

The cost of the investment is $350,000. The expected returns in terms of cash flow into the cricket business are shown in Figure 3.24.1.

Using accounting conventions, each cash inflow or outflow takes place at the end of a year. In the figures for cash flow above, there is a cash inflow of $60,000 at the end of Year 1 (then $90,000 at the end of Year 2, etc.).

Calculating the average rate of return (ARR)

The simplest way of calculating returns on investments is to use the average rate of return method. This method focuses on the profits arising from the project:

$$\text{ARR} = \frac{\text{average annual profit}}{\text{average cost of investment}} \times 100$$

Using the example of expanding the capacity of the cricket stadium, we need to compare the initial costs of the investment in the stadium with the profits that arise from its expansion within our chosen planning horizon (which is five years) to give us the average rate of return.

If the return is high enough, the building will go ahead. If there are competing projects, the one with the highest return is likely to be chosen.

Calculating average annual profit

We can calculate the average annual profit in the following way:

Average annual profit
  = Average income per year − Average cost of capital per year

Figures in the calculations below are shown in $000s.

$$\text{Average income per year} = \frac{60 + 90 + 120 + 200 + 100}{5 \text{ years}} = 114$$

$$\text{Average cost of capital per year} = \frac{\text{Cost of capital}}{5 \text{ years}}$$

$$= \frac{350}{5} = 70$$

The average annual profit is $44,000 a year, i.e. = 114,000 − 70,000

Calculating average cost of investment

Now that we have calculated the average annual profit, we need to calculate the average cost of investment:

Average cost of investment
$$= \frac{\text{Total amount of capital invested}}{\text{Period over which it was invested (i.e. 5 years)}}$$

An assumption is made (using the **straight-line method**) that during the five years, the value of the investment will depreciate by the same amount each year (i.e. by one-fifth of the original investment), which is $70,000 a year.

A quick way of calculating the average cost of the investment (taking into account depreciation) is therefore:

Average capital invested
$$= \frac{\text{Start capital + End capital (\textit{less} Depreciation)}}{2}$$
$$= \frac{350 + 0}{2} = 175$$

Calculating average rate of return

We can now work out the average rate of return.

$$\text{Average rate of return} = \frac{\text{Average annual profit}}{\text{Average cost of investment}} \times 100$$

$$= \frac{44}{175} \times 100 = 25.1\%$$

Assessing the average rate of return

Is this a good rate of return? It depends on:

- how much it costs to borrow the original $350,000 for the investment – the higher the rate of interest on borrowing money, the higher the ARR would need to be
- the rate of return on competing projects – if the ARR on investing in new floodlights is 30 per cent then this might be more attractive
- whether the rate of return is regarded as a good rate of return by those carrying out the investment project.

Summary table

Calculation	Explanation
Average rate of return	Calculates average profit made each year as a percentage of the average capital invested
Average profit per year	Calculated by deducting annual depreciation cost from the annual cash inflow
Average capital invested	Calculated by adding start capital to end capital and dividing by 2

Straight-line method: the simplest way of calculating the depreciation of a fixed asset. Using a given planning horizon (e.g. five years), the asset is depreciated by an equal value each year. Over a five-year period it is depreciated by one-fifth of the capital invested at the end of each year.

Did you know?

The average rate of return method of appraisal is based on profits. All other ways of calculating return on investment that we will look at are based on cash flow. ARR is the only method that takes into account depreciation.

Summary questions

1 Using the cricket stadium example outlined in this section, the cricket organisation also wants to investigate investing in floodlights at the stadium. Investing $350,000 in new floodlights would yield the cash flows shown below.

Year	$000
1	60
2	180
3	240
4	20
5	20

2 Work out the ARR for this alternative investment project. Which of the two projects is more attractive in terms of ARR?

3.25 Analytical methods of appraisal: payback period

Specific objective

On completion of this section, you should be able to:

- assess the payback method for appraising investment.

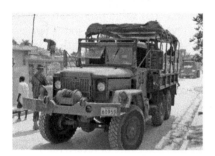

Figure 3.25.1 *The government often uses payback techniques when investing in military equipment*

Did you know?

The relevant year is the year in which cash flow becomes positive. The 'deficit remaining' is the deficit that remained at the start of the year. In the example shown (Figure 3.25.2) cash flows of $20,000 were generated in Year 3, while the deficit at the start of the year was $5,000. It would therefore take three months (one-quarter of the year) to pay off this remaining deficit.

What is payback?

This is a commonly used investment appraisal technique that assesses the time period required for an investment project to 'pay back' an initial investment. Payback is a useful method of appraising investments that become dated very quickly. For example, computers are replaced rapidly by new models, so a business needs to know how quickly it can pay back an initial investment in technology so that it knows when it can invest in a new model. The military often use payback techniques when investing in armoured vehicles and aircraft, for example, because they want to keep their equipment up to date. The quicker they can pay back their investment, the better.

A weakness of the payback method is that it ignores the timing of cash flows and any cash flows that take place after the payback period.

Calculating payback

The calculation is based on cash flow and net profit.

The annual cash flows are cumulated (added up) and the payback period is reached when the cumulative cash flow reaches zero. If you look at Figure 3.25.2, you can see that the payback time will come somewhere in the third year. The initial investment in the project was $45,000.

	Year	Project cash flow $	Cumulative cash flow $
Investment in fixed asset	0	−45,000	−45,000
Net inflows of cash	1	15,000	−30,000
	2	25,000	−5,000
	3	20,000	15,000

Figure 3.25.2 *Payback for Project A*

The formula for payback can be set out in the following way:

Payback period =

$$\text{Years with negative cumulative cash flow} + \frac{\text{Deficit remaining}}{\text{Cash flow in relevant year}} \times 12 \text{ months}$$

Using the information in Figure 3.25.2, we can calculate payback as follows:

We know that the payback of the initial investment of $45,000 will take place between Year 2 and Year 3 – because we can see this visually (from looking at the cumulative cash flow column).

$$\text{Payback period} = 2 \text{ years} + \frac{5{,}000}{20{,}000} \times 12 \text{ months}$$
$$= 2 \text{ years and } 3 \text{ months}$$

The payback method is helpful when comparing alternative projects. The project with the shortest payback period is the best investment proposition, as the shorter time scale reduces the risk of unforeseen circumstances affecting returns.

The payback method

Using payback, we can assess two investment possibilities (Project A and Project B), each costing $15,000, and decide which one is the best investment proposition:

	Project A ($)	Project B ($)
Initial cost in Year 0	(15,000)	(15,000)
Year 1 cash receipts	+3,000	+1,000
Year 2 cash receipts	+3,000	+3,000
Year 3 cash receipts	+4,000	+3,000
Year 4 cash receipts	+5,000	+5,000
Year 5 cash receipts	+3,000	+9,000

Project A repays the initial cost by the end of Year 4, whereas Project B does not repay until sometime in Year 5. Using the payback method, we would choose Project A.

1 Why may Project A be a good choice?

2 What are the advantages of selecting Project B?

Did you know?

Some businesses may use payback as a method of testing the viability of potential investments. For example, one of the business's criteria for investment may be that initial investment is paid back within four years. If the investment meets this criterion, then the business may use other appraisal methods to determine investments.

Summary table

What is the payback period?	The time required for a project to repay the original investment The calculation is based on cash flows
How is it calculated?	Cash flows are cumulated and the payback period is reached when cumulative cash flow is zero

Summary questions

1 Calculate the payback period for the two investment projects (A and B) outlined in Figure 3.25.3. The table shows the capital invested in Year 0 and the cash inflows in Years 1, 2 and 3. You need to calculate the cumulative cash flow before calculating the payback period.

2 Why might project B be more attractive than Project A even though the payback period is longer?

Year	Project A cash flow $	Cumulative cash flow $	Project B cash flow $	Cumulative cash flow $
0	−30,000		−30,000	
1	20,000		2,000	
2	10,000		12,000	
3	6,000		24,000	

Figure 3.25.3 Cash flows for two investment projects (A and B)

3.26 Analytical methods of appraisal: net present value

Specific objective

On completion of this section, you should be able to:

- assess the net present value method for appraising investment.

KEY TERMS

Opportunity cost: the next best alternative that we sacrifice when we take a particular action. For example, when we put $50 into our savings account we are sacrificing the next best alternative on which we could have spent the money. When a company engages in capital investment, it is committing funds that it could have used for other purposes.

Compound interest: interest added to the initial sum borrowed or lent. From that moment on, the interest that has been added also earns interest.

Did you know?

The NPV approach involves calculating the present value of all the flows arising from a project and taking the net value. A negative NPV would result in a decision not to go ahead, and a positive NPV would result in a decision to undertake the project.

The net present value (NPV) method is an alternative method for appraising investment that deals with the disadvantage of the payback method (see 3.25). The net present value of an investment is the present value of cash inflows less the present value of cash outflows. (The value of cash inflows and outflows is measured in terms of the monetary value of these flows today.)

In order to understand and calculate net present value, firstly you need to understand the principle of discounted cash flow.

Discounted cash flow

The discounted cash flow approach is a way of valuing future returns on investment in terms of their present value. For example, we all know instinctively that $1 in the hand today is worth more than a promise of $1 in the future. This is because:

- there is always a risk that unforeseen circumstances will prevent you receiving the amount you have been promised
- inflation (rising prices) may reduce the real value of money
- the money cannot be put to constructive use immediately – the delay in payment therefore incurs an **opportunity cost**
- the 'time value' of money (the idea that money available now is worth more than the same amount in the future) is often represented by a composite annual percentage rate.

Discounted cash flow works on the same principles as **compound interest**.

We can use the example in Figure 3.26.1 to show how discounted cash flow can be calculated. A sum of $100 is invested in a savings account that yields interest at 10 per cent per annum. Assuming that the interest is left in the account at the end of each year, the savings account balance for the next four years will be:

Year	10% interest	Balance
0	–	100.00
1	10.00	110.00
2	11.00	121.00
3	12.10	133.10
4	13.31	146.41

Figure 3.26.1 *The value of $100 today in terms of future balances (with interest at 10 per cent per annum)*

What does this mean in terms of net present value?

These calculations show us how much a business would need to invest in the future. For example, for $100 that a business might invest now, it would need to invest:

- $110.00 in a year's time
- $146.41 in four years' time.

By reducing all future cash flows to a common measure in this way, comparisons can be made between different investment projects.

If a business is going to invest capital, it needs to be able to appraise the value of the returns from the investment in today's money values. The net present value of a future cash flow is found by multiplying it by a discount factor. The size of the discount factor depends on two things:

- the discount rate used (cost of capital)
- the number of years involved.

The easiest way of finding a discount factor is to look it up in an NPV table, like the one shown in Table 3.26.1.

Table 3.26.1 shows that cash in four years' time discounted at 10 per cent should be multiplied by a factor of 0.6830.

Did you know?

Discount tables can be found on the internet. Search for discount tables that are used to calculate the NPV of money.

Table 3.26.1 *A simple discount table for different rates of interest and time periods*

Year	Interest rate											
	5%	6%	7%	8%	9%	10%	11%	12%	13%	14%	15%	20%
1	0.9524	0.9434	09346	0.9259	0.9174	0.9091	0.9009	0.8929	0.8850	0.8772	0.8698	0.8333
2	0.9070	0.8900	0.8734	0.8793	0.8417	0.8264	0.8116	o.7972	0.7831	0.7695	0.7561	0.6944
3	0.8638	0.8396	0.8163	0.7938	0.7722	0.7513	0.7312	0.7118	0.6931	0.6750	0.6575	0.5787
4	0.8277	0.7921	0.7629	0.7350	0.7084	0.6830	0.6587	06355	0.6133	0.5921	0.5718	0.4823
5	0.7835	0.7473	0.7130	0.6806	0.6499	0.6209	0.5935	0.5674	0.5428	0.5194	0.4972	0.4019
6	0.7462	0.7050	0.6663	0.6302	0.5963	0.5645	0.5346	0.5066	0.4803	0.4556	0.4323	0.3349
7	0.7107	0.6651	0.6227	0.5835	0.5470	0.5132	0.4817	0.4523	0.4251	0.3996	0.3759	0.2791
8	0.6768	0.6274	0.5820	0.5403	0.5019	0.4665	0.4339	0.4039	0.3762	0.3506	0.3269	0.2326
9	0.6446	0.5919	0.5439	0.5002	0.4604	0.4241	0.3909	0.3606	0.3329	0.3075	0.2843	0.1938

Calculating the discount factor

It is also possible to calculate the discount factor without having to rely on NPV tables.

The calculation is:

$$\text{NPV discount factor} = \frac{1}{(1 + r)^n}$$

Where: r = discount rate
n = number of years

For example, cash received in four years' time discounted at 10 per cent is calculated as follows:

$$\text{NPV discount factor} = \frac{1}{(1 + 0.1)^4}$$

Compare the answer to the NPV figure in Table 3.26.1.

Calculating NPV using discount factors

Figure 3.26.2 shows how discount factors are used to calculate NPV, using the same figures that we used for the payback method.

	Year	Project cash flow $	10% discount factor	Calculation $	NPV $
Investment in fixed assets	0	−45,000	1.000	$\frac{-45,000}{(1 + 0.1)^0}$	−45,000
Net inflows of cash	1	15,000	0.909	$\frac{15,000}{(1 + 0.1)^1}$	13,636
	2	25,000	0.826	$\frac{25,000}{(1 + 0.1)^2}$	20,661
	3	20,000	0.751	$\frac{20,000}{(1 + 0.1)^3}$	15,026
Total		**15,000**			**4,323**

Figure 3.26.2 *Calculating the NPV of a project*

Measuring the cash returns in terms of NPV yields a much lower figure than would have been the case if the time value of money had not been taken into consideration.

The NPV here is positive ($4,323) and therefore investment should go ahead. Where a number of projects are competing for investment, the project with the highest NPV is likely to be selected.

A good way of illustrating net present value is by using a personal example. Consider $100 which you could place in a savings account with an interest rate of 10%. What return would you receive?

Year 1	$100 @ 10% = $110
Year 2	$110 @ 10% = $121
Year 3	$121 @ 10% = $133
Year 4	$133 @ 10% = $146

Figure 3.26.3 *Returns on savings with an annual interest rate of 10%*

According to the above calculation, $100 invested today is worth $146 in four years' time. However, $146 in four years' time is only worth $100 today. So although an investment may have a cash inflow of $150 in four years' time it is actually only worth just over $100 at today's values. The cash is converted into today's values by discounting the future inflows.

A business would want to calculate future returns on investment in today's values. This would enable the business to make rational decisions about how it would use the funds which it has available to it today.

Did you know?

The discounting process assumes that all cash flows occur at the end of the relevant year.

Did you know?

A business needs to decide on how to choose a discount rate in order to make an NPV calculation. If the business is already using cash that it has in a bank, the obvious rate would be the interest that the business is earning at present from the bank. This is the opportunity cost of the funds (the amount of opportunity lost by using the funds to invest in the project). Similarly, if the business has to borrow money, the simple approach is to use the interest rate on the money being borrowed.

Summary table

What is NPV?	A method of appraising investment that takes into account the fact that money values change with time
How is it calculated?	NPV is the present value of discounted cash inflows less the present value of cash outflows If it is positive then the project is financially viable
What is the discount factor?	The percentage rate used to calculate the present value of future cash flow (e.g. if capital is borrowed for an investment at 5% interest, the present value of future earnings should be discounted by 5%, as future earnings will be worth less due to the interest payable)
When should investment take place?	When the NPV of an investment is positive (i.e. earnings are at a higher rate than the cost of capital)
What is the 'time value' of money?	The concept that money available now is worth more than the same amount in the future because of its current capacity to earn rewards for the owner

Summary questions

1 Why is money a business has today valued more highly than the same amount of money received in the future?

2 What are discount tables used for?

3 Why should an investment project have a positive NPV?

4 A friend offers to lend you $100 but says that if you are going to pay him back in one month's time then he will want more than $100 in repayment. Is he being fair to you? What might be a reasonable sum to repay him and how did you arrive at this calculation?

Did you know?

If you look at the price of many products five or 10 years ago and compare them with today's prices, you will find that many of them were cheaper. As time passes prices increase so that the value of money falls. Business returns on investment take place in the future when the money value of the returns on investment will be worth less than an equivalent sum of cash today.

On completion of this section, you should be able to:

- compare different appraisal techniques.

Stages in investment appraisal

Figure 3.27.1 shows the four stages that a business is likely to have gone through during the investment appraisal process.

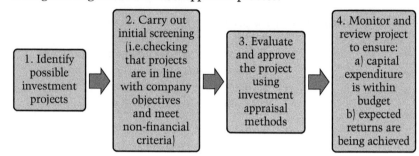

Figure 3.27.1 *Stages in investment decision making*

Advantages and disadvantages of investment appraisal techniques

Table 3.27.1 shows the advantages and disadvantages of the different investment appraisal techniques.

Table 3.27.1 *The advantages and disadvantages of the different investment appraisal techniques*

Technique	Advantages	Disadvantages
Average rate of return (ARR)	■ Method of appraisal is the same as profit and loss reporting (using the income statement), so relatively easy to understand	■ Not based on cash flows, so subject to the different ways in which company accountants present accounts (e.g. how they report profit)
Payback	■ Simple to calculate ■ Easy to understand ■ Bias towards early payback minimises risk	■ Takes no account of timing of cash flows other than within or outside payback period ■ Does not consider cash flows after the payback period ■ Does not consider the cost of capital
Net present value (NPV)	■ Theoretically 'correct' as it considers timing of all cash flows, inflation and cost of capital	■ Calculations are complex ■ Results are highly sensitive to assumptions, such as the discount rate and the planning horizon

CASE STUDY

Prizewinning Colour Printers Ltd

Prizewinning Colour Printers Ltd has to refuse work because it has insufficient print capacity. A new printing press would cost $400,000 but would enable the business to process additional work to the value of $500,000 each year. The additional annual running costs would be two operatives at $25,000 each and materials amounting to $100,000.

1 Calculate the payback period of the printing press.

2 Calculate the net present value, assuming the company's policy is to discount four years of cash flows at 20 per cent per annum. (Use the discount table shown in 3.26 to make your calculation.)

3 What are the benefits of making the decision using the payback method? What are the benefits of making the decision using the NPV approach?

Racecourse improvements

On an ongoing basis, a racecourse invests in improvements to the spectator facilities and to the race track itself. Managers review possible improvements periodically. This is the first stage of identifying possible investment projects. The next step is to carry out an initial screening. Some projects may be essential on health and safety grounds (e.g. for the safety of spectators and competitors), whereas other investments may be less essential (such as increasing luxury viewing boxes). The important thing is to identify which of the possible projects best fits with the long-term objectives of the racecourse authorities.

The next stage is to evaluate and approve the projects. Detailed financial analysis is employed at this point. With a short-term planning horizon, a payback approach can be taken. However, it is more likely that a net present value approach would be taken because this would enable the project sponsors to calculate the returns on the investment in financial terms and to assess whether the cost of capital is being covered in an appropriate way. In addition the decision makers will need to consider non-financial factors (e.g. the effects of investments on the image of their world-famous venue).

Once an investment project is approved, planning (budgeting) and financial control measures come into play. It is necessary to monitor progress to ensure that capital expenditure is within the allocated budget. Once the project has been completed, it needs to be reviewed on an ongoing basis to ensure that the expected returns are being achieved.

1 For a sports or leisure venue with which you are familiar, identify some possible investment projects.

2 How might the payback approach be used to screen some of the alternatives that you have outlined?

3 What are the benefits of using the net present value approach for the investment projects that you have outlined?

Summary table

Average rate of return	A method of investment appraisal that measures the profit earned on an investment as a percentage of the average investment.
Payback	A simple and frequently used method of capital investment appraisal. Payback measures the length of time required for a stream of cash proceeds from an investment to recover the initial cash outlay on the investment.
Net present value	A method of investment appraisal that uses the present value of net cash flow (cash inflows minus cash ouflows at today's price levels), less the initial investment. Provided the net present value of the investment is positive then you should go ahead with the investment.

Summary questions

Prizewinning Colour Printers (see case study) has another investment opportunity. Currently, the work of cutting out card from printed sheets has to be done by an external supplier. To do the work internally they would need a die-cutting machine, which would cost $300,000. Although the machine would cost $100,000 a year to run, it would remove the supplier's annual cutting charges of $325,000.

1 Calculate the payback period of the die-cutting machine.

2 Calculate the net present value based on a 20 per cent discount rate.

3 Unfortunately the company does not have sufficient financing facilities to fund both the printing press and the die-cutting machine. Which investment opportunity should the company pursue based on the results of the different investment appraisal methods?

Did you know?

The average rate of return is also frequently referred to as the accounting rate of return.

Section 1: Multiple-choice questions

1 From where would you derive information to calculate the ratio comparing operating profit with revenue?

   A The statement of financial position and the income statement

   B The statement of financial position only

   C The income statement only

   D The trading account of the income statement only

2 A business has current assets of $30 million and current liabilities of $24 million. This shows that it has access to enough short-term liquidity to meet pressing liabilities. Which of the following ratios represents this position?

   A 54 : 30   B 30 : 30

   C 5 : 4   D 5 : 5

3 What does the term 'payback period' mean?

   A The period up to the point at which a project becomes profitable

   B The time taken for the initial investment in a project to be repaid with subsequent cash inflows

   C The time allowed before the bank must be repaid

   D The net present value of cash used in an investment

4 Which of the following is most likely to be classified as a current asset?

   A Stock (inventories) waiting to be sold

   B A mortgage that a company has taken out on a building

   C The company's premises

   D A bank loan that the company has taken out

5 Which of the following budgets would typically be created first?

   A The raw materials budget

   B The labour budget

   C The production budget

   D The sales budget

6 Which of the following is retained in a business to generate wealth over time?

   A Current assets

   B Stock (inventories)

   C Trade receivables

   D Fixed assets

7 Company A is funded principally by equity whereas Company B is funded principally by debt. Which of the following statements is therefore correct?

   A Company A and Company B will have broadly the same level of gearing.

   B Company A is more highly geared than Company B.

   C Company A's gearing position is more risky than that of Company B.

   D Company A is less highly geared than Company B.

8 Which of the following institutions is part of the capital market?

   A The stock exchange

   B A commercial bank

   C A credit union

   D The money market

9 Net profit is calculated by:

   A taking away the cost of sales from sales

   B taking away net interest from gross profit

   C taking away all costs and expenses from sales

   D adding taxes to gross profit

10 Earnings per share is calculated by:

   A dividing net profit by the average number of shares on offer

   B dividing gross profit by the number of shares

   C dividing the dividend per share by the market price per share as a percentage

   D dividing total dividend per share

Section 2: Structured questions

11 Rose Wood Furniture manufactures and sells classic wooden beds. Demand for the beds seems to peak in the period between November and January, while other months are relatively quiet. The sales manager has calculated that sales in 2014 are likely to be 200 units per month in the busy months, but only 150 per month in quieter months. The production manager has constructed a production budget that involves producing 200 units per month throughout the year.

a Identify the order in which the company should produce budgets to make sure that there are enough beds to meet customer demand. [3]

b Explain TWO reasons why the company should follow the lead given by the sales manager rather than the production manager. [4]

c What are the THREE main benefits that Rose Wood Furniture can reap from engaging in a detailed budgeting exercise? [9]

d In reality, the actual sales figures show that there are adverse variances in the busy months (November, December and January) while there are favourable variances during the remainder of the year. Identify THREE key implications of these variances in the sales budgets for other budgets. [9]

12 Below are the financial statements for Sea Island Hotels for the year ended 31 March 2013.

Income statement for year ending 31 March 2013

	$000
Sales	5,000
Cost of sales	(2,000)
Gross profit	(a)
Expenses	
Marketing	(750)
Administration	(1,500)
Net profit	(b)

Balance sheet for Sea Island Hotels as at 31 March 2013

	$000	$000
Fixed assets		30,000
Current assets		
Stock (inventories)	800	
Trade receivables (debtors)	720	
Cash	480	
Creditors due within one year	(1,200)	
Net current assets		(c)
Creditors due in more than one year		(8,000)
Total net assets		(d)
Shareholders' funds		
Opening capital		(e)
Net profit		(f)

a Calculate the value of the each of the letters in brackets (a) to (f). [6]

b Compute, correct to one decimal place, the following ratios for the year ended 31 March 2013:
  i current ratio
  ii return on capital employed
  iii net profit margin
  iv acid test ratio
  v stock turnover. [15]

c i Outline ONE reason for the difference between the gross profit and the net profit of a business. [2]
  ii Explain the difference between a current asset and a fixed asset. [2]

Further exam questions and examples can be found on the accompanying CD.

Glossary

Words in **_bold italic_** are not listed as key terms in this study guide but have been included here as useful financial terms to help you to develop a better understanding of some of the main terms used in finance and accounts.

A

Accountability: being answerable for actions taken and tasks performed.

Accounting system: a set of methods and procedures for organising, interpreting and using accounting information.

Accrual concept: an accounting principle which involves recording a transaction in the period to which it relates rather than when it is paid.

Acid test ratio: a ratio measuring those assets that can be most easily turned into cash in the short term (cash + debtors) against the short-term liabilities of a business:
Acid test ratio = (Cash + Debtors) : Current liabilities

Administration expenses: costs that are not associated with producing and delivering goods and services to the customer (e.g. preparing financial accounts for the company).

Appropriation account: part of an account that describes how profit is used (e.g. to show that funds are paid out as dividends or retained as reserves).

Assets: items of value that a business owns which generate future economic benefits.

Authorised capital: the sum of capital that relevant authorities, such as the Stock Exchange, authorise a business to raise through the issue of shares. The business may only raise part of the authorised capital, referred to as the issued capital. The business can then issue more capital later up to the total value of the authorised capital.

Authority: legitimate rights associated with a specific role.

B

Balance sheet (statement of financial position): one of the main financial statements, showing the financial situation of a business at a particular date. It summarises the assets and liabilities of a business as well as the owner's capital.

Bank loan: money lent by a bank for which the bank charges interest.

Bank overdraft: the amount in a bank account when the money withdrawn exceeds the money paid in.

Benchmark: a standard that other organisations or parts of an organisation seek to emulate.

Break-even point: the level of output at which total revenue equals total costs.

Budget: a plan for the future, usually set out in numbers.

Budget officer: individual responsible for administration of a budget.

Budgetary control: the comparison of actual figures with budgeted figures. Managers may then need to take action to control costs or adjust the budget.

Business ethics: principles that incorporate a sense of 'doing the right thing'. A business that takes ethics seriously will make business decisions that benefit the wider society.

Business plan: a detailed description of a business and its plans for the next one to three years. A business plan explains what the business does (or what it will do if it is a new business): that is, what it will produce or services it will provide. It also provides financial assessments and forecasts to demonstrate the business's viability.

C

Capital: see **Financial capital** or **Physical capital**.

Capital employed: the value of the investment in an entity (usually a business).
Capital employed =
　Fixed assets + (Current assets − Current liabilities)

Capital expenditure: money spent on fixed assets.

Capital market: a financial market for the buying and selling of long-term debt. Institutions in the capital market include those trading shares on the stock exchange, investment banks and private equity firms.

CARICOM: the Caribbean Community and Common Market is an organisation made up of 15 Caribbean nations and dependencies that promotes economic integration and operates as a free trade area/single market.

Cash flow statement (statement of cash flows): describes and measures the various types and values of cash flows into and out of a business over a particular period of time.

Certificate of Incorporation: states that a company has been incorporated as a company.

Certificate of Trading: states that a company can commence trading.

Chain of command: successive links from top to bottom in a hierarchy showing lines of responsibility.

Change agents: individuals with a key role in championing the change.

Change objectives: what the change will achieve and by when.

Change plan: a plan showing the activities that will enable the organisation to achieve the change.

Charity: an organisation set up for charitable purposes (that is thereby exempt from some or all taxes) and which does not seek to make a profit.

Closed system: a system whose operations are not impacted by the external environment.

Closing stock: the value of stock that a company holds at the end of a trading period.
Closing stock = Value of the opening stock
　+ Value of purchases of new stock − Value of sales

Commercial banks: high street banks that provide bank accounts, loans and other forms of finance to personal and business customers.

Communications escalator: a way of illustrating the progressive (rising) intensity of communications required to engage individuals and groups involved in delivering change processes.

Company: a business that is owned by shareholders, who contribute capital in return for a share in the company and its profits. The US term for company is corporation.

Competency: a characteristic of an individual or a skill that they possess that enables them to do something within a job effectively or successfully.

Compound interest: interest added to the initial sum borrowed or lent. From that moment on, the interest that has been added also earns interest.

Consistency concept: a concept that involves treating similar items consistently from one period to another (e.g. if assets are depreciated using one method of calculating depreciation one year then the same method of depreciation should be used in the following year).

Contingency approach: an approach to management based on the idea that there is no one best way to manage and that the approach needs to vary according to the context or situation.

Continuum: a continuous sequence that blends from one to another seamlessly.

Control system: methods, such as target and performance indicators, used to identify whether a business is on track to achieve its objectives and, where it is not, taking actions to put it back on track.

Control tool: a mechanism for controlling an activity (e.g. a budgetary control system compares actual performance against the budget, enabling management to take action as appropriate).

Convertible debenture: a document stating that the company has received a loan from an individual that will be paid in the future by converting the loan into shares in the company.

Corporate governance: the processes by which the board of directors ensures accountability, fairness and transparency in an organisation. Good corporate governance involves directing a business in an efficient and responsible way.

Corporate social responsibility: the responsibility of a company to society and the environment.

Corporation tax: a tax on company profits.

Cost centre: part of the business organisation for which costs are collected and reported (e.g. the marketing department).

Cost effective: carrying out activities in a way that provides value for money.

Cost of sales (cost of revenue): the cost of goods sold (inclusive of materials and other direct costs).

Cost of sales = Opening stock plus purchases − Closing stock

Creditor: a supplier who provided goods but has not yet received payment for them.

Current assets: assets that will be used up in the everyday trading of the business.

Current liabilities: sums owed that are repayable in the next 12 months.

D

Debentures: long-term loans with fixed repayment dates. Interest is usually paid annually.

Debt: capital that is borrowed from outside the business, which must be repaid with interest.

Debtor: a customer who bought on credit but who has not yet paid their debt.

Delegation: trusting someone (usually a subordinate) to carry out duties.

Depreciation: the process of gradually decreasing the value of a fixed asset over its economic life.

Disbursement: money paid out or spent.

Discount factor: the percentage rate used to convert future cash flows into their present value.

Distribution costs: the cost of moving a firm's product from the factory to the customer.

Dividend: the return (reward) paid to a shareholder out of the profits made by a company.

Dividend cover: shows the extent to which the profit that a company makes is greater than the dividend it pays out. It shows how 'safe' the dividend payment was in terms of how many times the current year's profit could have covered the dividend payout.

$$\text{Dividend cover} = \frac{\text{Net profit}}{\text{Ordinary dividend paid}}$$

Dividend yield: assesses the cash return to shareholders (dividends) compared with the amount of money they have invested to earn the cash return.

$$\text{Dividend yield (\%)} = \frac{\text{Dividend per share}}{\text{Market price of share}} \times 100$$

Drawings: money or assets that owners of the business take from the profits.

E

Earnings per share: shows how much profit a company makes for each share in the company (e.g. 40 cents per share).

$$\text{Earnings per share} = \frac{\text{Net profit}}{\text{Average number of shares on offer}}$$

Ease of Doing Business Index: an index created by the World Bank to show the ease of doing business in particular countries.

Efficiency ratio: a ratio that shows how well a business is using its assets (e.g. the stock turnover ratio shows how efficiently a business is turning over its inventory).

Entropy: the natural tendency for a system to decline.

Equity: owner's capital – in the form of ordinary shares.

Expectancy theory: the belief that rewards can be achieved for working hard (high expectations).

Expenses: costs a business incurs in order to generate revenue (e.g. costs of marketing activities or administration costs).

External recruitment: recruitment from candidates who are not currently working for the company.

Extrinsic motivation: factors in the external environment that encourage motivation, such as pay and other rewards (external motivation).

F

Factoring: selling off debts at a discount to another company who is then responsible for collecting the debts. Factors are businesses that provide finance for another business's trade debt by advancing a given percentage of the value of invoices outstanding to it, with the remainder becoming payable when customers pay at the end of their credit periods. Factors then receive interest on the finance they advance.

Fair trade: a trading partnership based on dialogue between partners, transparency (about who gets what), respect and equality.

Final accounts: accounts produced at the end of a period (e.g. an income statement).

Finance director: the head of the finance department who also sits on the company's board of directors.

Financial accounts: an accounting statement prepared to satisfy legal reporting requirements for **Published accounts**.

Financial capital: the funds used for investment in a business. The term 'capital' is also used in accounting to refer to the value of the owner's investment in a business.

Fixed assets: the tools of the trade that remain in the business.

Fixed costs: any costs that do not vary with the level of output or sales.

Fixed liabilities: include outstanding liabilities of a company that need to be repaid. There is a minimum of 12 months before payment becomes due.

Forecast: an estimate of what is likely to happen in the future.

Foreign direct investment (FDI): the investment of capital by a business in one country into another country (e.g. through investment in plant and equipment in another country, or by buying shares in overseas companies).

Formal leadership: where a person is officially designated as the leader of a group.

For-profit organisation: any business that seeks to make a profit for its owners.

Franchise: a business that operates under the name of a well-known business and pays the company a fee or royalty for using its name and branding.

Franchisee: the person who has been granted the franchise. The franchisee usually contributes a sum of capital to take on the franchise and pays regular royalties or fees related to sales.

Franchisor: the company or person granting the franchise.

Functional (constructive) conflict: a moderate level of disagreement that can improve a team's performance and help it achieve its goals through open discussion.

Functions: specialist parts of an organisation (e.g. marketing, finance and human resource management).

Funds flow analysis: involves the study of how funds are allocated between different forms of assets and projects in order to identify the best uses for which the funds can be used.

Furniture, fixtures and fittings: miscellaneous fixed assets, such as desks, shelving and electrical tools.

G

Gap in the market: an opportunity to meet existing and potential customer requirements that nobody else has spotted.

Gearing: the proportion of capital on which fixed interest payments are charged.

Gearing ratio: the ratio of debt to capital employed.
Gearing ratio =

$$\frac{\text{Long-term debt}}{\text{Capital employed}} \times 100$$

Globalisation: the process whereby products, people and capital are highly mobile across the globe.

Going concern concept: the concept that a company will continue trading in the foreseeable future.

Government grant: a sum of money provided to businesses and other organisations by the government to fund specific targeted activities (e.g. to set up a new business). The grant is not expected to be repaid.

Gross profit: profit calculated as the sales of a business minus the costs associated with making those sales.

$$\text{Gross profit (\%)} = \frac{\text{Gross profit}}{\text{Sales revenue}} \times 100$$

Group: a loose collection of individuals who come together for a specific purpose.

Group cohesiveness: the level of attachment of members to a group.

H

Hawthorne effect: employees are more motivated and apply more effort if they are being studied or if someone is taking an interest in them.

Hawthorne experiments: a series of experiments, conducted by Elton Mayo and his fellow researchers, at the Western Electric Company in Chicago between 1927 and 1932.

Hierarchy: the different levels within an organisation representing the degree of authority and responsibility.

High-performance team: an effective team based on collaboration, shared goals, shared accountabilities and shared responsibility. Members of the team are committed to each other and to achieving the team's goals.

Hire purchase: a financial arrangement that enables businesses and individuals to hire vehicles and equipment, through the payment of instalments (with interest factored in) over an agreed period of time (e.g. three years). When all the instalments have been paid, ownership of the item passes to the business.

Historical cost: stated at cost value (i.e. the cost of the asset when it was originally purchased).

Human relations approach: a management approach that recognises that humans respond to a personal approach. The human relations approach recognises individuals' needs.

Human resource management: management of an organisation's workforce. HR managers look for ways of recognising the needs and aspirations of workers.

Hygiene factors: factors that need to be present in the workplace to ensure basic satisfaction (e.g. safe and clean working conditions and reasonable pay). Without these factors employees would be unmotivated.

I

Income statement: one of the main financial statements, showing the revenues, cost of sales, expenses and income of a business over a period of time.

Inflation accounting: method by which adjustments are made to the account to reflect changes in price levels.

Informal leadership: leadership by a person who is not officially recognised as a leader. Members of a group 'appoint' him or her as a leader.

Intangible assets: valuable items that have no physical form (e.g. patents and goodwill).

Internal recruitment: recruitment from amongst a firm's existing employees.

Interest: payment to compensate the lender for their sacrifice of the ability to use the loaned money for other purposes.

Intrinsic motivation: motivation that comes from within an individual (self-motivation).

Inward investment: the inflow of investment capital into an area. For example, the Bahamas has recently benefited from considerable inward investment in its international airport (Lynden Pindling Airport) and a sophisticated modern road and transportation network.

Investment: the purchase of fixed assets, such as buildings and equipment, in the present for benefits in the future.

Investment appraisal: methods of calculating the likely returns on an investment, which can be used to compare different investment options.

Invoice: a document showing goods sold and their prices. Both sellers and buyers use invoices for their records.

Issued capital: the number or value of shares that a company issues at a particular moment in time. A company may not always have issued shares to the full value of its authorised capital.

J

Job analysis: identifying the requirements of a job.

Job enrichment: the process of making a job more interesting and challenging by increasing the range of tasks. Job enrichment should improve motivation.

Joint venture: a new business venture set up by two existing businesses for a specific purpose.

K

Key performance indicators (KPIs): performance indicators that are used to measure important aspects of business performance (e.g. sales, profit, market share, employee turnover, employee satisfaction and volume of work recycled).

Knowledge-based economy: economies in which specialised knowledge and information that people and companies possess have become a new form of a highly valued and saleable product.

L

Learning: a relatively permanent change of behaviour that occurs as a result of practice or experience.

Lease: a contract to allow the lessee (borrower) to use an asset leased (e.g. machinery) from a lessor (lender).

Liabilities: sums of money that a business owes to an individual or other organisation. In accounts, liabilities (i.e. negative numbers) are put in brackets to show that they need to be subtracted from the business's assets.

Limited liability: a restriction on the amount of debt in a company that owners can be expected to pay. Liability is limited to the value of their shares.

Line manager: a manager directly responsible for someone else.

Line of control: the reporting and responsibility structure within an organisation. For example, individuals report to a line manager or supervisor who is responsible for them. The higher up the line an individual is, the greater their seniority and responsibility.

Liquid assets: an asset that can be converted into cash. The most liquid asset is therefore cash itself. Short-term debtors (accounts receivable) also provide a company with liquid assets because they will pay in cash.

Liquidity: the extent to which liquid assets are available to pay debts.

Liquidity ratios: ratios that measure the ability of a business to pay off current liabilities by using cash and other assets that can be turned into cash.

Loan stock: loans that can be bought and sold in the same way as shares in a company.

Long-term finance: finance typically taken over five years or longer.

Long-term liabilities: liabilities due for settlement over one year from the date of the balance sheet.

M

Management accounts: accounting information prepared for managers of a business organisation.

Marginal cost: the cost of producing the additional unit of output (i.e. one extra good).

Marginal revenue: the revenue from selling an additional output.

Market price per share: the price at which shares in a company are currently being bought and sold.

Market research: the systematic gathering, recording and analysis of data about the market for a good or service.

Matrix structure: an organisational structure with two or more reporting lines and two or more lines of control.

Medium-term finance: finance typically taken over one to five years.

Mission: the purpose of an organisation. An organisation's mission is often set out in a mission statement.

Mixed economy: an economy comprising a combination of public sector and private sector enterprises.

Monetary assets: assets with an obvious cash value (e.g. trade debtors who will pay in the next month or so).

Money market: a market made up of organisations that channel short-term finance (provided by savers) into businesses and other borrowers.

Motivational needs: internal psychological motivators, such as the need for power or the need to be accepted (affiliation).

Motivators: the reasons why an individual takes certain actions.

Multi-criteria decision analysis (MCDA): an organisation uses a range of criteria to make a decision. The criteria are weighted to reflect their relative importance.

Multinational: a company that operates in at least two countries and has operating units in other countries.

N

Nationalisation: the taking over and running of a business or industry by the government.

Net book value: the value of an asset as recorded in a business's accounting records.

Net book value =
Cost of fixed asset − Asset's accumulated depreciation

Net current assets: the value of current assets once current liabilities have been deducted (also known as working capital).

Net current assets = Current assets − Current liabilities

Net profit: the profit of a business after the cost of sales and other expenses have been deducted.

Net profit after tax: the profit remaining after expenses and tax have been deducted from gross profit.

Net profit after tax = Gross profit − Expenses − Tax

Net profit to sales ratio: net profit over sales.

Net wealth: the value of assets once liabilities have been deducted.

'**New broom' approach**: changes introduced by a new manager that encourage greater participation in decision making.

Nominal share value: par value (value of a share as set out on the share certificate when the share is first issued) of a share unrelated to its market value.

Non-governmental organisation: an organisation independent of government with a humanitarian focus.

Not-for-profit organisation: an organisation that pursues objectives other than making a profit.

O

Open system: a system that is impacted by the external environment.

Opening stock: the value of stock that a company holds at the start of a trading period.

Operating activities: the business of satisfying customer needs as opposed to incidentals such as earning interest on surplus cash. Operating activities are associated with the typical operations of a company rather than other flows.

Operating profit: the profit remaining after expenses are deducted from gross profit.

Operating profit = Gross profit − Operating expenses

Operations: the grass-roots activities put in place to ensure that tactics and strategies are implemented.

Opportunity cost: the next best alternative that we sacrifice when we take a particular action. For example, when we put $50 into our savings account we are sacrificing the next best alternative on which we could have spent the money. When a company engages in capital investment, it is committing funds that it could have used for other purposes.

Ordinary share capital: the value of shares that are issued to the owners of a company.

Organisational culture: the accepted way of behaving and interacting in an organisation.

Owner's capital: finance that the owners provide to the business.

P

Performance appraisal: a method by which the job performance of an employee is evaluated.

Person specification: document setting out the skills and qualities that a candidate needs to have in order to be selected.

PESTLE analysis: stands for political, economic, social, technological, legal and ecological analysis and refers to a method of reviewing the external environment in which a business operates.

Physical capital: goods that are used to make other goods (e.g. machinery and equipment).

Planning horizon: the period over which the benefits and costs of an investment are calculated.

Plant and machinery: equipment used in the production of a business's goods.

Preference shares: shares that earn fixed dividends that are paid before those on ordinary shares.

Pressure group: an organisation that seeks to bring about change by putting pressure on political decision making.

Price earnings ratio: shows how many times larger the current market price of a share is compared to the annual earnings of that share. A high price earnings ratio indicates that the investors have high confidence in the future prospects of the company because the price that investors are willing to pay for the share is considerably higher than the dividends being paid on that share.

$$\text{Price earnings ratio} = \frac{\text{Market price per share}}{\text{Earnings per share (after tax)}}$$

Primary inputs: settings that control the operation of the system (e.g. the speed of a production line, the temperature at which processes take place, and the amount of time for which the line runs).

Private equity: money invested by wealthy individuals and institutional investors to purchase businesses. Typically, they improve the performance of a business that they have acquired before selling it on.

Privatisation: the transfer of businesses from government ownership to private ownership.

Profit centre: a part of a business organisation for which both sales revenues and costs are collected and reported.

Profit margin: indicates how many cents of profit are made for every $1 of sales.

$$\text{Profit margin} = \frac{\text{Net profit (before interest and tax)}}{\text{Sales}}$$

Prudence concept: an accounting principle where a profit is recognised when it is realised but a loss is recognised as soon as possible.

Psychological contract: an unwritten, informal agreement between an employer and employees based on mutual commitment.

Public corporation: a state-owned business or industry that is set up for a specific purpose (e.g. to run the telecommunications service or to provide utility services such as water or gas).

Published accounts: financial statements that a company produces and makes available for wider scrutiny (e.g. a statement of financial position and an income statement).

Q

Qualitative information: descriptive information that is based on views and perceptions rather than facts.

Quantitative information: information that is measurable and quantifiable. It can be analysed mathematically.

Quaternary industries: knowledge-based industries (i.e. industries that add value through knowledge and human intelligence e.g. processing and selling electronic data and information to other organisations).

R

Ratio analysis: expressing one variable in relation to another and comparing the result with other firms, years and budgets.

Reserves: the accumulated funds of a business; generally, the amount of profit not paid out to shareholders as dividends.

Residual value: estimated value of a fixed asset at the end of its economic life (e.g. scrap).

Responsibility: duty to carry out tasks according to the level expected.

Responsibility centre: unit within an organisation that takes responsibility for variances.

Return on capital employed (ROCE): shows how much profit is made for every $1 of capital employed.

$$\text{ROCE} = \frac{\text{Operating profit}}{\text{Total capital employed}} \times 100$$

Revaluation reserve: an account that shows the amount by which a company's assets have increased in value when compared to the historical cost value of those assets.

S

Sales: turnover or revenue obtained as a result of a company selling its goods or services.

Scientific management: a classical approach to management based on using scientific methods to identify the 'one best way' of doing a job.

Secondary inputs: resources (e.g. the raw materials and ingredients that are processed).

Secured loan: a loan where the borrower pledges an asset to secure the loan. The lender then has the legal right to be repaid out of the proceeds of the asset if the borrower is unable to repay the loan.

Self-motivation: intrinsic characteristics that motivate an individual.

Share: ownership of a company is split into a certain number of issued shares.

Share premium: the difference between the amount received and the nominal value when a company issues new shares.

Share premium account: proceeds of a share issue in excess of the nominal share value.

Shareholder: someone who owns shares in a company. A share represents a portion of the total capital of the company. A shareholder therefore part owns the company.

Shareholder return: the total return received by a shareholder (dividend plus change in share price) over a period of time, calculated as a percentage of the initial share price.

Shareholders' funds: nominal share value shares plus reserves.

'Sleeping' partner: an individual who contributes capital to a business but who is not involved in the day-to-day decision making or running of the business.

'Soft loans': loans that have easy repayment terms (e.g. low or no interest spread over a longer period of repayment than other forms of borrowing).

Sole trader: a business owned by one person. The sole trader may, or may not, employ other people.

Solvency: the ability of a company to cover all of its pressing liabilities (short-term liabilities) with short-term assets, so that it can carry on trading.

Span of control: number of employees accountable to a manager.

Stakeholder: an individual, organisation or government with an interest in the decisions that a company makes.

Statutory board: an organisation set up by the government, through legislation, with the aim of performing certain functions, such as managing a port or providing clean and regular water supplies. It reports to a specific government minister.

Stock: goods bought (whether worked or not) for resale, that is, normal trade.

Stock turnover: a measurement of how many times a company's inventory (stock) turns over (is replaced) in a given time period.

$$\text{Stock turnover} = \frac{\text{Cost of sales}}{\text{Stock}}$$

Straight-line method: the simplest way of calculating the depreciation of a fixed asset. Using a given planning horizon (e.g. five years), the asset is depreciated by an equal value each year. Over a five-year period it is depreciated by one-fifth of the capital invested at the end of each year.

Strategies: plans that an organisation puts in place to meet objectives. Strategies have major resource implications for the organisation as a whole.

Style theories: theories that state that leaders have a preferred style of management (e.g. autocratic or democratic), which they apply in a range of situations.

Synergy: the relationships between the parts of a system that collectively make it more effective than if the individual parts were working alone.

Systems approach: a management approach that looks at organisations and parts of an organisation as systems in which inputs are processed into more desirable outputs. In particular, it focuses on identifying more effective systems and processes.

T

Tactics: broad approaches that an organisation takes to deliver strategies.

Takeover: where a company buys at least 51 per cent of the shares of another business in order to secure a controlling interest.

Tangible assets: assets that are physical items (that can be touched).

Team: a group of people with a shared purpose and responsibility for the output of the team.

Team development: the stages that a team goes through to become an effective, high-performing team.

Top-down approach: a management approach where decisions and directions are communicated downwards from the top management.

Trade liberalisation: the removal or reduction of trade barriers or restrictions (e.g. import and export taxes) to make it easier for countries and firms to trade across international frontiers.

Trading account: the part of the income statement which shows the sales, cost of sales and gross profit for a trading company i.e. a company that buys in goods to resell them.

Traits: personal and psychological characteristics of individuals. Trait theories of management assume that leaders possess one or more specific traits (e.g. above average intelligence) that make them more suited to leadership.

Transformational leadership: a type of leadership that establishes a clear vision and enables others to share that vision. Transformational leaders encourage followers to behave in a positive way (e.g. working more collaboratively with others to make well-informed decisions).

Turnover: revenue obtained as a result of a company selling its goods or services (see **Sales**).

U

Unlimited liability: situation in which owners of a business have no limits on the sums that they may be required to pay to settle the debts of their business.

V

Value Added Tax (VAT): a tax levy for each sale/purchase.

Variance: the difference between what actually happens and what is budgeted to happen.

Venture capitalists: businesses and individual entrepreneurs who provide capital to other businesses (often start-up businesses and small businesses seeking to expand) in return for a share in the equity of the business.

Virtual organisation: a network organisation in which the components of the organisational structure (including people) are linked electronically so that they can operate from different physical locations.

Vision: an aspirational picture of what an organisation would like to become in the future. A company's vision is often set out in a vision statement.

W

Working capital: the capital required to purchase stock (inventories). A more technical definition is:
Working capital = Current assets − Current liabilities

Working capital ratio: compares the value of assets that will be turned into cash in the short period (under one year) with the value of liabilities (that need to be paid) in the short period (under one year).

$$\text{Working capital ratio} = \frac{\text{Current assets}}{\text{Current liabilities}}$$

Z

Zero-based budget: a budget where every activity is questioned as if it is new. Each plan of action is justified in terms of total costs involved and benefits to accrue, with no reference to past activities.

Index

A

accountability 67
accounting 134–55
    accounting information 134–5
    finance 120–1
    financial statements 136–55
accounting ratios 144–55
    efficiency ratios 150–1
    gearing ratio 152–3
    investor/shareholder ratios 154–5
    liquidity ratios 146–7
    profitability ratios 148–9
acid test ratio 147
ARR *see* average rate of return
assets 122
authority 67
average rate of return (ARR), investment
    appraisal 168–9

B

balance sheets (statements of financial
    position) 138–9, 142–3
banks/banking
    commercial banks 41, 126
    cooperative banks 11
    FirstCaribbean International Bank 68
    motivation 75
benchmarks 144
budgets/budgeting 156–65
    benefits 162
    budget officers 165
    budgetary control 164–5
    cash budgets 158–9
    labour budgets 161
    limitations 162–3
    materials budgets 161
    production budgets 160–1
    purpose 156
    sales budgets 159
    types of budget 156–7
business ethics 3, 24–7
    corporate governance 26–7
    corporate social responsibility (CSR)
        24–5
    stakeholders 26
business objectives 20–3
    hierarchies 22–3
    key performance indicators (KPIs) 21
    SMART objectives 20–1
business organisation 6–17
    companies 8–9
    cooperative enterprises 10–11
    franchises 12–13
    joint ventures 13
    not-for-profit organisations 16–17
    partnerships 7
    private limited companies 8
    for-profit organisations 17
    public limited companies 8–9
    public sector organisations 14–15
    sole traders 6
business plans 2

C

capital, financial 122–3
capital markets 130–3
Caribbean Examinations Council (CXC),
    business objectives 22–3
CARICOM, globalisation 38–9, 44–5
cash budgets 158–9
cash flow statements 140–1
centralisation, organisational structure 68
Certificate of Incorporation 8–9
Certificate of Trading 9
chain of command 66
change 96–101
    managing 96–101
    nature of change 96–7
    resistance to change 98–9
    strategies 101
change agents 101
change objectives 100
change plans 100
charities 16–17
closed systems 55
commercial banks 41, 126
communication 102–9
    barriers 108–9
    channels 104
    communications escalator 103
    formal/informal 106–7
    lines of communication 106–7
    methods 104–5
    networks 107
    stages 102–3
companies
    business organisation 8–9
compensation
    human resource management (HRM)
        116–17
competency 117
compound interest 172
conflict 92–5
    causes 92–3
    management strategies 94–5
contingency approach, management
    theories 55
continuum 80
contract manufacturing, joint ventures 13
control systems 57
convertible debentures 125
cooperative banks 11
cooperative enterprises, business
    organisation 10–11
corporate governance 26–7
corporate social responsibility (CSR) 24–5
cost-effective 28
credit unions 11
cruise industry 43
CSR *see* corporate social responsibility
current assets 122

D

debt 6, 124
decentralisation, organisational structure
    68–9
decision making 28–35
    factors affecting 34–5
    key performance indicators (KPIs) 30–1
    PESTLE analysis 34–5
    qualitative information 30–1
    quantitative information 30–1
    stages 32–3
    takeovers 31
delegation 67
depreciation, straight-line method 169
development/training, human resource
    management (HRM) 114–15
disbursements 158–9
dividends 8

E

Ease of Doing Business Index 39
economic activity 4–5
efficiency ratios 150–1
entropy 55
equity 124
ethics, business *see* business ethics
expectancy theory 70
external recruitment 112
extrinsic motivation 71

F

fair trade 11
farming cooperatives 10
FDI *see* foreign direct investment
finance
    accounting 120–1
    criteria for seeking 126–7
    financial capital 122–3
    long-term finance 128–9
    medium-term finance 128–9
    short-term finance 126–7
    sources 124–31
financial capital 122–3
financial statements 136–55
    accounting ratios 144–55
    balance sheets (statements of financial
        position) 138–9, 142–3
    cash flow statements 140–1
    income statements 136–7
    statements of comprehensive income
        142–3
financial strategies, motivation 76–7

fixed assets 122
fixed liabilities 139
Fordism 51
foreign direct investment (FDI) 130
formal leadership 84–5
for-profit organisations 17
franchisees 12–13
franchises 12–13
franchisors 12
functional conflict 92
functions 60
    management functions 56–61
funds flow analysis 165

G
gaps in the market 2
gearing 124
gearing ratio 152–3
globalisation 36–45
    benefits 40
    CARICOM 38–9, 44–5
    consumer behaviour 40–1
    disadvantages 40–1
    domestic business 42–3
    government's role 38–9
    impact 40–5
    multinational companies 36–41
    opportunities 42
    threats 43
    trade liberalisation 44–5
government grants 128
gross profit 136
group cohesiveness 90–1
groups 86
    see also teams

H
Hawthorne effect 52
Hawthorne experiments 52
Herzberg's hygiene theory, motivation 73
hierarchies 66
high-performance teams 87
hire purchase 127
HRM see human resource management
human relations approach 53
human relations model, management
    theories 52–3
human resource management (HRM) 53,
    110–17
    compensation 116–17
    development/training 114–15
    hard HRM 111
    performance management 117
    recruitment 112
    selection 113
    soft HRM 110–11
    training/development 114–15
hygiene factors, motivation 73

I
income statements 136–7
industry types 4–5
informal leadership 84–5

internal recruitment 112
intrinsic motivation 71
investment 166
investment appraisal 166–77
    average rate of return (ARR) 168–9
    comparing methods 176–7
    need 166–7
    net present value (NPV) 172–5
    payback period 170–1
investor/shareholder ratios 154–5
inward investment 37

J
Jamaica Stock Exchange (JSE) 132–3
job analysis 113
job enrichment 74
joint ownership, joint ventures 13
joint ventures 13
JSE see Jamaica Stock Exchange

K
key performance indicators (KPIs)
    business objectives 21
    decision making 30–1
knowledge based economies 4
KPIs see key performance indicators

L
labour budgets 161
leadership 78–85
    effective leadership 83
    formal leadership 84–5
    informal leadership 84–5
    leadership styles 80–1
    leadership theories 78–9
    transformational leadership 82–3
learning 114
liabilities 124
licensing, joint ventures 13
limited liability 7
line managers, organisational structure
    66–7
line of control 60
liquidity ratios 146–7
long-term finance 128–9

M
management functions 56–61
management theories 48, 50–5
    classical model 50–1
    contingency approach 55
    human relations model 52–3
    systems approach 54–5
market research 29
Maslow's theory of motivation 72
materials budgets 160–1
matrix structures, organisational structure
    62–3
MCDA see multi-criteria decision analysis
medium-term finance 128–9
missions 22
mixed economies 14
monetary assets 147

money markets 130
motivation 70–7
    factors influencing 70–1
    financial strategies 76–7
    Herzberg's hygiene theory 73
    Maslow's theory of motivation 72
    motivational needs 71
    motivators 73
    non-financial strategies 77
    theories 72–5
multi-criteria decision analysis (MCDA) 28
multinational companies 36–41

N
nationalisation 18–19
net present value (NPV), investment
    appraisal 172–5
net profit 137
network structures, organisational
    structure 64–5
'new broom' approach 98
NGOs see non-governmental organisations
non-financial strategies, motivation 77
non-governmental organisations (NGOs)
    17
not-for-profit organisations 16–17
NPV see net present value

O
objectives, business see business objectives
open systems 55
operations 23
opportunity cost 172
organisational culture 95
organisational structure 60–9
    centralisation 68
    characteristics 66–9
    decentralisation 68–9
    FirstCaribbean International Bank 68
    functions 60
    geography 61
    line managers 66–7
    matrix structures 62–3
    network structures 64–5
    organisational charts 66
    products 60–1
    virtual organisations 65

P
partnerships, business organisation 7
payback period, investment appraisal 170–1
performance appraisal 76
performance management, human
    resource management (HRM) 117
person specifications 113
PESTLE analysis
    decision making 34–5
    managing change 97
physical capital 20
planning horizon 167
preference shares 124
pressure groups 17
primary inputs 54

private equity 131
private limited companies, business
    organisation 8
privatisation 18–19
production budgets 160–1
profitability ratios 148–9
psychological contracts 111
public corporations 14–15
public limited companies
    business organisation 8–9
public sector broadcasting 15
public sector organisations 14–15

Q
qualitative information, decision making
    30–1
quantitative information, decision making
    30–1
quaternary industries 4, 5

R
recruitment, human resource management
    (HRM) 112
responsibility 67
responsibility centres 164
retail cooperatives 11

S
sales budgets 159
scientific management 50
secondary inputs 54

selection, human resource management
    (HRM) 113
shareholder return 154
shareholders 8
'sleeping' partners 7
SMART objectives 20–1
'soft' loans 128
sole traders 6
solvency 135
span of control 66
stakeholders 26
statements of financial position (balance
    sheets) 138–9, 142–3
    see also financial statements
statutory boards 14
stock exchange, Jamaica Stock Exchange
    (JSE) 132–3
straight-line method, depreciation 169
strategies 23, 76–7, 94–5, 100–1
style theories, leadership theories 78–9
synergy 55
systems approach 54
    management theories 54–5

T
tactics 23
takeovers
    decision making 31
teams 86–91
    advantages/disadvantages 91
    characteristics 88

composition 88
    group cohesiveness 90–1
    team development 87
    team working 63
television cooperative 10
top-down approach, management theories
    52
trade liberalisation, globalisation 44–5
training/development
    human resource management (HRM)
        114–15
traits 78
transformational leadership 82–3

U
unlimited liability 6

V
variance 156
variance analysis 164–5
venture capitalists 123
virtual organisations 65
    organisational structure 65
vision 22

W
workers' cooperatives 10
working capital 123

Z
zero-based budgets 165